One Course Two Visions

A Comparison of the Teachings of the Circle of Atonement and Ken Wapnick on *A Course in Miracles*

Robert Perry Greg Mackie Allen Watson

Book #27 in a Series of Commentaries on
A Course in Miracles

THE CIRCLE OF ATONEMENT

This is the 27th book in a series, each of which deals with a particular theme from the modern spiritual teaching, *A Course in Miracles*. The books assume a familiarity with the Course, although they might be of benefit even if you have no acquaintance with the Course. If you would like a complete listing of these books and our other publications, a sample copy of our newsletter, or information about the Circle of Atonement, please contact us at the address below.

The Circle of Atonement
Teaching and Healing Center
P.O. Box 4238, West Sedona, AZ 86340
(928) 282-0790 Fax: (928) 282-0523
E-mail: info@circleofa.com
Website: www.circleofa.com

The ideas presented herein are the personal interpretation and understanding of the authors, and are not necessarily endorsed by the copyright holder of *A Course in Miracles*: Foundation for *A Course in Miracles*, 41397 Buecking Dr., Temecula, CA 92590. Portions from *A Course in Miracles* © 1975, *Psychotherapy: Purpose, Process and Practice* © 1996, and *Song of Prayer* © 1996, reprinted by permission of the copyright holder.

ISBN 1-886602-22-0

Published by The Circle of Atonement Teaching and Healing Center

Cover art by Phillips Associates UK Ltd
Design and layout by Phillips Associates UK Ltd

Library of Congress Cataloging-in-Publication Data

Perry, Robert, 1960-
  One Course, two visions : a comparison of the teachings of the Circle of Atonement and Ken Wapnick on a Course in miracles / Robert Perry, Greg Mackie & Allen Watson.
    p. cm. -- (A series of commentaries on a course in miracles ; bk. #27)
  Includes bibliographical references and index.
  ISBN 1-886602-22-0
  1. Course in miracles. 2. Wapnick, Kenneth, 1942- 3. Circle of Atonement
(Organization) I. Mackie, Greg, 1963- II. Watson, Allen, 1940- III. Title.
IV. Series.
  BP605.C68P46 2004
  299'.93--dc22
                                        2004008877

All references are given for the Second Edition of the Course, and are listed according to the numbering in the Course, rather than according to page numbers. Each reference begins with a letter, which denotes the particular volume or section of the Course and its extensions (T=Text, W=Workbook for Students, M=Manual for Teachers, C=Clarification of Terms, P=*Psychotherapy*, and S=*Song of Prayer*). After this letter comes a series of numbers, which differs from volume to volume:

T, P, or S-chapter.section.paragraph:sentence; e.g., T-24.VI.2:3-4

W-part (I or II).lesson.paragraph:sentence; e.g., W-pI.182.4:1-2

M or C-section.paragraph:sentence; e.g., C-2.5:2

CONTENTS

Introduction

We feel this book needed to be written. The specific catalyst for it is that we have been asked by students for years to clarify the relationship between Ken Wapnick's teaching and our own. For most of that time we chose not to, because we were concerned that the confusion and misunderstanding it would stir up might outweigh whatever good it did. However, in the last few years, we have received so many such requests that we finally decided to respond to what appears to be a widespread need. We initially planned a newsletter, but when we went to write the articles we planned, we found we simply couldn't do them justice in the space allotted. The articles turned into long essays and the newsletter became a book.

We see this book, however, as fulfilling an important need beyond the need to understand how the Circle's teaching relates to that of Ken Wapnick. Therefore, before you embark on reading it, we want to clarify the purpose for which it was written. Although responding to the views of an influential thinker is completely normal in the world, there are as yet no such established conventions around *A Course in Miracles*. Hence, we would like to begin by making the purpose of this book clear.

In it we discuss the teachings of Ken Wapnick and how those teachings relate to our own. As you will see, we often differ with his teachings and openly explain our reasons why. The book, however, is not intended as a personal attack on Wapnick. We fully acknowledge that he has had an immensely important role in relation to *A Course in Miracles*. In addition to being the third member of the original Course family (after Helen Schucman and Bill Thetford), he helped edit the Course for publication, and since then has been its most prominent interpreter. If one believes that the writing and publishing of the Course was driven by a higher plan—which we at the Circle do—it is difficult to deny that Wapnick was an important part of that plan; that he was, in essence, handpicked by Jesus to play a pivotal role. One also cannot help but respect the depth of his devotion to the Course. He has dedicated his life to it and worked tirelessly to serve its students. He has taught things and done things that we do not agree with, but our perspective is that even these came out of his drive to honor the purity of the Course. His influence, in fact, has pulled the entire Course world toward a greater respect for the Course's unique and radical elements than would have been there without him. We all owe a debt of gratitude to Ken Wapnick.

This book is not meant to deny that debt. It is meant, very simply, to address Wapnick's *views*.[1] They have been very influential among Course students, and we believe that discussion of those views by other teachers of the Course will be helpful to many students. Where we attempt to refute his views, we will do so in a respectful manner; that is, with evidence from the Course, never with speculation about the supposed biases, projections, and character flaws that gave rise to those views.

We realize this book is not for every Course student. It is written especially for those who put a great deal of stock in things like logical arguments and rules of evidence in deciding for themselves what the Course teaches. In writing this book, we particularly had in mind those who teach the Course to others. They have a special responsibility to come to informed views of the Course rather than simply passing on views that may appear popular or authoritative but are not grounded in the Course.

This book is also not intended to stir up controversy. It is extremely easy to use any issue, especially that of differences in Course interpretation, as an excuse to get caught up in controversy and take our focus off the real issue: that of living the Course. That is why this is the only book the Circle has ever written about differences in interpretation. Our main focus has been and always will be on helping students to understand the Course's teaching and apply its practice. We hope that this book will help students clarify for themselves what the Course actually does teach, so that they can more effectively follow its teachings in their lives.

This book is based on two premises:

1. How one understands what the Course says is a crucial issue for Course students.

2. Hearing Course interpreters respond to the views of other interpreters can put us in an ideal position to make up our own minds about what it says.

The first premise should be self-evident. *A Course in Miracles* is a book that lays out an entire spiritual path. If the Course is your path, then how you understand and practice your personal path is determined by how you interpret this book. In this sense, the Course is analogous to a cookbook. How you read the instructions determines what kind of dish you cook. If you interpret a cookbook differently than someone else, then you end up cooking a different dish. For example, one of us once had soup that a housemate made for the household. He hadn't done a lot of cooking and so he thought that "2 t. salt" meant two *tablespoons* of salt. He interpreted the cookbook instructions differently and the result was an incredibly salty pot of soup.

How we interpret the words of the Course matters. Different interpretations amount to different recipes for the spiritual life, and consequently turn out different dishes—different kinds of spiritual seekers. If you think the Course trains you in meditation, for instance, your path will be different than that of someone who believes that meditation is at odds with the Course's radical teaching. If you think the Course sends you out into the world to help strangers in need, your path will be different than that of someone who believes that such "help" makes the separation real.

Words get a lot of bad press in Course circles. Barely a week goes by when we do not hear someone quote, "Words are but symbols of symbols. They are thus twice removed from reality" (M-21.1:9-10). Yet imagine how shocked you would be if you purchased the Course only to find that it *had* no words, nothing but blank pages. These words tell us what to do in the "kitchen" of our spiritual life, what ingredients to put in, in what measure and what order, and how long to bake the dish. In the end, we are meant to go beyond words, but the Course's strategy is to *use* words to tell us *how* to go beyond them.

Thus, how we understand the Course's words makes a huge difference. Yet few of us—perhaps none of us—have the time, ability, and inclination to piece together the Course's entire thought system by ourselves. Most of us can therefore benefit from skilled interpreters who have devoted their lives to understanding this teaching. Not only can we benefit, we already *do* benefit. I think there are few long-term Course students who have not been influenced by interpreters. The Course is so massive and so multifaceted that students tend to be hungry for simple concepts that can condense major aspects of the Course into a small package. So hungry are we that when such a simple concept comes along we often soak it up like a sponge without even realizing it. A great example of this is the notion that *A Course in Miracles* is a self-study course. This is one of the most accepted pieces of "wisdom" about the Course and yet nowhere does the Course itself say that it is a self-study course. Someone came up with that idea and we all just took it in and passed it around without any actual evidence for it. In other words, we have all been influenced by that interpreter, whoever it was.

In our experience at the Circle, many of the simple concepts through which students see the Course come from the teachings of Ken Wapnick. He has a knack for reducing the Course to a series of simple concepts and then repeating those concepts again and again. The result is that many students have taken in elements of his framework without remembering, or even knowing, where those elements came from. Others have taken those elements in *because* they came from him—they believed that he was the authority on the Course and that what he said was the final word. Still others have taken those elements in because they found Wapnick's presentation genuinely persuasive, but perhaps they might not have if there existed a true marketplace of ideas, in which there were multiple options which were in public dialogue with each other.

This is why we believe issues of Course interpretation need to be discussed out in the open. Two factors are relevant here. Students in the end have to make up their own minds; they must decide for themselves what they believe the Course teaches. Yet they also need the help of interpreters, of experts—people who have devoted their lives to understanding the Course. Both of these factors are true, but together they present us with a difficulty: if you need an expert but you yourself are *not* an expert, how do you know how to evaluate what the expert says? One of the oldest and best answers to this question is that *you listen to different experts commenting on each other's views.* To pick an extreme example: if you hear about a radical new theory in the field of cosmology, and you yourself are not qualified to evaluate it (which is most probably true), you naturally want to hear what professional cosmologists say about it.

Evaluating interpretations of the Course is not as specialized as evaluating theories in cosmology, yet the same basic need exists. When a Course student confronts the teachings of Ken Wapnick, there is an obvious power differential. That student knows that he or she is only a mere student, whereas Ken Wapnick was close to Helen Schucman, helped edit the Course, heads up a large center, has written a pile of books on the Course, and even owns the copyright. This power differential puts the student at a distinct disadvantage. The student may not feel convinced by what Wapnick says, but may think, "Who am I to question Ken Wapnick?" The time-honored way to equalize the situation is for students to hear what other qualified interpreters have to say about Wapnick's teachings. Then the student is in a good position to make a truly informed decision, even if that decision ends up being that his or her inner sense was wrong and that Wapnick was right after all.

That is the very simple idea behind this book. Ideally, it would be a true dialogue between Wapnick and the Circle. However, Wapnick declined our request to respond to the essays in this book and for many years has declined our repeated invitations to engage in public dialogue. To our knowledge, he does not publicly dialogue with anyone about the question of what the Course teaches.[2] We therefore had to do the next best thing: respond to his views by ourselves. This, of course, leaves us open to misrepresenting his views. For this reason, we have done our utmost to be fair. We have based our representations of his views on quotes from his own writings and have done our best to keep from caricaturing his views.

Addressing the ideas of an influential thinker in any field is, as we all know, standard procedure in the world. It is an integral part of how human understanding moves forward. Yet some of the feedback we received when we published two of this book's essays in our newsletter said that we shouldn't be talking about differences. Not talking about differences in Course interpretation can sound spiritual, but can you imagine that being standard practice in other fields? Can you imagine the field of psychology, for example, if it were taboo to respond to the ideas of Freud? In fact, while Helen Schucman was taking down the early chapters of the Text, the author of the Course himself responded to the ideas of Freud, freely expressing both agreements and disagreements. He was not at all shy about addressing differences.

Another frequent response to that newsletter was the claim that both Wapnick and the Circle are really saying the same thing; that in effect, there are no differences. This seemed to stem, at least in part, from a discomfort with the possibility that someone was right and someone was wrong. While we acknowledge that differences in views are often more apparent than actual, the simple fact is that not all views can be right. If someone claimed that the Course's message is to hate your brother, would we really want to say, "Well, that's right, too"? If we want the real truth, we must be willing to identify what is not true. Otherwise, the truth gets lost amidst all those falsehoods we are so open-mindedly affirming. Likewise, if we want to know what the Course really says, we must be willing to identify what it does *not* say. If a view is false—if it does not reflect the Course—we should let it fall by the wayside, not with anger, but with dispassion. On the road to the truth we must be willing to let a thousand views fall by the wayside. All that matters is the truth.

For this same reason, the Course is not shy about saying that we are wrong, something it does many, many times. Our egos take it as a terrible insult, and they are in a sense right: admitting that you are wrong is a little death of the ego, a little part of its total relinquishment. Yet that relinquishment is the whole goal of the spiritual path. That is why the Course says, "Be glad, then, that you have been wrong" (T-9.IV.10:5). We invite you, therefore, not to be shy in facing the differences between our view of the Course and Ken Wapnick's, and even in deciding that one or both of us is wrong.

This is the spirit in which we at the Circle try to approach our own views. Our views are not sacred. We can be wrong and have been— many times. There are probably views of ours in this very book that we will eventually decide are wrong. When we find that we have been wrong, rather than trying to make our earlier view and new view *both* right, we try to simply say, "We were wrong," and talk about it with each other and with our students here. Putting our previous view in the best possible light, making it somehow right too, just gets in the way of moving on from it. It was wrong. Who cares about it anymore?

The value we place on admitting when we are wrong is part of our aim of getting it right. And we *do* want to get it right. We place a high value on Course scholarship. We do a lot of in-house scholarship that we do not publish, and one of our long-term goals is to found a genuine tradition of scholarship around the Course. We see this as the special function of one of our writers, Greg Mackie, who contributes heavily to this volume.

Our emphasis on closely examining the words of the Course and taking them literally most of the time has led a few people to label us "fundamentalists." We, however, do not think that term applies to us at all. While fundamentalists claim to take scripture literally, the term itself refers to far more than this. Fundamentalism began as a label for currents within 20th century American Protestantism, but the word is now often used to describe movements in various traditions around the world. Karen Armstrong, in her book *The Battle for God: A History of Fundamentalism*, describes fundamentalist movements as "embattled forms of spirituality" that have emerged to fight against what they see as the encroaching evil of secular modernity:

> Fundamentalists do not regard this battle as a conventional political struggle, but experience it as a cosmic war between the forces of good and evil. They fear annihilation, and try to fortify their beleaguered identity by means of a selective retrieval of certain doctrines and practices of the past.[3]

The notion of "selective retrieval" is particularly important. Fundamentalists are not truly devoted to drawing out and following the original meaning of their scriptural writings. Speaking of Christian fundamentalists, L. William Countryman comments in his book *Biblical Authority or Biblical Tyranny?*:

> They often speak of Scripture as inerrant. In fact, however, they have tacitly abandoned the authority of Scripture in favor of a conservative Protestant theology they buttress with strings of quotations to give it a biblical flavor, but it predetermines their reading of Scripture so thoroughly that one cannot speak of the Bible as having any independent voice in their churches.[4]

Given the above descriptions, it is difficult to see much if any resemblance between fundamentalism and the Circle. We prefer instead to think of ourselves as "purists." Our whole intent is to approach the Course on its own terms and thereby give it a truly "independent voice," independent of our preconceptions and preferences. Perhaps with other scriptures such an attempt to follow "the letter of the law" stifles "the spirit of the law" and leads to a stale and restrictive spiritual life. Our experience with *this* scripture, however, is that the more minutely we go into the "letter" the more deeply we get in touch with the spirit; the more practical, alive and transformative the Course becomes for us. In the case of the Course, we believe, the "letter" genuinely serves the "spirit."

In conclusion, we have written this book in as neutral a tone as possible and we invite you to read it in that same spirit. This is not a boxing match. It is an exploration of what the Course teaches. What matters is not who is right or who is wrong; what matters is coming to a better understanding of the Course's teaching, so that we can live that teaching in our lives. Our goal here is to put you in the position of making a truly informed decision about what the Course teaches. We therefore urge you to approach it in that spirit. Do not decide something is true just because *we* say it. We don't want the Circle to turn into another unquestioned authority. Try not to get caught up in drama and controversy. Look at the evidence, look at the arguments, and decide for yourself.

Notes

[1] In keeping with standard scholarly practice for referring to a thinker, we will refer to Ken Wapnick throughout the book by his last name.

[2] Wapnick has published a dialogue with Fr. W. Norris Clarke entitled *A Course in Miracles and Christianity: A Dialogue*. However, in this book, Wapnick and Fr. Clarke do not dialogue about the question of what the Course teaches. Rather, they dialogue about how the Course relates to Christianity, with Wapnick playing the representative of the Course. The dialogue thus assumes that Wapnick's understanding of the Course is correct; at no point in the dialogue is his understanding of the Course challenged.

[3] Karen Armstrong, *The Battle for God: A History of Fundamentalism* (New York: Knopf, 2000), p. xiii.

[4] L. William Countryman, *Biblical Authority or Biblical Tyranny?* (Harrisburg, PA: Trinity Press International, 1994), pp. ix-x.

The Relationship between the Circle's Teachings and the Teachings of Ken Wapnick

We at the Circle, particularly those of us who write for the Circle (Robert Perry, Allen Watson, and Greg Mackie), have for years been regularly asked by students to clarify the relationship between our teachings and those of Ken Wapnick. These students know that both Ken Wapnick and the Circle of Atonement seek to accurately represent the Course, yet they are also aware that we see the Course differently. This presents a confusing situation for students, many of whom regard both the Circle and Ken Wapnick as authoritative sources of teaching.

We have finally decided to address this issue, briefly in this newsletter and more fully in an upcoming book. What follows in this article will be a list of similarities and a list of differences between our teaching and Wapnick's. This list will not be exhaustive, but we have tried to make it as accurate as possible. It is difficult to summarize someone's views as briefly as we have here. To be as faithful as possible in representing Wapnick, we have frequently quoted his own words. Further, in areas where he teaches different (and seemingly incompatible) things, we have tried to capture his main emphasis. Introducing the list of similarities and the list of differences will be a brief account of where, in our view, those similarities or differences come from.

One more point: the purpose of this essay is not to present reasoning and evidence in support of our views (which is why there are no Course references attached to our views below). In the other essays in this book, we explain and support our views more fully, but this introductory essay merely aims to present our views and Wapnick's views as objectively and neutrally as possible.

1

SIMILARITIES

The similarities between Wapnick's teaching and the Circle's seem to be the result of our both holding a common value: fidelity to the Course. Both of us strongly believe in honoring the Course as it is, sticking to what it says, not mixing it with other teachings, and not compromising its views just because they seem too radical or extreme. Both of us believe in trying to represent the Course purely, without distortion or dilution. The following are the main similarities we have identified:

- There is only one reality, the oneness of Heaven. There is nothing outside of that.

- The world, including the entire universe of space and time, is illusory.

- The world is not the creation of God, but the projection of our insanity, the result of our attack on God.

- The world of space and time is the result of the separation, an event in which one or more members of Heaven went insane.

- Jesus is (in some sense) the author of the Course.

- It is a crucial aspect of the Course's path to acknowledge the darkness of the ego's thought system; looking at and letting go of that darkness is vital to our salvation.

- This letting go happens in forgiveness, which is the Course's central teaching.

- Forgiveness takes place in the context of our interpersonal relationships.

- The Course is an educational program (or curriculum) in spiritual awakening. It presents a process of learning, an "integrated curriculum,"[1] in which each volume plays a role.

- The Text is the theoretical foundation of *A Course in Miracles*. Intellectual study of the Text is crucial for Course students.

- The Workbook is for the purpose of practically applying the thought system we studied in the text, to train our minds "along the lines the text sets forth" (W-In.1:4).

- The Course is written symphonically. It introduces themes, sets them aside, then reintroduces and develops them.

- The Course is a unique, sufficient, and complete spiritual path.

2

Mixing the Course with other teachings and methods generally clouds it and waters it down. It asks its students to practice its methods, rather than the methods of other paths. Yet it also asks them to honor those paths as other forms of the universal course.

DIFFERENCES

The differences (at least the significant ones) come down to a single issue: Should one interpret the Course as being primarily literal or primarily metaphorical? At the Circle, we approach it as primarily literal. We see it as a "course…that means exactly what it says" (T-8.IX.8:1). Though Wapnick uses this same quote to support his way of interpreting the Course, his main emphasis is quite different. He teaches that anything in the Course which implies what he calls "duality"—which amounts to the majority of the Course's language ("Jesus' teachings come largely within a dualistic framework")[2]—should be seen as a metaphor. What is duality? It is anything that seems to suggest that there are two realities: the oneness of Heaven *and something else.* Duality, as Wapnick treats it, seems to include the following ideas:

• anything that suggests that God or Heaven is aware of the separation and responds to it

• anything that seems to imply that the physical world is real

• anything that seems to imply that engaging in certain forms or physical behaviors, or aiming at certain external results, yields salvation

As you can see, all of these ideas at least *could* be taken to imply that there is something *in addition* to the oneness of Heaven. According to Wapnick, all passages that imply this must be reinterpreted in light of the Course's non-dualistic metaphysics, which says that the only reality is the oneness of Heaven. On the surface, those passages seem to speak of duality, but their *real* meaning (according to this view) is always non-dualistic. Therefore, we need to reach down beneath their surface to find an underlying meaning that can actually be the opposite of the surface meaning. "Taking the words of *A Course in Miracles* literally [can have] the result…that conclusions are drawn that are the exact opposite of what Jesus is actually teaching in his Course."[3]

3

Oddly enough, therefore, that common value of fidelity to the Course takes off in two different directions. For the Circle, being "pure Course" means closely adhering to what the Course says. For Wapnick, it means closely adhering to those passages in the Course that express the pure truth, and then reinterpreting the rest of the Course's passages in light of that pure truth—in essence, "purifying" those passages. To simplify it further, in our approach all of the Course is "pure Course," while in Wapnick's approach only selected portions of the Course are "pure Course"—in the sense that only those portions *openly* express the pure truth which the Course is really teaching. These two different versions of fidelity to the Course quite naturally yield two different visions of the Course itself, as can be seen in the following series of contrasts.

As you go through these contrasts, it will be natural to note where you agree with the Circle, where you agree with Wapnick, and where you agree with neither. We urge you, however, to try to keep an open mind as well. All of these issues should be decided in light of careful examination and exploration of what the Course itself teaches. As students of the Course we have all quite naturally formed our own ideas about its teachings, but these should ideally be open to being modified in light of what the Course itself says. No one's views are sacred. The primary allegiance of Course students, we believe, should not be fidelity to the Circle's views, to Wapnick's, *or to their own*, but to the Course itself.

Heaven and the Separation

The Circle	Ken Wapnick
God can accurately be described as an infinite, formless Person (without the form and limits of what we normally call a person). The personal aspects of God that the Course describes—His fatherly care for us, His desire to lift us out of our painful sleep, His yearning for our awakening—are real. The Course may be using the language of	"The God of *A Course in Miracles*...is not a person."[4] "He is thoroughly impersonal."[5] When the Course speaks of God's personal qualities, when it "speaks of God *doing* anything,"[6] for instance, it is telling us a "fairy tale,"[7] because we are still children. "You do not tell little children ...that they do not have to be afraid since

4

our human experience to express something beyond our comprehension, but that "something" is really there.

Daddy does not even know that they exist."[8] God "certainly does not experience Himself in relationship to His creation."[9]

The separation occurs when God-created parts of the Son of God (called Sons) withdraw their awareness from the oneness of the Sonship and retreat into a private state of sleep, in which they dream of separation.

The separation occurs when the one Son falls asleep. Only later does this one Son, in an attempt to elude expected punishment from God, split apart into many. "Then the Son of God—still unified as *one* Son—[tries to] confuse his wrathful pursuer by fragmenting into billions and billions of pieces."[10]

Each of us is one of these God-created parts or Sons. You experience yourself as a human being, but the "you" who is so convinced it is a human, the "you" who chooses (most of the time) to reinforce that conviction, is a Son of God, asleep in Heaven. The "you" to whom the Course is addressed is this sleeping Son of God.

Each one of us "is an illusion,"[11] a projected fragment of the one split mind. "We all are— including, we may add, the person we identify as ourselves— projected images of a split mind."[12] The one who makes our choices is the decision-maker, an illusory part of our separated mind that is outside time and space. "The 'you' [to whom the Course is addressed] is the decision-maker."[13]

God is aware that His Sons have fallen asleep. He knows that they are neither receiving His Love and joy nor extending them. He is not aware, however, of the specific content of their dream.

God is not aware that His Son has fallen asleep. "*A Course in Miracles'* position...is that God does not even know about sin, separation, and the dream."[14] "If God knew about the 'tiny, mad

5

The Circle	Ken Wapnick
	idea,' it would have to be real."[15]
God responds to the separation by creating the Holy Spirit in order to awaken His Sons.	God does not create the Holy Spirit; He knows of no reason to do so. "God, strictly speaking, does not truly 'give' an Answer—the Holy Spirit—to the birth of the thought of separation."[16]
God hears our prayers and answers every one. He does so through the Communication Link He set up: the Holy Spirit. This link allows God to stay in communication with His Sons, both giving communication *and* receiving it.	"God does not hear our prayers."[17] How could He hear the prayers we utter in our separated state when He isn't aware of the state itself?

The Holy Spirit

The Circle	Ken Wapnick
The Holy Spirit is an extension of God's Being, and is therefore a created Being like the Christ.	"We can better understand the Holy Spirit to be the memory of God's perfect Love that 'came' with the Son when he fell asleep. In this sense then the Holy Spirit is not really a Person Who was specifically and intentionally created by God."[18]
The Holy Spirit, being a creation of God, is real and eternal.	The Holy Spirit is "an illusion,"[19] "a symbol,"[20] that was not created by God, but is merely a "projected split-off part of our self."[21]

6

The Circle	Ken Wapnick
The Holy Spirit is active. He acts in our minds: teaching, guiding, and healing our minds. And He acts in the world: guiding our decisions, supplying us with needed things, designing our special function, and planning the events of our lives.	The Holy Spirit, being only an illusion, cannot act, either in our minds or in the world. "The Holy Spirit does not really do anything."[22] His apparent actions are really the product of our own minds. "What we ask for...we do receive, *but not from God*. It is the power of our minds that gives us what our minds request."[23]
Asking the Holy Spirit for guidance is a major emphasis in the Course. As we study the Text, we are taught the importance of Him guiding our lives. As we practice the Workbook, we are trained to quiet our minds and hear His Voice. Once we have gained this ability, the Manual then urges us to let Him make all the decisions for our earthly function as teachers of God. As we ascend up the ladder of development, He increasingly becomes the One in charge of our minds and our lives.	Asking the Holy Spirit for specific guidance is "extremely helpful and necessary on the bottom rungs of the ladder,"[24] where students need to believe in the "fairy tale"[25] of God helping them in this world. As they move up the ladder, however, this asking becomes counterproductive, becomes an ego "defense against the experience of [God's] love."[26] As they ascend, they increasingly recognize that the Holy Spirit is only a symbol and that God is not present in the dream.[27]

Jesus and the Bible

The Circle	Ken Wapnick
The Bible can be characterized as an impure or distorted	"The Bible...is the ego's story, with the character of God being

revelation, in which genuine teaching from the Holy Spirit was filtered through the lens of human egos. As such, the Bible contains both pure elements (which speak of a God of Love) and impure elements (which speak of a God of wrath). The Course emphasizes the pure elements in the Bible and corrects or reinterprets the impure.

the ego's self-portrait"[28] "*A Course in Miracles*...and the Bible are fundamentally incompatible."[29] To say that the Course corrects the Bible is inappropriate, for "to correct something implies that you are still retaining the basic framework of what you are correcting. *A Course in Miracles*, on the other hand, directly refutes the very basis of the Christian faith, leaving nothing on which Christians can base their beliefs."[30]

The gospel accounts of Jesus are flawed, but they do contain some historical truth, both in terms of Jesus' *words* and his *deeds*. The gospels can therefore give us a glimpse (especially with the help of New Testament scholars) of the Jesus of history, a glimpse that reveals remarkable parallels with the Jesus of the Course.

The Course's Jesus "is definitely the same Jesus who appeared in the world two thousand years ago."[31] This Jesus, however, has nothing to do with the Jesus we are told about in the gospels. That Jesus is nothing but "the collective projections of the various authors of the gospels."[32] For this reason, "the Jesus of the Bible and the Course are mutually exclusive figures, with only the common name linking them together"[33]

Jesus as a personal presence is actively and constantly present with every single person, is available to help us with our thoughts and with our lives, and

Jesus does not do anything, for he, like the Holy Spirit, "is an illusion,"[34] "a symbol."[35] When it appears as if some form in our lives has come from him, it was

The Circle	Ken Wapnick
invites us to have a genuine two-way relationship with him.	really our own mind putting form onto his formless, inactive love. "Jesus is understood as not operating in the world."[36]
Jesus actively designed the words and ideas of *A Course in Miracles* and dictated these to Helen Schucman. In order to reach Helen, he intentionally used forms with which she was familiar (English language, Christian symbology, Freudian psychology, curricular format, and Shakespearean blank verse).	Jesus did not actively author the Course, nor did he specifically intend that it be written. He exists as a kind of reservoir of formless, inactive love beyond time and space. Helen's mind rose to make contact with this love, which then flowed into her mind like water filling an empty glass. This is how the Course was produced. It contains so many of Helen's forms because they made up the "glass" that imposed a shape onto his shapeless love. "Thus it was Helen's mind that gave the Course its form."[37] Jesus only provided the content of formless love (and did so without specifically intending to).

Relationships

The Circle	Ken Wapnick
When we forgive other people, we do this not just for ourselves but also as a gift to them. We intend to release them, both from *our* projections of guilt and from their *own* self-condemnation.	Forgiveness is metaphorically described as occurring within the dualistic framework of two people having a relationship, but it really "has nothing to do with our brother."[38] "In truth, there *is*

This egoless, loving intent is at the heart of why forgiveness benefits us, for it proves to us that something genuinely divine lives within us.

no person outside us, since we are all…projected images of a split mind….That is why the penultimate meaning of forgiveness is that, through the Holy Spirit's help, we learn to forgive ourselves."[39]

Extending love and forgiveness to others, in thought, word and deed, is crucial to our own awakening. Watching love come forth from us, seeing the healing effect it has on others, and feeling their gratitude (when offered), convinces us that the Holy Spirit resides in us and that we therefore must be holy. We accept the Atonement for ourselves *so that* it can then flow through us in the form of miracles that we extend to others.

Our job is solely to accept the Atonement for ourselves. "Salvation of the world depends on [us] simply doing just that *and only that*."[40] The light in our minds will then automatically brighten the mind of the entire Sonship. Trying to help people outside us in the world is falling into the trap of believing that there is something really out there. "One cannot heal others because ultimately, if the world is an illusion, who is there to help?"[41]

For each one of us, the Holy Spirit designs a special form of extending to others, one especially suited to our strengths and the particular time and place in which we find ourselves. This is our special function. It is our particular part in the overall plan for the salvation of the world. As part of this special function, the Holy Spirit brings us into contact with those whom we are to help.

Our "special function" is simply the generic function of forgiveness.[42] The Holy Spirit does not call us to do a particular work in the world ("No one is really called by Jesus or the Holy Spirit to do anything").[43] To think we are called to a particular work is the ego trying to enhance its own specialness. "What better way to witness to [the ego's] reality than to be

10

specially chosen to do *holy, special, and very important work in this world.*"[44]

In the Course, a special relationship is always a relationship with *another person*, in which both people are actively participating. Our ego-based "relationships" with things besides people (with alcohol, for example) are called by another name: *idolatry*. Moreover, the term "special relationship" (along with "unholy relationship") virtually always refers to special *love* relationships, relationships that are outwardly loving but have an underlying content of hate. The Course contains only one fleeting reference to the "special hate relationship."

A special relationship—like any relationship—exists in one person's mind alone. For this reason, a person can even have a "special relationship" with inanimate objects like the Workbook.[45] The Course describes two subcategories of special relationships: special love relationships (outwardly friendly relationships) and special hate relationships (outwardly antagonistic relationships).

Joining with others in a genuinely common goal (and even a common function) is crucial to our own salvation. We cannot get back to God alone. Only by joining can we learn that we are not these separate selves. Only by joining can we learn that who we really are encompasses the other person as well.

Trying to join with others on a behavioral level is "an example of magic."[46] It is "the very antithesis of what Jesus is really teaching us in *A Course in Miracles*."[47] "It cannot be said too often that the only true joining—and the real focus of Jesus' teachings in *A Course in Miracles*—is the joining with him or the Holy Spirit in our minds."[48]

11

The Circle	Ken Wapnick
The holy relationship is one in which two people have joined in a mutually held common goal. Once this happens, holiness enters the relationship and leads the two through a process of gradually transcending their egos, increasingly uniting with each other, and entering into a joint special function together.	The holy relationship is not a *mutual* joining *between* two people but a condition that exists only in the mind of one, whenever that one forgives the other. "A holy relationship...can only exist in the *mind* of the perceiver of the relationship. Relationships are not holy in *form*, but only in *purpose*. And purpose exists, once again, in the individual's mind."[49]

The Program

The Circle	Ken Wapnick
The Course is an educational program in accepting healed perception into our minds and extending it to others. Each volume represents a different primary activity (Text = study, Workbook = practice, Manual = extension), and a different phase in the overall program. Together, they guide us through a single process of progressively internalizing healed perception, a process that deepens with each successive volume.	The Course is an educational program in accepting healed perception into our own minds *and nothing else*. Each of the Course's volumes does have a somewhat different focus, "making a unique contribution to the student's learning and growth."[50] However, the volumes do not represent different phases of an ascending process, nor does each volume correspond to a different activity on the student's part. For the most part we do the same basic activities as we go through the volumes: primarily the study of the teaching (especially the

301748

CUSTOMER'S ORDER NO.				DATE	3/1/09	

NAME

ADDRESS

CITY, STATE, ZIP

SOLD BY	CASH	C.O.D.	CHARGE	ON ACCT.	MDSE. RETD.	PAID OUT

QUAN.	DESCRIPTION	PRICE	AMOUNT	
1	after balightment		14	95
2	Mentreluthier		9	95
3	One Course		4	50
4				
5				
6				
7				
8				
9				
10				
11				
12				

RECEIVED BY

metaphysics), and the practice of looking at our egos with the Holy Spirit or Jesus.

The Course was not intended by Jesus to be a self-study course. In those few places where he refers to new students of *A Course in Miracles*, he always depicts them as the *pupils* of a Course *teacher*. He portrays them as walking this path under the loving guidance and supervision of a more experienced student. This is not the only way of doing the Course, but it seems to be the author's *preferred* way.	*"A Course in Miracles* is inherently a self-study curriculum."[51] "The central process of studying the Course and following its particular spiritual path is an individualized one….Since all students of *A Course in Miracles* are capable of being guided specifically by the Holy Spirit, it would certainly be presumptuous for [teachers] to tell them how they should approach the Course."[52]
The basic technique of Course study is to read slowly and carefully and pay close attention to the literal words, interpreting each line *primarily* in light of its immediate context. Any statement that is not clearly a metaphorical image should be taken as straight teaching.	The basic technique of Course study is to look past the literal words (which are largely "dualistic")[53] to a deeper, "non-dualistic" meaning, revealed by interpreting each line in light of the broad context of the Course's non-dualistic metaphysics. "A student should always evaluate any particular statement in the Course in light of the Course's overall metaphysical teaching."[54]
The Workbook is a training manual in the Course's method of spiritual practice, a manual which aims to ground in us a	The Workbook is not meant to train us in a particular method of spiritual practice but "simply to orient the student on the right

lifelong habit of regular, frequent Course practice rooted in the practice methods taught to us in the Workbook.

path with the right teacher."[55] After we have completed the Workbook, we move on from its specific methods of practice. "These are only meant for a one-year period."[56]

The Workbook's practice instructions should be followed as closely as possible. Jesus asks us to do this knowing that we need the structure the Workbook provides in order to train our minds.

While some structure is necessary early in our training, there is a great danger in trying too hard to follow the Workbook's instructions. Our attempts to do "*exactly* what Jesus says" are rooted "in the magical and usually unconscious hope that [we] will please the Authority."[57] Moreover, the Workbook's structure "*could easily lend itself to ritual*"[58]— wherein we believe the mere *form* of practice yields salvation. This leaves "the content...totally sabotaged and undermined."[59]

The Workbook offers us a rich variety of different lessons and practices, and doing those specific lessons and practices as instructed is the vehicle for the shifts in perception the Course seeks to bring about in us.

Doing the Workbook's instructed practice has value in teaching us that we have a mind that can choose. However, the main value of the practice is that it flushes our ego to the surface when we *don't* do it. The Workbook lessons simply "provide a classroom in which the student's ego can 'act up,' so that its thought system can at last be recognized and chosen

14

against."[60] *This* practice—the practice of looking at the ego with the Holy Spirit or Jesus, "the essence of the Atonement"[61]—is the primary vehicle for shifting our perception.

When we fail to do the Workbook's required practices, we should forgive ourselves, because this keeps us from giving up on practicing (due to guilt) and enables us to return immediately to our practice schedule. Forgiving ourselves, then, serves the primary goal of *doing the practice.*

When we fail to do the Workbook's required practices, we should forgive ourselves, because forgiving ourselves for *not* doing them is the whole point of the Workbook. "The purpose of the workbook lessons [is] to forgive oneself when one inevitably fails to do the lesson perfectly."[62]

Meditation is an integral part of the Course's program (the Course does not call it "meditation"—except once—but that is clearly what the Course is teaching). It was discussed (by name) with Helen and Bill during the early scribing of the Course. It plays a very important role in the Workbook, which teaches three distinct meditation techniques (among its many techniques of spiritual practice). Finally, the Manual teaches that one is to continue a twice-daily practice of meditation after completion of the Workbook.

While all the Workbook lessons can be looked upon as "meditations" of a sort,[63] there is nothing in the Course that asks one to continue with meditation after the Workbook. "Meditation as such is not an integral part of the Course's curriculum"[64] Students should feel free to meditate if they so choose, but they should beware of making an idol of it and should not believe that all students of the Course should meditate.

Most of us will probably benefit from going through the Workbook more than once. We are ready to go beyond the Workbook when we can practice in the way it taught us under our own power, without needing an outside voice to *tell* us to practice, and this will probably take more than one pass through. Once we have reached this point, the Course recommends that we do post-Workbook practice, practice that is still within the basic structure of practice laid out in the Workbook, but is tailored to what we have found meets our needs.

As a general rule, we should not go through the Workbook more than once. Further, it "probably should be done relatively early in a student's work with the Course."[65] Our desire to do the Workbook more than once is very likely the voice of the ego "urging repeated run-throughs of the Workbook exercises in the magical hope that 'this time, I'll get it right.'"[66] After the Workbook there is no more need to do structured practice. We simply "spend the rest of our lives having [the Holy Spirit] be our Teacher of forgiveness."[67]

The Manual represents the final phase of the student's development: extension to others. Its primary purpose is to serve as an instruction manual for experienced Course students who have gone through the Text and Workbook, and are now ready to take up their function of extension. Its secondary purpose is to serve as a summary of some of the Course's teachings, for both the Course teacher (or mentor) and his Course pupil.

The Manual's primary purpose is to serve as "a summary of *some* of the themes and principles of the text."[68] As such, it is essentially an appendix to the Text and Workbook, "a most useful adjunct ['adjunct' is defined in the dictionary as 'something added to another thing but not essentially a part of it'] to the other two books."[69] It does not represent a distinct phase in the Course's program or in the student's development, nor is it meant for Course "teachers" (in the sense of "mentors") or for "pupils" of those teachers.

The term "teacher of God"—the person to whom the Manual is addressed—refers to someone who, having reached a particular stage of development, is ready to teach (or extend to) others. He reached this readiness by seeing truly common interests with another person, and (in the Course's system) by completing the Course's Text and Workbook.	The term "teacher of God" does not refer to someone who is ready to teach (or extend to) others, but is just "Jesus' term for his students,"[70] a generic term "for those who pursue *A Course in Miracles* as their spiritual path."[71]
While the teacher of God's role of extending to others can take many forms, the Manual specifically describes and focuses on two forms: teacher of pupils (a Course mentor to less experienced Course students) and healer of patients (a Course-based spiritual healer). These forms are literal roles that some people will be called upon to fulfill in this world.	Since active extension to others is not a part of the Course, the Manual does not literally advocate any specific role like those of teacher of pupils or healer of patients. The belief that it does is a form of "spiritual specialness": "The ego's need to make the world and itself special will distort the [Manual's] words to mean that the Course student...is asked by Jesus *behaviorally* to teach other students, heal the sick, or preach to the world."[72]

Miscellaneous

The holy instant is a moment in which we temporarily set aside our normal mental framework, which is rooted in the past, and	"The holy instant is not a period of meditation wherein the student has a 'good experience,' and feels the presence of Jesus or

enter into the timeless present. We shift into another state of mind in which we experience the lifting of the barriers of time and space, the unawareness of the body, a sense of joining with Jesus or the Holy Spirit (and all our brothers), and sudden feelings of peace, joy, and love.

the Holy Spirit. On the contrary, the holy instant is the Course's term for the *instant*—outside time and space—when we choose the Holy Spirit as our Teacher instead of the ego."[73]

In the Course, focusing on the light and looking at our darkness *both* play an important role. It is crucial to expose and look calmly at our ego's darkness, despite our resistance to doing so. Yet it is also crucial to repeatedly dwell on the light (as most Workbook lessons have us do). Only when both are present in our minds can God's light shine away our darkness.

The Course is not a course in love and light, but a course in looking at our ego's darkness. "Overly emphasizing the lovely truth about ourselves short circuits the process of undoing, by placing our sleeping guilt under the heavy blanket of denial....To assert that the central teaching of *A Course in Miracles* is love and oneness is not only to fly in the face of the Course's own words, but also to deny ourselves access to the healing opportunity it offers us. In this regard...students of *A Course in Miracles* may fall into the...category of *blissninnyhood*."[74]

The Course is a radical teaching and it makes many unique contributions to world spirituality, and these contributions should be celebrated. Yet we should also

The Course is so unique that not only is it "totally incompatible"[75] with the Bible, but this same thing can be said "regarding any other spiritual path."[76] What makes the Course so unique is its

18

celebrate the Course's many and profound similarities with other spiritual traditions. In fact, part of the Course's uniqueness is its ability to incorporate diverse elements found in other traditions, elements which appear to be mutually exclusive yet which the Course weaves together into a unity (e.g., its emphasis on the *illusory* nature of the world and its emphasis on *saving* the world).

teaching that the world is an illusion that God did *not* create and "that God is in no way involved in the illusory and unreal world."[77] This makes for a purer non-dualism than we find in either Advaita Vedanta (a form of Hinduism) or Gnosticism.[78] Attempts to liken the Course to other spiritualities are "subtle ego ploys to minimize the radicalness of the Course."[79]

CONCLUSION

As you can see, after some essential similarities, the Circle's vision and Wapnick's vision take off in very different directions. They are quite simply two different visions of *A Course in Miracles*, so different that we at the Circle do not see how a student could seriously pursue both at the same time. How should we regard these differences? First, with tolerance. It is inevitable that such differences arise; it is human nature. Second, with a sincere desire to discover what the Course really says on these issues. It does not matter who is right. What matters is finding out what the Course actually teaches and putting that into practice in our lives. We hope that this article will serve to contribute to that process.

Notes

[1] *The Message of 'A Course in Miracles,' Volume Two: Few Choose to Listen* (1997), p. 13. All of the works cited below as sources of Ken Wapnick's views are published by the Foundation for *A Course in Miracles*, located in Temecula, California. All of the works were written by Wapnick; one work, *The Most Commonly Asked Questions about 'A Course in Miracles,'* was co-written with his wife Gloria, and another work, *'A Course in Miracles' and Christianity: A Dialogue*, is the transcript of a dialogue with W. Norris Clarke, S.J., Ph.D.

[2] *Ibid.,* p. 95.

[3] *The Most Commonly Asked Questions about 'A Course in Miracles'* (1995), p. 85.

[4] *Ibid.,* p. 4.

[5] *'A Course in Miracles' and Christianity: A Dialogue* (1995), p. 29.

[6] *Ibid.,* p. 8.

[7] *Few Choose to Listen,* p. 69.

[8] *The Most Commonly Asked Questions about 'A Course in Miracles'* (1995), p. 72.

[9] *'A Course in Miracles' and Christianity: A Dialogue* (1995), p. 29.

[10] *The Message of 'A Course in Miracles,' Volume One: All Are Called* (1997), p. 66.

[11] *Few Choose to Listen,* p. 114.

[12] *Ibid.,* p. 95.

[13] *Commonly Asked Questions,* p. 33.

[14] *'A Course in Miracles' and Christianity: A Dialogue* (1995), p. 43.

[15] *Commonly Asked Questions,* p. 101.

[16] *All Are Called,* p. 35.

[17] *Commonly Asked Questions,* p. 120.

[18] *All Are Called,* p. 33.

[19] *Few Choose to Listen,* p. 88.

[20] *Ibid.,* p. 124.

[21] *Ibid.,* p. 108.

[22] *All Are Called,* p. 339.

[23] *Ibid.,* p. 315. "Our minds, which are rooted in the ego's plan, thus interpret *our* change of mind as being done for us by the Holy Spirit" (*All Are Called,* p. 314).

[24] *Few Choose to Listen,* p. 114.

[25] *Ibid.,* p. 69. "Jesus would have us believe instead, in these early stages of our journey of awakening, in the God of his corrected fairy tale Who truly loves us, independent of what we believe we have done to Him....But if these words are taken literally, we would find ourselves back in our childhood world of fairy godmothers, Santa Claus, and a Sugar Daddy for a God."

[26] *Ibid.,* p. 117.

[27] *Ibid.,* p. 120. "It is the Course's emphasis on undoing the ego, and *not* on hearing the Voice of the Holy Spirit, that makes it so unique in the world's spiritual literature" (*Few Choose to Listen,* p. 142).

[28] *All Are Called,* p. 57.

[29] *Forgiveness and Jesus: The Meeting Place of 'A Course in Miracles' and Christianity,* 6th ed. (1st ed. 1983; 6th ed. 1998), p. xiv.

[30] *ACIM and Christianity,* p. 2.

[31] *Commonly Asked Questions,* p. 102.

[32] *Ibid.,* p, 102.

[33] *Ibid.,* p. 102-103.

[34] *Few Choose to Listen,* p. 114.

[35] *All Are Called,* p. 35.

[36] *'A Course in Miracles' and Christianity: A Dialogue* (1995), p. 39.

[37] *Absence from Felicity: The Story of Helen Schucman and Her Scribing of 'A Course in Miracles,'* 1st ed. (1991), p. 480.

[38] *Commonly Asked Questions,* p. 78.

[39] *Few Choose to Listen,* p. 95.

[40] *Ibid.,* p. 32.

[41] *Ibid.,* p. 32-34.

[42] "This special function of forgiveness belongs to everyone." (*All Are Called,* p. 340).

[43] *Few Choose to Listen*, p. 137.

[44] *Ibid.,* p. 137.

[45] *All Are Called*, p. 329.

[46] *Few Choose to Listen*, p. 182.

[47] *Ibid.,* p. 166.

[48] *Ibid.,* p. 169.

[49] *Ibid.,* p. 81.

[50] *Ibid.,* p. 3.

[51] *Commonly Asked Questions*, p. 131.

[52] *Few Choose to Listen*, p. 181-182.

[53] *Ibid.,* p. 95.

[54] *Ibid.,* p. 67.

[55] *Commonly Asked Questions*, p. 116.

[56] *Ibid.,* p. 74.

[57] *Few Choose to Listen*, p. 24.

[58] *All Are Called*, p. 329.

[59] *Few Choose to Listen*, p. 25.

[60] *Ibid.,* p. 27.

[61] *Glossary-Index for 'A Course in Miracles,'* 4th ed., p. 137.

[62] *Few Choose to Listen*, p. 26.

[63] *Commonly asked Questions*, p. 74.

[64] *Ibid.,* p. 74.

[65] *Ibid.,* p. 116.

[66] *Few Choose to Listen*, p. 22.

[67] *Commonly Asked Questions*, p. 116.

[68] *Few Choose to Listen*, p. 31.

[69] *Ibid.,* p. 31.

[70] *Ibid.,* p. 13.

[71] *Ibid.,* p. 16.

[72] *Ibid.,* p. 32.

[73] *Commonly Asked Questions*, p. 76.

[74] *Few Choose to Listen*, p. 202; "The central teaching of *A Course in Miracles*...is not the love and unity that is our reality in Heaven, but rather the identifying and undoing of the guilt and fear." *Love Does Not Condemn*, p. 553.

[75] *Commonly Asked Questions*, p. 112.

[76] *Ibid.,* p. 112.

[77] *All Are Called*, p. 9.

[78] *Ibid.,* p. 9.

[79] *Few Choose to Listen*, p. 189.

Course Metaphysics

by Robert Perry

The issue of Course metaphysics is foundational to examining the relationship between the Circle's teachings and Wapnick's, just as it is foundational to the Course itself. Metaphysics is always foundational, for it is the branch of philosophy which deals with the question of what is ultimately real. It seeks, in other words, to discover *the* foundation, the foundation of reality.

In my essay "How Metaphoric Is the Language of the Course?" I say that Wapnick's basic approach to interpreting the Course says that we must reach below the surface, literal meaning of the Course's words to the real, underlying meaning. Why? The metaphysics require it, says Wapnick. In his view, the literal meaning of most of the Course's words, if taken seriously, would violate the Course's metaphysics. This requires us to search for a subsurface, nonliteral meaning that is in *harmony* with the metaphysics. The "real" meaning we find in this way can actually be the opposite of the apparent meaning: "Taking the words of *A Course in Miracles* literally [can have] the result…that conclusions are drawn that are the exact opposite of what Jesus is actually teaching in his Course."[1]

Thus, according to Wapnick, the metaphysics forces us to radically reinterpret much of the Course's language. This raises the question: just what is the Course's metaphysics? If we understand the metaphysics in Wapnick's way, we have to reinterpret the majority of the Course's words so that they fit the metaphysics. What if we view the metaphysics differently, however? The way we at the Circle understand the metaphysics, we are not forced to reinterpret the Course's words, for there is no conflict between those words and the metaphysics.

This essay, therefore, will examine the issue of the Course's metaphysical teachings. Just what does the Course teach about ultimate reality? One note: the issue of the origin and nature of the physical world is an important issue in Course metaphysics, but I do not plan to cover it in this essay. The reason is that when Wapnick says we have to reread the language of the Course in light of the metaphysics, he is usually referring to metaphysical issues other than the making of the world, to things that happened (or didn't happen) right before the making of the world.

THE CIRCLE'S VIEW OF THE METAPHYSICS

The Circle's understanding of the Course's metaphysics is based on a straightforward reading of the Course. Words, of course, cannot capture the transcendent realities of which the Course speaks, but we must use them nonetheless. Please keep in mind, therefore, while reading the following, that the words are just a rough approximation.

God is the Creator of Heaven, a realm that is totally unified and undifferentiated. It consists of an infinite expanse of formless, changeless spirit. It is the only reality. Nothing outside of Heaven exists. In Heaven abides God's Son, the Christ. God created the Christ by extending His Being. As a result, Christ is of the same substance as God, united with God, and part of God. Yet Christ is still the effect, the created; God is the Creator.

Although the Son is one, this one Son contains within Himself an infinite number of parts, parts which are *not* the product of the separation but are Thoughts of God: "Creation is the sum of all God's Thoughts, in number infinite" (W-pII.11.1:1). These heavenly parts are referred to hundreds of times in the Course by various names: Sons, children, creations, aspects, parts, minds, Thoughts, brothers. Though they are called parts, they are not like parts in this world, for each part is one with the whole and even *contains* the whole. In this world, the whole is made of its parts. In Heaven, each part is literally made of the whole. Further, rather than being different selves, the parts all share the same Self, the Christ.

These parts are crucial to the Course's picture, for they are the ground on which the separation takes place. According to the Course, the parts fell into a dream of separation, apparently by over-identifying with their "part-ness" at the expense of their oneness. As a result, they retreated into a private state, in which they dreamt of living as

24

completely separate beings. What God created as completely unified parts seemed to become discrete, separate parts. Thus, when the separation occurred and Heaven shattered (T-18.I.12:2), it didn't shatter like normal glass, but like *safety glass*: it shattered along fracture lines that, though invisible, were already potential in the pre-separation Heaven.

We are these Sons, these parts. Just as we can lie in bed and dream we are somewhere else and even some*one* else, so we are each in Heaven at this very moment, dreaming we are in this world. We are each a perfect Son of God dreaming that we are a fallible human being. The dreamer is not some buried element in our mind that is puppeting our conscious mind. The dreamer is the very "I" that is directing our eyes to read these words right now, the very "I" that finds the Course so challenging, the very "I" that is unfulfilled and afraid most of the time. That "I" is actually a Son of God in Heaven who simply has a severe case of amnesia, and thinks he is some*one* else and some*where* else.

This also means that behind every physical body we see is another one of these divine dreamers. The body we see is an illusion that lies outside of us, but the being who identifies with that body is a real Son of God, another part of the Sonship. Thus, reaching out to that being with love and healing is no empty gesture. By doing so, we are bringing healing to a real aspect of reality.

God was aware that His Sons fell asleep. Hundreds of passages in the Course assume this by speaking of God in some way responding to the separation. Two key passages in particular (T-4.VII.6 and T-6.V.1) tell us that God is aware that His Sons are not communicating fully with Him, that they are not receiving and extending His Love, and that they are not in complete joy. As we will see later, the first of these passages says that God *knows* our joy is incomplete. He knows because His Being is directly experiencing what we are experiencing, so that *our* incomplete joy actually becomes *His* incomplete joy. God therefore directly experiences the *essential mood*, you might say, of our separated condition, even though He is unaware of the specific details.

In order to remedy the situation, God created the Holy Spirit. The Holy Spirit is spoken of as an *extension* of God—as God's Voice—and as a created Being Who *represents* God—as the Voice *for* God. He is an intelligent Spirit Who has a Mind, a Will, awareness, intention and

25

feeling. A Spirit Who thinks, feels, and wills can rightly be called a Being, and so we at the Circle are comfortable referring to Him that way. His role requires Him to be fully conscious in Heaven and yet specifically aware of everything in the dream. This enables Him to perceive everything in the dream *in light of* the reality of Heaven, and this perception is the root of everything He does. His goal is to lead us to the complete healing of our minds, the restoration of our sanity. He is constantly at work in our minds, mostly at a level below consciousness. He seeks to teach us new beliefs, to guide our thoughts, and to heal our perceptions.

He does not confine Himself to our beliefs, thoughts, and perceptions, however. He also has a plan for our external lives. He will guide our every decision if we let Him and He also designs a function—a life purpose—especially for us. Finally, He is engaged in a constant orchestration of the events and encounters of our lives, so that in every moment we are in the right place at the right time for the sake of our journey home. He does not inject the pain and suffering into our life events; we are responsible for that. But in the midst of each painful situation that we dream, He builds into that situation a doorway out of the nightmare. In every situation He places the potential for something holy to take place, a potential that, though often nearly invisible, is always within our reach.

WAPNICK'S VIEW OF THE METAPHYSICS

Wapnick's understanding of the metaphysics has significant commonalities with the Circle's. Like us, he sees reality as a transcendental realm of pure spirit. Like us, he sees time and space as the result of the thought of separation. And like us, he sees the physical universe, not as God's wonderful creation, but as the illusory outpicturing of our insane attack on God.

The two views are at their most similar in their views of the pre-separation Heaven. Like us, Wapnick sees Heaven as the only realm there really is. He teaches that God is pure, formless spirit and that God creates a Son, the Christ, Who is one with God and like God. Like us, Wapnick sees the Christ as being one, yet also paradoxically containing an infinite number of parts or Sons: "Christ consists of infinite Rays (Sons of God), all perfectly united and indivisible."[2] In other places, however, he seems to take a contrary position: "There can be only one Son, since Unity can only create unity, and multiplicity cannot originate from oneness....Therefore the term *Sons of God* is used for convenience while Jesus is addressing his students as they *believe* they are."[3]

The differences between our view of the metaphysics and Wapnick's mainly come in with the separation. Here, Wapnick is guided by a foundational idea, an idea which informs all of his teaching: "[The Course's] basic metaphysical premise is that God does not even know about the dream."[4] It is crucial that God not know about the separation because, according to Wapnick, "If God knew about the 'tiny, mad idea,' it would have to be real."[5]

This appears to be Wapnick's primary concern in the constructing of his theories: to preserve the unreality of the separation. He says that if God were to know about the dream and respond to it, that "would be violating the Course's 'prime directive' (to borrow a term from *Star Trek*), which is not to make the error [the separation] real."[6] This overriding concern for the unreality of the separation profoundly shapes how Wapnick sees Course metaphysics. We can see this concern displayed especially in how Wapnick frames God and the Holy Spirit, but I think this same concern also influences how Wapnick characterizes the Son of God and his relationship with the separation. Let me now go through and summarize Wapnick's view of all three Persons of the Trinity and their relationship with the separation:

God

In Wapnick's system, as we saw above, God has no awareness of the separation. God does not have the slightest idea that anything has happened. As far as He is concerned, no one has fallen into a dream of separation, no one feels separate from Him. This lack of awareness of the separation on God's part is pivotal, for it rules out any possibility of a heavenly response to the separation. If no one knows that you are missing, there will be no search party. Wapnick says:

> This God [the God of *A Course in Miracles*] does not even know about the separation...and thus does not and cannot respond to it.[7]

> Above all, it is always essential to keep in mind that God has no true response to the thought of separation, even though, as we have already seen, the metaphoric language of *A Course in Miracles* often portrays it so.[8]

27

To rephrase the second quote: The Course talks as if God responds to the separation, but that language is just a metaphor. In truth, He does not respond.

The Holy Spirit

Since, in Wapnick's view, God is unaware of the separation and does not respond to it, then it is impossible for Him to create the Holy Spirit as a means of healing the separation. Wapnick is quite clear that the Holy Spirit is *not* a creation of God: "The Holy Spirit is not really a Person Who was specifically and intentionally created by God."[9] If the Holy Spirit is not a creation of God, what, then, is He? Wapnick answers:

> We can better understand the Holy Spirit to be the memory of God's perfect Love that "came" with the Son when he fell asleep.[10]

The Holy Spirit, therefore, is our own memory of the heavenly state. Wapnick, in fact, often calls the Holy Spirit the "memory of God" (a Course term that the Course itself never applies to the Holy Spirit). Notice how this takes the causation of the Holy Spirit out of God's Hands. The Holy Spirit is there as a result of *our* function of *memory*, not as a result of *God's* function of *creation*.

Wapnick, however, has another way of talking about the Holy Spirit. He says that the Holy Spirit is "an illusion,"[11] "a symbol and not reality,"[12] that He is merely a "projected split-off part of our self."[13] These two ideas seem quite different: the Holy Spirit is our memory of God and the Holy Spirit is an illusion we project from a split-off part of our self. I am not completely certain how they go together, but this quote from Wapnick gives us a clue:

> The figures of Jesus or the Holy Spirit are really the projections (reflections) of the memory of a non-dualistic God within our dualistic minds. The problem, however, is that this projected split-off part of our self is actually *believed* and *experienced* to be real.[14]

This quote contains both versions of the Holy Spirit (Holy Spirit as unreal projection and Holy Spirit as memory of God) and describes how they are related: the Holy Spirit as unreal symbol is *projected from* our buried memory of God. So, one version of the Holy Spirit (unreal symbol) is projected from the other version of the Holy Spirit (memory of God). As an analogy, let's say you have a memory of the ideal spring day. The sun was out, the air was warm, the flowers were budding, the birds were singing, and you hadn't a care in the world. This day was so beautiful, it stayed in your mind as a lovely memory. Then one night, years later, you have a dream, and in this dream a person shows up that vaguely reminds you of that spring day. This person, in fact, is the very embodiment of that day. Everything about him is reminiscent of that day. The person, of course, is not real. He is just a dream symbol. Where did he come from? He is the manifestation of your memory of that perfect spring day. He is that memory expressed in symbolic form. He is that memory projected in personified form.

This is how I think Wapnick is seeing the relationship between the Holy Spirit as memory of what is real and the Holy Spirit as illusory symbol. The Holy Spirit is actually just a memory. The appearance that the Holy Spirit is a real Spirit or Being is just a symbol, a moving picture that has been projected from that buried part of our mind that contains this memory. This Spirit is just a personification of our memory, a personification we project and which is no more real than the dream person I described above. This, at least, is what the above quote from Wapnick seems to indicate.

What is clear from Wapnick's description of the Holy Spirit is that there is no actual Being in Heaven called the Holy Spirit. There is no Spirit Who is aware of our dream of separation and acts within it. The Holy Spirit has been completely stripped of being-status. In effect, then, there is no Holy Spirit. There is only our memory of being with God, a memory that, when projected, gives rise to the illusory image of an active, caring Spirit, an image that is no more real than the pictures on a movie screen.

Christ, the Son of God

Wapnick has a very complex view of the relationship between the Son of God and the separation, a view which involves the Son going through a series of four splits, which I will now attempt to summarize:

First split. The story begins with the one Son in Heaven. The thought of separation, the "tiny, mad idea," appears to enter the Mind of the one Son, with the result that this one Mind apparently splits into two: "the Mind of Christ, still united with its Creator…and the separated mind of the Sonship, now seemingly split off from its Source."[15]

29

Second split. This single separated mind now splits into three parts: the wrong mind (which contains the voice of the ego), the right mind (which contains our memory of being with God), and the decision-maker (which chooses between the wrong and right mind).

Third split. The one separated mind feels overwhelming guilt for its attack on God. To escape this guilt it submerges the self that both carried out the attack and carries the guilt over the attack. Wapnick calls this guilt-ridden, victimizer part of the mind "self A." In a further attempt to get rid of its guilt, the now-submerged self A then projects the guilt outward. This produces an external image of a victimizing God. The Son now sees outside himself a sinful, wrathful God bent on punishing him for his sins, yet this God is just self A's sinfulness and guilt seen as external. This God is called "self C." Finally, the Son now identifies with a third self, "self B," a self that seems to be free of sinfulness and guilt. This self seems innocent only because he has buried all the sinfulness and guilt deep in his unconscious (where self A is) and projected it outside himself (onto self C). He therefore seems to be a harmless, good self (self B), a self with no hidden, lurking evil within (self A), a self who is the innocent victim of a wrathful God (self C).

Fourth split. It is important to understand that all of this has taken place within the one mind of the separated Son. It is only now, in the fourth split, that this one Son splits "into an almost infinite number of fragments, each one retaining the ego's thought system of individuality, sin, guilt, fear, and the template of the third split: A – B – C."[16] The one separated Son carries out this fragmentation because he assumes that if he can hide himself in all these pieces, he is more likely to escape from God, Whom he believes is bent on executing him for his sin. "Then the Son of God—still unified as *one* Son—[tries to] confuse his wrathful pursuer by fragmenting into billions and billions of pieces."[17]

We, of course, are these pieces, in this view. We are the fragments of the one split mind. "We all are—including, we may add, the person we identify as ourselves—projected images of a split mind."[18] According to Wapnick, "each fragment carries within it the entirety of the ego's thought system, and the Holy Spirit's as well for that matter."[19] Furthermore, according to Wapnick, we are illusions, which makes sense given that we are pieces of one big illusion. Speaking of Jesus, Wapnick says, "It is only near the top [of the ladder of development] that students can truly know that he is an illusion, along with themselves."[20] Here is how Wapnick describes these illusions:

> Recall that we are speaking of hallucinatory figures within a dream that can have no reality at all, and are but the projections of delusional thoughts within the split mind of the dreamer that ultimately have no reality either.[21]

I understand all that (I think). What I do not understand is why, given this view, Wapnick still calls us the Son of God, speaks of "Who we really are as Christ,"[22] and says that "we are not truly here, but are dreaming that we are."[23] To my mind, *either* we are mere illusions on earth *or* we are the real Son of God in Heaven, merely dreaming that we are here. I do not see how both go together, nor does Wapnick appear to explain how they do.

The first thing that strikes me about this picture is the tremendous distance it puts between the Son of God in Heaven and ourselves here on earth. There are just so many things in between. By the time the four splits are done, you are an illusory fragment on earth who is separated from Christ in Heaven by a whole series of things: a split mind, a wrong mind, a right mind, a decision-maker, self A, self B, and self C. The Son of God is real, you are an illusion, and in between the two lies a whole series of other illusions.

This is not the way the Course talks. It talks as if there is a much more direct relationship between you and the Son of God. It "establishes you as a Son of God" (W-pI.38.1:3) who is asleep in Heaven, dreaming he is a human being in this world. "You are at home in God, dreaming of exile" (T-10.I.2:1). In this view, there is no distance whatsoever between you and God's Son. "The Son of God is you" (T-11.III.1:8 and W-pI.64.3:4). The world may be an illusion, your body and personality may be illusions, but the "you" that identifies with them is a real Son of God. As Lesson 132 has you repeat, "I am real because the world is not" (W-pI.132.15:3). In you, then, pure reality and complete illusion meet. You are a real part of Heaven who is directly experiencing the world of illusion.

If this is the way the Course talks, then why does Wapnick inject so much distance between you on earth and the Son of God in Heaven? I do not know, but I suspect it is because of his "prime directive" of not making the separation real. I suspect that for him the idea of a real part

31

of Heaven who is directly experiencing the world of illusion would imply that the illusion is real. If the illusion is having an experiential effect on a real part of Heaven—if it is having an impact on true reality—doesn't that imply that the illusion is real?

I suspect that this concern is at least part of what has motivated Wapnick to depart from the way the Course talks (i.e., we are real Sons of God directly experiencing the illusion) and instead inject so much distance between us and the Son of God (i.e., we are illusions separated from the Son of God by a series of intermediary illusions). By placing we who are in the illusion at such a distance from the Son in Heaven, it is as if the illusion itself has been kept at a distance from the Son in Heaven, so as not to make the illusion real.

This is all just speculation on my part, yet if it is accurate, then this is a strategy that does not work. For even in Wapnick's four splits there is a real part of Heaven that has direct contact with the illusion. This occurs in the very first split. There, one side of the Son's split mind experiences itself as separated from its Source. This part of the Son's mind, therefore, is aware of the separation and responds to it. This part of the Son's mind directly experiences the illusion.

This fact, it seems to me, raises an important question for Wapnick's view of Course metaphysics. If one real part of Heaven— the Son—can be aware of and respond to the illusory separation, then why can't God be aware of it and respond to it? After all, in Heaven everything is one. It seems to me that by allowing that the Son can be aware of and respond to the separation, this naturally opens the possibility that God can as well.

ARE WE ILLUSORY FRAGMENTS OF THE ONE SPLIT MIND OR SLEEPING SONS OF GOD IN HEAVEN?

I will spend the main part of this essay addressing the issue of whether God is aware of and responds to the separation. However, before getting into that, I want to address the teaching I just discussed above, in particular the idea that we are all illusory fragments of a single, collective split mind. This issue is a bit peripheral to the main thrust of this essay, but I want to address it because of its immense practical implications. If you are told that everyone out there is just an illusion, what rationale is there for reaching out to them with help and healing? There really isn't any. We can see this in the following two quotes from Wapnick:

> One cannot heal others because ultimately, if the world is an illusion, who is there to help? The Sonship cannot be understood quantifiably...because the student needs to understand that the appearance of many conceals the underlying oneness of the Sonship. There is, in the end, only one Son.[24]

> "Releasing" one's brother has nothing to do with our brother...because in truth it is our dream, and he is but a figure in our dream....Therefore, there is no one to forgive because, again, all the people in our lives are simply made-up figures in our dream.[25]

To put these two together: there is only one Son; the apparent Sons outside us are just made-up figures in our dream. They are just illusions. In effect, then, no one is really out there. Why would you try to help if no one is there? If you are helping, that is a sign that you just don't get it.

Obviously, then, this view has some hefty practical consequences, and this fact has not been lost on many of the students I have spoken to. Under the influence of this view, it becomes difficult for them to see what importance there could be in reaching out to others with help and healing. They still do it, but they see little support for their acts from the Course.

Let's look closely, then, at this theory of Wapnick's. The crucial issue to examine is: does the Course teach that there was a single collective split mind which then fragmented into the billions of people we see now? Or does it teach that there is a plurality of God-created Sons in Heaven, a plurality which fell asleep and which now appears as billions of human beings (and other living things) on planet earth? To put this more succinctly: *are we the illusory pieces of a vast ego-mind or are we the real parts of God's Son?*

Evidence that we are real parts of God's Son

To answer that, I will first provide the evidence for what we at the Circle believe—that we are the real parts of God's Son. It is easy to present the evidence for this view, for this is quite simply the way the Course talks throughout. I'll summarize the evidence for this in the following four points:

33

1. There is a plurality of Sons in Heaven.

The Course speaks countless times of a plurality of God-created Sons in Heaven. For example, in speaking of the heavenly state, the Course says, "God, Who encompasses all being, created beings who have everything individually, but who want to share it to increase their joy" (T-4.VII.5:1). These Sons are not separate. Paradoxically, there is a many that is perfectly one. We see that paradox in the following passage, which emphasizes one Son but then speaks of this one Son as a whole which contains a plurality of creations, Sons, or parts:

> It should especially be noted that God has only *one* Son. If all His creations are His Sons, every one must be an integral part of the whole Sonship. The Sonship in its oneness transcends the sum of its parts. (T-2.VII.6:1-3)

2. The separation itself depended on the prior existence of this plurality of Sons.

The Course says that the separation began when you asked God for special love: "You were at peace until you asked for special favor" (T-13.III.10:2; see also T-16.V.4:1-2). You asked God to "single out" (T-13.III.12:1), to "set you apart" (T-13.III.12:2), to make you His favorite Son. What can this mean, though, except that before the separation there were many Sons? How can you ask for special favor if you are already the only one? This means that the separation is actually inexplicable without the pre-separation existence of many Sons.

3. We separated as multiple Sons, not as one Son.

Did we separate as one Son or many Sons? The Course often speaks of what separated from God in terms of multiple Sons. We see this in the two passages that speak directly of God's awareness of the separation. I'll quote from both of them:

> The constant going out of His Love is blocked when His channels are closed, and He is lonely when the minds He created do not communicate fully with Him. (T-4.VII.6:7)

> What God does know is that His communication channels are not open to Him, so that He cannot impart His joy and know that His children are wholly joyous....God's extending outward, though not His completeness, is blocked when the Sonship does not communicate with

Him as one. So He thought, "My children sleep and must be awakened." (T-6.V.1:5,7,8)

Notice all the plurality in these passages. What separated from God? "His channels," "the minds He created," "His communication channels," "His children," "the Sonship," "My children." All of these are plural terms. These passages do not say: The constant going out of His Love is blocked when His channel is closed, and He is lonely when the mind He created does not communicate with Him.

4. The plurality of Sons shows up as a plurality of people.

The Course speaks of this same plurality of *Sons* as what shows up on earth as a plurality of *people*. In speaking to us on earth, the Course constantly calls us God's Sons, sometimes even calling us His "separated Sons." For instance: "You may still think this [total commitment to the Atonement] is associated with loss, a mistake all the separated Sons of God make in one way or another" (T-2.II.7:2). Clearly, in this passage, "you" are one of the separated Sons of God. Your body and personality may be illusions, but the "you" who identifies with them is a real Son of God.

The conclusion that we at the Circle have drawn from these four points is simple and obvious: The plurality of Sons that God created is the same plurality of Sons that asked for special favor, the same plurality of Sons that fell into the dream of separation, and the same plurality of Sons that shows up on earth in the form of billions of human beings.

Is there evidence that we are illusory pieces of a vast split mind?

The above four points represent the way the Course consistently talks. In the face of this, Wapnick's theory is going to need extremely strong evidence, given how different it is from this model. Yet herein lies the problem. Wapnick's theory, so far as I can see, doesn't have any evidence behind it. I have never been able to find even a single line of support for it in the Course. What we are looking for is some place in the Course that suggests that there first arose a single collective split mind (what Wapnick, I believe, used to call the primordial ego), which only later (three splits later) fragmented into billions of separate pieces. My claim is that there is no such place.

There is, however, some material in the Course that might be interpreted as evidence for this view. First is this passage, which is the only passage I can find that Wapnick quotes as support for his view:

> You who believe that God is fear made but one substitution. It has taken many forms, because it was the substitution of illusion for truth; of fragmentation for wholeness. It has become so splintered and subdivided and divided again, over and over, that it is now almost impossible to perceive it once was one, and still is what it was. (T-18.I.4:1-3)

This passage, however, is not talking about the original split mind dividing into different minds. Rather, it is talking about the original *thought of fear* taking countless different forms—the fearful phenomena of this world. The surrounding paragraphs in this section provide a list of these forms: fear-based behaviors (3:4), special relationships (4:6), the frightening events of this world (7:1), and the physical world itself (6:4). But we are not forms, we are minds. What is not mentioned in this section is the original error taking the form of the different *minds* in this world. Nowhere does it say that *we* are the fragments of this original thought of fear. Wapnick presents this passage as one that teaches his view that we are "the fragments of the one split mind of God's Son,"[26] but there is no sign of that in the passage itself or in the surrounding context.

One might also use the Course's talk of the heavenly Sonship fragmenting into separate pieces as support for Wapnick's view. There are many passages that speak of this. Here are two:

> And what are you who live within the world except a picture of the Son of God in broken pieces, each concealed within a separate and uncertain bit of clay?
> (T-28.III.7:5)

> The Holy Spirit's function is to take the broken picture of the Son of God and put the pieces into place again. This holy picture, healed entirely, does He hold out to every separate piece that thinks it is a picture in itself. To each He offers his Identity, Which the whole picture represents, instead of just a little, broken bit that he insisted was himself.
> ...The forms the broken pieces seem to take mean

nothing. For the whole is in each one. And every aspect of the Son of God is just the same as every other part.

(T-28.IV.8:1-3, 9:5-7)

Passages like these, however, do not support Wapnick's view. They do not speak of a collective split mind fragmenting, but rather of the actual *Son of God* fragmenting (or apparently fragmenting). As a result, the broken pieces are not illusions. The forms they take may be illusory, but (as the second passage above tells us) behind the form is a *real* aspect of the Son of God, an aspect that is the same as other aspects, that is one with the whole and that even *contains* the whole. This is the Course's typical language about the real parts of God's Son. These passages, in other words, support the Circle's view that each of us is one of those Sons whom God created, who asked for special favor, who fell into a dream of separation, and who now appears to be a human being. They do not support the view that each of us is an illusory fragment of a larger illusory mind.

I mention these passages about the Son of God fragmenting only because one *could* see them as support for Wapnick's view. However, I can find no instance of Wapnick himself citing them as such support. The really strange thing about Wapnick's view is that he doesn't appear to even *try* to demonstrate that the Course teaches it. He mentions again and again "the fragmentation of the ego's thought of separation into an almost infinite number of parts,"[27] but, so far as I can see, doesn't provide texts from the Course to back this up. We are apparently supposed to take him at his word. The only exception I can find is him quoting that passage about the original thought of fear becoming "splintered and subdivided and divided again" (T-18.I.4:3), which doesn't provide any support, given that it is talking about something else entirely.

My conclusion about Wapnick's view remains that it simply has no support in the Course. Instead, the Course always talks as if the one Son of God contained an infinite number of Sons at creation, that these Sons are what fell asleep, and that these Sons are who we are. On a practical level, this means that behind each body is a real aspect of God's Son, who has fallen into the misery of separation, and *who needs our help.*

37

IS GOD AWARE OF THE SEPARATION AND DOES HE RESPOND TO IT?

This question, as I mentioned earlier, will be the primary focus of this essay, for it seems to me that Wapnick's answer to this question is absolutely foundational for his view of the metaphysics and of the Course itself. Before we begin, then, let's get clear on just what his view is. The following statement of his captures it nicely: "If God knew about the 'tiny, mad idea,' it would have to be real."[28]

The logic behind this is not hard to fathom: God is the Creator of reality. He is the One Who decides what is real. If He were aware of the separation, He would be acknowledging it as real, and therefore it *would* be real. I'm not saying I agree with this reasoning, but this I think is Wapnick's reasoning.

If God is not aware of the separation, He obviously cannot *respond* to it. Earlier I quoted Wapnick saying that "God has no true response to the thought of separation."[29] In light of that, I will summarize Wapnick's principle in this way:

> God cannot be aware of the separation in any way, for that would make it real. And therefore, He cannot respond to it.

Throughout the rest of this essay, when I refer to "Wapnick's principle," this is what I am referring to. The crucial question to ask is: *Does the Course teach this?* Does the Course itself say that if God knew about the separation or responded to it, it would be real? No, it does not. I say this with confidence for four reasons:

1. The Course puts forward another principle that is directly incompatible with Wapnick's. It is this: if God did not respond to the separation by creating a remaining Communication Link (the Holy Spirit), the separation would have been real.

2. The Course directly states and indirectly implies countless times that God is aware of and responds to the separation.

3. There are only a few Course passages that could be taken to support the idea that God is not aware of the separation, but looked at closely, they are fully compatible with the idea that God *is* aware of the separation.

4. There are no passages in the Course that express the idea that God is not aware of or does not respond to the separation.

The next four sections will cover these points one by one.

1. The Course puts forward another principle that is directly incompatible with Wapnick's. It is this: if God did not respond to the separation by creating a remaining Communication Link (the Holy Spirit), the separation would have been real.

This principle and Wapnick's principle are not only different, they are mutually exclusive. Since Wapnick's says that if God responded to the separation, it would have to be real, and since creating the Holy Spirit is a response to the separation, his principle amounts to this:

> If God had created the Holy Spirit, the separation would be real.

This stands in direct contrast to the principle I believe the Course teaches:

> If God had *not* created the Holy Spirit, the separation would be real.

Clearly, only one of these principles can be true. If, therefore, I can show that the Course teaches the one I claim it does, this simultaneously establishes that it does not teach Wapnick's principle.

In order to establish the principle I am referring to, it is important to remember the nature of the separation. "The separation was...a failure in communication" (T-6.IV.12:5). We can see this connection between separation and communication failure in many places in the Course. Here are two:

> You have regarded the *separation* as a means for *breaking your communication* with your Father.
> (T-14.VI.5:1; my emphasis)

> So will the world of *separation* slip away, and *full communication be restored* between the Father and the Son. (T-14.V.5:2; my emphasis)

The separation, then, was our act of breaking off communication with God. This makes sense in terms of our experience. When suddenly we cannot communicate with a loved one (the most extreme example of this being death), how do we feel in relation to that person? Separate. In the context of a relationship, separation always has to do with a disruption in or breaking off of communication. That is what *the* separation with God was: a break in communication between Father and Son.

This simple fact helps us appreciate the significance of God creating the Holy Spirit. The Course often calls the Holy Spirit our "Communication Link" with God, through which God communicates with us and we with Him. Significantly, three times the Course adds onto this description the word "remaining": The Holy Spirit is our "remaining Communication Link" with God (T-10.III.2:6 and C-6.3:1) or simply, our "remaining communication" with God (T-5.II.8:3). This word "remaining" is important, for it captures the purpose of the Holy Spirit's creation. He was created to ensure that at least some communication between God and His Sons still *remained*.

To summarize these points so far:

- Separation equals cessation of communication. The separation was our act of breaking off communication with God.

- In response God created a Communication Link, the Holy Spirit, to ensure that at least some communication remained.

It is obvious now what God was doing in creating the Holy Spirit. He was keeping communication from ceasing entirely. And since separation means the cessation of communication, *He was preventing the separation from becoming real.*

This is a different version of the separation being real than we are perhaps familiar with, yet the Course has several versions of what would make the separation real. One is that if we actually tore ourselves from the Mind of God and literally went somewhere else, the separation would be real. Another is that if we could keep ourselves *permanently* asleep (even while still inside the Mind of God), the separation would be real. Another is that if we could succeed in cutting off all communication with God, the separation would be real. This last version, of course, is what I am arguing for now, and to show that it is an actual Course principle, I will present three Course passages that express this idea. Here is the first:

> The Communication Link [the Holy Spirit] that God Himself placed within you, joining your mind with His, cannot be broken. You may believe you want it broken....Yet His channels of reaching out cannot be wholly closed and separated from Him.   (T-13.XI.8:1-3)

Look at the final sentence, which says that we cannot be separated from God ("His channels" refers to us; see, for instance, T-6.V.1:5). This is another way of saying that our separation from God cannot be real. That is a familiar Course thought, but what does it mean in this particular context? It has to be read in light of the preceding sentences. Let me slightly rephrase the sentences and the connection will become clear:

1. The Communication Link that joins you with God cannot be broken.

2. You may believe you want it broken.

3. Yet you cannot be wholly separated from God.

If I reorder the thoughts a little, the connection will become even clearer:

- You may believe you want to break the Communication Link that joins you with God.

- But it cannot be broken; you cannot be wholly separated from God.

Clearly, breaking the Communication Link is being *equated* with being wholly separated from God. The implication is clear: without the Holy Spirit as Communication Link, we *would* be wholly separated from God. This is another way of stating the principle I am arguing for: if God had not created the Holy Spirit, the separation would be real. Here is another passage that expresses the same idea:

> And the truth is that the Holy Spirit is in close relationship with you, because in Him is your relationship with God restored to you. The relationship with Him [God] has never been broken, *because* the Holy Spirit has not been separate from anyone since the separation.
>
> (T-17.IV.4:5-6; my emphasis)

This is the same idea in different language. Instead of broken communication it speaks of broken relationship. Our relationship with God is not broken, it is still intact. Why? Because we all have a relationship with the Holy Spirit, and *via* that relationship we are still in relationship with God. Again, because God created the Holy Spirit,[30] we are not separated from God. Let's look at one final passage:

> He [the Holy Spirit] is your remaining communication with God, which you can interrupt but cannot destroy.
>
> (T-5.II.8:3)

41

As with so many sentences in the Course, there is more here than is initially apparent. To understand this sentence, you first have to realize that what can be interrupted but not destroyed is our "communication with God." Second, when it says "which you can interrupt but cannot destroy," what is implied is that we *have* interrupted it and have *attempted* to destroy it. We can therefore capture this sentence's content with the following three points:

- You tried to destroy your communication with God,
- but God created a Communication Link, the Holy Spirit.[31] Through Him, communication with God remains,
- thus demonstrating that you cannot sever your communication with God.

As in the other passages, the fact that through the Holy Spirit we still have communication with God is equated with the fact that we cannot break communication with God. This obviously implies that without the Holy Spirit communication with God *would* be broken. And since broken communication equals separation, without the Holy Spirit, we *would* be separate from God. Thus, we see the same thing here that we saw in the other two passages: if God had not created the Holy Spirit, the separation would be real.

We have now seen this principle set forth in three different passages. These passages firmly establish that this principle *is* taught in the Course. And this means that Wapnick's principle—if God was aware of and responded to the separation, it would be real—is not taught in the Course (assuming that the Course does not contradict itself, an assumption I do make), for the two principles are mutually exclusive. Whereas Wapnick's principle says that if God created the Holy Spirit, the separation would be real, the Course says that if God did *not* create the Holy Spirit, the separation would be real.

This principle I am arguing for makes a great deal of intuitive sense. First, think of a time when you felt you experienced some sort of communication with God through the Holy Spirit; perhaps a time when you experienced genuine guidance from the Holy Spirit, or when you felt that you saw the Holy Spirit working in your life, or when you were convinced a prayer of yours was answered. Wasn't some of that experience's impact the implicit message it conveyed that you and God are communicating, that He has reached down and touched you, that you are not cut off from Him, *that you are not separate from Him*? That is what the Holy Spirit is there for: to keep communication going between God and us, so that we are not separated from Him.

Now think of the reverse scenario. Imagine for a moment that Wapnick's scenario is true. Imagine that you succeeded in breaking off communication with God. As a result, you are now in a condition in which you and He do not communicate in any way. God does not speak to you. He does not give you guidance. He does not work in your life. And He does not hear your prayers. You are on one side of a gulf; He on the other. And no communication crosses this gulf. If you were in this scenario, wouldn't you feel cut off from Him? Wouldn't you feel separate? I have met many students of Wapnick's who report struggling with these exact feelings.

The Course, I believe, would say that in this scenario you would have very good reason to feel separate. For we now can say (based on the above passages) that such a scenario, from the Course's standpoint, would indeed make the separation real. Without God creating a Communication Link to establish at least some remaining communication, communication would have ceased and separation would have been achieved.

Thus, under one definition of what would make the separation real—if we had literally separated from God's Mind—Wapnick is very clear that it is not real. Yet under another definition of what would make the separation real—if we had succeeded in breaking off communication with God—Wapnick's teaching inadvertently makes it real.

This is an extremely ironic situation for Wapnick. He has overruled countless passages in the Course which suggest that God does respond to the separation, based on a single, all-important principle: if God was aware of and responded to the separation, that would make it real. How ironic, then, that God not responding to the separation doesn't *save* it from being real, but rather *makes* it real. For without God responding to the separation, He does not create the Holy Spirit, and without the Holy Spirit as Communication Link, the separation *would* be real.

2. The Course says countless times that God is aware of and responds to the separation.

There is overwhelming support in the Course for the idea that God is aware of the separation and responds to it. This theme is everywhere in the Course. As a test of this, I examined 50 pages drawn randomly from the Course, four pages for every hundred pages in the Course (this amounted to 26 from the Text, 20 from the Workbook, and 4 from the Manual). With each of these 50 pages, I searched the page for sentences that spoke of God the Father either being aware of our separated condition or responding to it in some way. To give you a sense of what passages I considered as qualifying, here are two of them:

> God, through His Voice, reminds you of it [your eternal place in His Mind]. (T-9.VIII.10:3)

> God's Answer to your forgetting is but the way to remember. (T-12.II.2:10)

Both of these passages speak of God acting in relation to our separated condition, doing something that has the intent of waking us up, something He wouldn't do if we had never fallen asleep. Here are the results of my survey:

- 26 pages (52%) with no references to God being aware of or responding to the separation (Text, pp. 27, 81, 86, 170, 314, 369, 392, 435, 440, 475, 563, 570, 613, 646; Workbook, pp. 6, 56, 80, 88, 182, 224, 248, 304, 386, 448; Manual, pp. 16, 40)

- 24 pages (48%) with one or more references to God being aware of or responding to the separation (Text, pp. 48, 117, 150, 179, 218, 243, 278, 291, 339, 482, 505, 506; Workbook, pp. 128, 143, 189, 272, 285, 303, 351, 422, 423, 457; Manual, pp. 5, 71)

- 38 separate references in those 24 pages ("separate references" means references separated from each other by at least one sentence)

Here is a summary of the many things these references say about God's response to our separated condition:

SUMMARY OF REFERENCES
God's response to our separated condition

He:

- offers us mercy (T-3.VI.6:1)

- gives us healing, through His Voice (T-7.IV.1:5)

- reveals His Will so we can learn of it (T-8.VI.8:3)

- reminds us of our eternal place in His Mind (T-9.VIII.10:3)

44

- answers our forgetting with a way to remember (T-12.II.2:10)
- calls us to Himself (T-13.III.8:2)
- lovingly guides us out of our isolation (T-14.III.18:3)
- leads us along the way, communicating all that He knows for us (T-14.III.19:2-4)
- teaches us how to see our guiltlessness (T-14.III.19:5)
- knows we will return, at which point He will take us in and replace our pain with the assurance of His Love (T-14.IX.4:2-3)
- builds with us the bridge that will lead us to knowledge (T-16.IV.10:1)
- makes sure that nothing interferes with those who serve His Will here on earth (T-22.VI.7:4)
- gives the Holy Spirit unlimited power to save us (T-22.VI.9:8)
- gives to our brother the key to our salvation (T-24.II.14:1)
- asks for our forgiveness (T-24.III.5:1)
- waits for us to bring our illusions to Him so that we can leave them behind (T-24.III.5:6)
- has a plan for our salvation (W-pI.73:9:1)
- guides our practice period, leading us to the light (W-pI.73:10:5-6)
- has a plan for our salvation (W-pI.80.1:8)
- gives an answer to our problem (W-pI.80.2:3, 4:2)
- assures us, through His Voice, that the Workbook lesson we repeat is true (W-pI.105.8:3)
- speaks to us, in order to heal us (W-pI.140.11:4-6, 12:3)
- elects those who will be His ministers in this world (W-pI.153.10:6)
- elects everyone to be His ministers (W-pI.153.11:2)
- assures us, through His Voice, that we are not a stranger to Him (W-pI.160.8:3-4)
- does His Will on earth as well as in Heaven (W-pI.186.1:5)

- trusts us to save the world (W-pI.186.3:2)

- assures us, through His Voice, that salvation needs our part (W-pI.186.5:4)

- assures us that we are His Son and like Himself (W-pII.255.1:2-4)

- wants us to achieve particular things today (W-pII.257.1:4-2:1)

- has chosen forgiveness as the means for our salvation (W-pII.257.1:4-2:1)

- gives us Christ's vision (W-pII.313.1:3)

- guides our future so that we don't have to (W-pII.314.2:2)

- establishes and completes a plan for the correction of separation (M-2.2:4)

- instantly gave an answer to the idea of separation (M-2.2:6)

- gives the Holy Spirit the power to translate our attacks into calls for help (M-29.6:5)

- does not allow our words to replace His; makes sure His Word replaces ours (M-29.6:8)

- has given us the means to realize that our weakness is His strength (M-29.7:5)

The overall result is that nearly half of the pages (48%) had a reference to God being aware of or responding to the separation. This percentage held for all three volumes (Text: 46%; Workbook: 50%; Manual: 50%). Further, 38 references in 50 pages (.76 references per page) yields an expected 948 references for the entire Course (.76 multiplied by 1,249 pages). That is a lot of references. The idea of God being aware of and responding to our separated condition is not a minor theme in the Course. We are not talking about a few scattered references; we are talking about a reference on every other page. We are talking about somewhere around a thousand references! This, in other words, is an absolutely massive theme in the Course.

Indeed, the Course portrays *itself* as a response of God's to the separation. In the fifth review in the Workbook, Jesus says the Workbook lessons that we review are thoughts he brought to us from the Holy Spirit, Who in turn got them from God (W-pI.rV.In.8:1). In fact, this same review includes a prayer to the Father in which we refer to the lessons we are reviewing as "the thoughts that You [God] have given us" (W-pI.rV.In.3:6). This prayer, then, claims that the Course consists of thoughts that God has given us to lead us out of our separated condition.

If you notice, the 38 references were really all about God's *response* to the separation. None of them were specifically about Him being *aware* of the separation. Now, obviously for Him to respond to the separation He must be aware of it. So all 38 references were implicitly about Him being aware of the separation. But are there any Course passages that explicitly mention Him being aware of it? I don't know how many such passages there are, but there are two important ones I want to highlight. Here is the first:

> Unless you take your part in the creation, [God's] joy is not complete because yours is incomplete. And this He does know. He knows it in His Own Being and its experience of His Son's experience. The constant going out of His Love is blocked when His channels are closed, and He is lonely when the minds He created do not communicate fully with Him. (T-4.VII.6:4-7)

This is a remarkable passage. It says that God *knows* our incomplete joy. How? His Being is directly experiencing our experience of being separated. He is experiencing our incomplete joy, which therefore becomes *His* incomplete joy. It also says when we do not communicate fully with Him, He is lonely. So, in two ways, it says that He is aware of our separated condition, and that this awareness has an experiential effect on Him (incomplete joy and loneliness). Here is the second passage:

> What God does know is that His communication channels are not open to Him, so that He cannot impart His joy and know that His children are wholly joyous. Giving His joy is an ongoing process, not in time but in eternity. God's extending outward, though not His completeness, is blocked when the Sonship does not communicate with Him as one. So He thought, "My children sleep and must be awakened." (T-6.V.1:5-8)

Just in case we thought that first passage was some kind of mistake, the Course repeats many of the same thoughts in the second passage.

47

Here is a table of the similarities

First passage (T-4.VII.6.4-7)	Second passage (T-6.V.1.5-8)
"And this He does know."	"What God does know"
"His channels are closed"	"His communication channels are not open"
"[your joy] is incomplete. And this He does know."	"so that He cannot...know that His children are wholly joyous."
"The constant going out of His Love"	"Giving His joy is an ongoing process"
"His Love is blocked...when the minds He created do not communicate fully with Him"	"God's extending outward...is blocked when the Sonship does not communicate with Him"

If we look just at what these two passages have in common, we get the following picture: the normal state of Heaven is that God constantly reaches outward through us, His Sons. We are the channels through which He extends His Love. Our job as channels (like any channel) is to be open: to receive His Love into ourselves and let it flow outward through us (to our creations). His Love—both receiving it and extending it—is our joy. Thus, as He gives His Love to us, He is also giving us joy. However, we as channels have closed down. We have stopped receiving and extending His Love, and as a result we are no longer in complete joy. And God *knows* this. He can feel that His outward extension is hitting a blockage. And He knows that His Sons are not wholly joyous.

This is probably as plain of a description of what is going on in Heaven as human language can manage. In fact, both of the above passages are quite clear and straightforward. I find them simply impossible to explain away. And yet these two passages constitute a mere part of the massive and overwhelming evidence that the Course does teach that God is aware of and responds to the separation.

3. There are only a few Course passages that could be taken to support the idea that God is not aware of the separation, but looked at closely, they are fully compatible with the idea that God is aware of the separation.

48

There are passages in the Course that seem to support Wapnick's position that God is not aware of the separation. I will present four passages that seem at first to support his argument. The first two are passages Wapnick cites to illustrate his claim that "the Course states clearly...that God does not even know about" the separation.[32] The second two are passages that I have no record of Wapnick citing as support for this idea (though for all I know he may); they have just always stuck in my mind as being some of the best support in the Course for his position. Between these four passages I think we have the strongest evidence in the Course for the idea that God was not aware of the separation. I'll first try to interpret all of them and then I'll discuss how they relate to this question of God's awareness of the separation.

Here is the first passage:

> Nothing can reach spirit from the ego, and nothing can reach the ego from spirit. Spirit can neither strengthen the ego nor reduce the conflict within it. The ego *is* a contradiction. Your self and God's Self *are* in opposition....They are fundamentally irreconcilable, because spirit cannot perceive and the ego cannot know. They are therefore not in communication and can never be in communication. (T-4.I.2:6-9, 11-12)

The thrust of this passage is that spirit (the Self God created as you) and the ego (the self you made) do not communicate. This passage seems weak to me in terms of what Wapnick wants it to support. To me, all it seems to say is that no communication passes back and forth between spirit and the ego. Yet, in my mind, this does not rule out the idea that spirit is *aware* of the ego. Can't you be aware of something even if you do not communicate with it?

This line of reasoning is strengthened by a passage which comes a chapter later. It refers again to the gulf between the ego and the spirit's knowledge, saying that one "is not understandable to another" (T-5.III.6:1). However, it then goes on to say something not included in the previous passage:

> The Holy Spirit is the Mediator between the interpretations of the ego and the knowledge of the spirit. His ability to deal with symbols enables Him to work with the ego's beliefs in its own language. His ability to look

49

beyond symbols into eternity enables Him to understand the laws of God, for which He speaks. He can therefore perform the function of reinterpreting what the ego makes. (T-5.III.7:1-4)

This passage claims that the apparently unbridgeable gulf between ego and spirit does indeed have a bridge across it: the Holy Spirit. He knows eternity but also can "work with the ego's beliefs in its own language." He spans the distance between the two sides. So the idea that nothing crosses the no man's land between ego and spirit is not entirely accurate, for the Holy Spirit does exactly that.

The second of our four passages is very interesting and seems to offer Wapnick much stronger support. It says, "Spirit in its knowledge is unaware of the ego" (T-4.II.8:6). Let's define the important terms in this sentence. "Spirit" is the "substance" of everything that God created. Spirit, in other words, is what your true Self is made of, just as the ocean is made of water. "Knowledge" is the state of mind that everything in Heaven shares, in which you know reality directly, without mediation. The "ego" is your belief that you are a separate identity. To say that "spirit in its knowledge is unaware of the ego" is to say, I believe, that when you are in Heaven, in the state of the direct knowledge of what is real, you do not know the ego because it is an illusion. This is almost the exact same meaning that is expressed in this line from the Workbook: "To know reality is not to see the ego and its thoughts, its works, its acts…." (W-pII.12.4:1).

The context of the passage is quite significant. I'll quote its fuller version:

> The ego's ceaseless attempts to gain the spirit's acknowledgment and thus establish its own existence are useless. Spirit in its knowledge is unaware of the ego. It does not attack it; it merely cannot conceive of it at all.
>
> (T-4.II.8:5-7)

Notice the very first line. It implies that if spirit would acknowledge the ego, the ego's existence would be established—*the ego would be real*. This is pretty close to Wapnick's principle that, if God were aware of the separation, it would be real (though, as we will see, this passage does not refer to God). If we put the whole passage together, we get something like this: the ego is not a part of what spirit knows, for if spirit acknowledged the ego as real (especially by attacking it), the ego *would* be real.

50

I will be saying more at the end about how this relates to God's awareness of the separation, but I will say a bit now. Everything hinges here on the word "spirit." That word is central to both of these first two passages. What, then, is spirit? I defined "spirit" in my *Course Glossary* in this way: "The substance of which God created His Son, of our true nature." As such, it refers to us, to the Son, not to God. We can see this in the Course's own definition of spirit: "*Spirit* is the Thought of God which He created like Himself. The unified spirit is God's one Son, or Christ." (C-1.1:3-4). According to this passage, spirit = Thought of God = creation of God = Son of God. We can also see it in Wapnick's definition of spirit from his *Glossary-Index*: "the nature of our true reality which, being of God, is changeless and eternal."[33] Spirit, in other words, as used in the Course, does not refer to God, only to His Son. One may think that spirit is a term that encompasses both the Son *and* God, but this is not so. Apart from unusual usages of the word, spirit refers to something *created by* God (I find eight references to spirit being a creation of God), rather than to an attribute *of* God. There are references to *God's Spirit* (as distinct from the Holy Spirit), but these are extremely rare. There are only three, and they are all capitalized. This is not to say that God is something other than spirit, that He is flesh, for instance (the passage I just quoted says that God created spirit "like Himself"). It is just to say that when the Course uses the term, that term refers to our true nature and not to God. This means, of course, that neither of the two above passages speaks about God. Even according to Wapnick's own definition of "spirit" they are not talking about God.

The third passage is found in "The Little Garden" section (T-18.VIII). This section provides an extended metaphor and then translates the metaphor into literal terms. In the metaphor, a sunbeam believes it is separate from the sun and a ripple thinks it is separate from the ocean. In presenting this metaphor, the Course specifically says that the sun and ocean "merely continue, *unaware* that they are feared and hated by a tiny segment of themselves" (T-18.VIII.4:2; my emphasis). The Course then gives us the literal translation of the metaphor, saying, "Like to the sun and ocean your Self continues, *unmindful* that this tiny part [of It] regards itself as you" (T-18.VIII.6:1; my emphasis).

What do we make of this? The section first speaks symbolically of our Self being unaware that we experience ourselves as separate. The

51

section next decodes its symbolic language and says that our Self is merely "unmindful" of our apparently separated condition. "Unmindful" is definitely softer than "unaware." According to the Merriam-Webster Dictionary, "unmindful" means, "not conscientiously aware, attentive, or heedful: inattentive, careless." Based on this definition, we could substitute "unheeding" for "unmindful": "Your Self continues, unheeding of the fact that this tiny part [of It] regards itself as you." This makes the sentence quite similar to this one from the Workbook: "The universe remains unheeding of the laws by which you thought to govern it" (W-pI.136.11:2). The emphasis seems to me to be less on our Self being unaware that we regard ourselves as separate, and more on our Self not taking it seriously.

What do we do, however, with that first sentence, the one about the sun and ocean, which suggests that our Self *is* truly unaware of our separated condition? My thought is that we have to take seriously *both* versions, the "unaware" version and the "unmindful" one (though especially the latter because its sentence is the literal one). In my view, to say that our Self can be described as either "unaware" of our separated state or merely "unmindful" of that state, suggests that the unawareness may not be a *total* unawareness, but perhaps just an *unmindful* unawareness.

One reason to suggest that our Self is not entirely unaware of the separation is that the Course speaks many times of our Self responding to the separation, acting in relation to it. In fact, this very section— "The Little Garden"—refers to this, saying that "your shining Self will lift the tiny aspect that you tried to hide from Heaven straight to Heaven" (11:6). How could our Self lift our separated minds back into Heaven unless It knew that we needed a lift? Unless it knew we experienced ourselves outside of Heaven? There are many passages in the Course that are even more explicit about this. For instance:

> Today we offer thanks that Christ has come to search the world for what belongs to Him. His vision sees no strangers, but beholds His Own and joyously unites with them….And He leads them gently home again, where they belong. Not one does Christ forget.
>
> (W-pI.160.9:1,2,5, 10:1)

As I said earlier, I believe that the Course is consistent, and therefore I assume that there must be a single perspective that can accommodate both of the views we see here—that Christ (our Self) is unaware of our separated condition and that Christ comes to lead us out of our separated condition. Somehow those two points of view must go together, and that is why I choose to stress "unmindful" more than simply "unaware." I'll say more later about how these two views might go together.

Here is the fourth passage:

> The tiny instant you would keep and make eternal, passed away in Heaven too soon for anything to notice it had come. What disappeared too quickly to affect the simple knowledge of the Son of God can hardly still be there, for you to choose to be your teacher. Only in the past,—an ancient past, too short to make a world in answer to creation,—did this world appear to rise. So very long ago, for such a tiny interval of time, that not one note in Heaven's song was missed. (T-26.V.5:1-4)

Let's look closely at this passage. It says the same thing in three different ways:

1. The separation ended "too soon for anything [in Heaven] to notice it had come."

2. The separation ended "too quickly to affect the simple knowledge of the Son of God."

3. The separation was so brief "that not one note in Heaven's song was missed."

My response to this is much like my response to the previous passages from "The Little Garden." I think that all three of the above versions need to be taken seriously and seen as different angles on a single phenomenon. The first one says that the separation was over so quickly that nothing in Heaven noticed it had come. But what is the significance of this? *Why* are we being told this? I think the second and third versions tell us that. Both say the same basic thing: the separation was too brief to compromise the state of Heaven (the Son's knowledge and Heaven's song are both ways of talking about the state of Heaven).

Further, I think we can safely assume that when this passage denies that "anything in Heaven" noticed the separation, it is referring to the *Sonship*, not to *God*. The second version of this statement, after all, specifically identifies "the simple knowledge of the Son of God." In addition, there are two good reasons for thinking that the phrase "anything in Heaven" does *not* include God. First, two paragraphs before this passage we were told that God answered the separation instantly and that is *why* it ended too soon for anything in Heaven to notice it (I'll discuss this more fully later). Obviously, to answer it, God must have noticed it. He therefore cannot be part of the "anything in Heaven" that *didn't* notice it. Second, this may be surprising, but God is not usually talked about in the Course as being *in* Heaven. Rather, Heaven is talked about as a *creation* of God. "Heaven is the home of perfect purity, and God created it for you" (T-22.II.13:6). And as with all of God's creations, "Heaven is…in God" (T-12.VI.7:7). Instead of God being in Heaven, Heaven is in God. This is another reason to think that "anything in Heaven" does not refer to God.

As a result, we can see that all four of our passages are really about the Son, not about God. The first two speak of "spirit"—a term which refers to the Son. The third speaks of our true Self, which of course is God's Son, the Christ. The fourth, as we just saw, appears to refer to the Son as well. Importantly, none of them is about God.

This puts us in a position to see the real import of all four passages. Taken as a whole, they all seem to be emphasizing that the state of being of God's Son is not truly affected by the separation, that the separation does not truly impact the awareness of the Son. The first says that the Son's knowledge does not receive communication from the ego, that the ego cannot reach to it. The second says that the Son's knowledge does not take in the ego as part of what it knows, does not acknowledge it as real. The third says that the Son is unheeding of the illusion of separation. The fourth says that the Son's knowledge has not been affected by the separation, that His song of love has not missed a beat due to the separation. We can boil them all down to the following simple theme: *the separation was too insignificant and unreal to make a dent in the Son's knowledge.*

Does this suggest a total unawareness of the separation on the part of the one Son, the Christ? I don't think so. Given the abundance of passages which speak of Christ responding to the separation, I think we have to posit something like this: The Son's eternal awareness— His permanent knowledge of Heaven—has not been affected at all by the separation. That awareness remains untouched. However, when the separation occurred, what I can only call (for want of a better term) an "additional awareness" arose. This was an awareness of the fleeting event of the separation (fleeting from the standpoint of eternity), an awareness that allowed Him to respond to the separation with help, and an awareness that presumably passes away when the separation itself does (see, for instance, T-17.II.7:3-5). Yet this awareness did not affect or color His eternal awareness in the slightest. In short, Christ's eternal awareness remained the same even while an additional, temporary awareness arose, one that was cognizant of the temporary event of the separation. This may sound deeply paradoxical, and it is, yet Heaven itself is deeply paradoxical, and it seems to me that we are forced into this particular paradox by the fact that the Course expresses two distinct views: Christ is unaware of our separated condition and Christ comes to lead us out of our separated condition.

Now let's get back to our real question: what do these passages imply about *God* being aware of the separation? Specifically, do they rule out the idea that God was aware of the separation?

I just don't see how they could. Despite the fact that there is something strange about allowing four passages to rule out a thousand, the simple fact is that these four passages do not directly conflict with the notion of God being aware of the separation. It is notable that not one of them says that *God* was not aware of the separation; they all speak about the Son. And none of them even comes close to saying that God did not *respond* to the separation. Not one of them says what Wapnick needs it to say.

The Course, in fact, just doesn't seem to see a conflict between the idea that the separation is too unreal to make a dent in the Son's knowledge and the idea that God was aware of (and responded to) the separation. Indeed, in the third passage above, the Course sees the two notions not as conflicting, but as *inseparable*. That passage said that the separation "passed away in Heaven too soon for anything to notice it had come" (T-26.V.5:1). Two paragraphs earlier, the reason that the separation "passed away" so quickly is given:

> God gave His Teacher to replace the one you made [the ego], not to conflict with it. And what He [God] would replace has been replaced....And in that tiny instant time was gone, for that was all it ever was. What God gave answer to is answered and is gone.
>
> (T-26.V.3:1-2, 6-7)

In other words, *because* God answered the separation instantly, it "passed away in Heaven too soon for anything to notice it had come." God's response to the separation is the *cause*; the separation passing away too soon to be noticed is the *effect*. To use this passage to support Wapnick's position, we would have to take the effect and use it to deny its cause: since nothing in Heaven noticed the separation (effect), the idea that God responded to the separation (cause) is impossible. But, of course, this is logically impossible. You can't use the effect to rule out the existence of its cause. That is like the child saying, "My existence is proof that my parents never existed."

Here in this passage we catch a glimpse of the real relationship between these two ideas (that the separation is too unreal to make a dent in the Son's knowledge and that God was aware of and responded to the separation). Rather than being enemies, they are allies. They are two sides of the same coin. Both are needed to make a single, all-important point.

Let's explore the import of the one idea, that the separation is too unreal to make a dent in the Son's knowledge. Why does the Course stress that idea? Isn't it because the apparent effect of the separation was that it *did* make a dent in our state of being? That it shattered our unity with the All and corrupted our nature forever? This idea, then, is meant to counteract our fear that we have truly changed our nature. Its import is that our true being is safe from the apparent effects of the separation.

Now let's explore the import of the other idea, that God was aware of and responded to the separation. Why does the Course stress that idea? Isn't it because we need to be reassured that we have not been left to our own devices, that there is Someone there to help us out of the mess we have made? We are afraid that we have dug ourselves into a hole that we can never get out of. We need to be told that our Father is aware of our predicament and will get us out. The import of this idea, then, is that we have God's help and so we are safe from the apparent effects of the separation.

Thus, both ideas have the same overall significance—that, *even in the face of the separation, we are safe.* And both ideas are needed to make this point fully true. If either of the two ideas is false, then our safety is deeply compromised. We need them both, which is why the Course emphasizes them both.

In conclusion, then, the four passages I explore above do not carry a message that *contradicts* the idea of God's awareness of (and response to) the separation—not one of them says that He was not aware of the separation. Instead, they carry a message that *complements* it.

4. There are no passages in the Course that express the idea that God is not aware of the separation or does not respond to the separation.

If the four passages I just explored are the best evidence in the Course for the idea that God is not aware of the separation (and I think they probably are), and if my interpretation of them is correct, then there simply are no passages in the Course that support this idea. And that, as far as I can tell, is the situation. I have been on the lookout for many years for passages saying that God was not aware of the separation, and I haven't found any. I don't think they are there.

Summary

The preceding four sections were designed to establish four points. To make an absolutely airtight case for those four points, the sections would need to be much longer. But even in this short space I hope they have provided a sense that there is a tremendous amount of support for those four points. And those points, if they are true, wipe away all possibility that the Course teaches that God is not aware of the separation and does not respond to it. For the sake of review, here they are again:

1. The Course puts forward another principle that is directly incompatible with Wapnick's. It is this: if God did not respond to the separation by creating a remaining Communication Link (the Holy Spirit), the separation would have been real.

2. The Course directly states and indirectly implies countless times that God is aware of and responds to the separation.

3. There are only a few Course passages that could be taken to support the idea that God is not aware of the separation, but looked at closely, they are fully compatible with the idea that God is aware of the separation.

4. There are no passages in the Course that express the idea that God is not aware of or does not respond to the separation.

CONCLUSION

In closing I must admit that Wapnick's metaphysical vision strikes me as quite bleak. In this vision, God does not know anything about our condition. As a result, we are adrift on a sea of suffering with no help from above. There is no Holy Spirit Who watches over us and can navigate for us. All we have to guide us home is our own distant memory of being with God. The brothers and sisters who cling to the same life raft we do are just projected images of a vast ego-mind. In essence, we are alone, for our companions on the journey are illusions. And eventually, as we progress on the journey, we will discover that we too are only an illusion.

This vision may inspire others, and for them it has value. But what strikes me about it is the bleakness of it. While viewing things from its standpoint, I feel as if I am simply cut off from reality while in this world of illusion. The various aspects of reality the Course says I have access to while here—the Holy Spirit, my own reality, the reality of my brothers—have all been removed from me. And I am left in a shadowland, a shadow myself, accompanied by shadows, while the only light lies on the other side of an immeasurable gulf.

I am sure that Wapnick is aware that his metaphysical vision may not be the most inspiring picture in the world. His point, though, is that this is what the Course teaches. And since metaphysics is foundational, we must interpret the rest of the Course in light of this metaphysical picture. Under its pressure, we must reinterpret the majority of the Course's words, for on the surface they do not reflect this metaphysics. We conclude, therefore, that those words must be metaphors, and then we go hunting for a presumed hidden meaning within them that *does* reflect the metaphysics.

On the face of it, all of that may sound reasonable. Yet here is the problem: at crucial points, Wapnick's metaphysics is *not* what the Course teaches. Key elements within his metaphysical vision are not grounded in the Course and even go against the Course. Establishing that has been the purpose of this essay. There are many points in his metaphysical vision that do reflect what the Course teaches (for instance, that Heaven is the only reality, that the universe is the product of the thought of separation, and that the world of time and space is an illusory outpicturing of our attack on God), yet his vision is profoundly skewed by a single questionable principle: if God were aware of and responded to the separation, it would be real.

This principle, in my opinion, is the real power in Wapnick's metaphysics; it is the guiding force. The Course's passages about metaphysics get fed through its filter, thus altering the meaning of many statements and simply discarding other ones. The result is the bleak metaphysical vision we have seen, a metaphysics that I believe is as much a product of Wapnick's principle as it is of the Course's teaching. Then, using this reshaped metaphysics, Wapnick is forced to reinterpret the rest of the Course in *its* light, which results in a significant reshaping of the entire Course.

All of this because of one foundational principle: if God were aware of and responded to the separation, it would be real. Given the power it carries, we would naturally assume that this principle is extremely well attested in the Course. Yet, as we saw, it is never mentioned, not once, while the idea that God is aware of and responds to the separation is mentioned hundreds of times. Furthermore, as we also saw, this principle doesn't *save* the separation from being real, but actually guarantees that it *would* be real. For if God was not aware of the separation, He could not create the Holy Spirit, and the creation of the Holy Spirit is what keeps the separation from being real. The end result is that the entire Course is skewed under the weight of a principle that *the Course doesn't teach*. The entire Course is reshaped in order to *save* the separation from being real, but, ironically, this reshaping *makes* it real.

As I have said, there are many things in Wapnick's version of Course metaphysics that I would affirm. Yet there are many elements that are simply not in the Course and that run contrary to the Course. Thus, when Wapnick comes to us and says that, because of the metaphysics, we have to treat most of the Course as metaphor that really means something else, we are justified in politely declining.

Notes

[1] *The Most Commonly Asked Questions about 'A Course in Miracles'* (co-written with Gloria Wapnick), p. 85.

[2] *The Message of 'A Course in Miracles,' Volume One: All Are Called*, p. 12.

[3] *Commonly Asked Question*, p. 13.

[4] *All Are Called*, p. 314.

[5] *Commonly Asked Questions*, p. 101.

[6] *Ibid.*, p. 90.

7 *Ibid.*, p. 4.

8 *Ibid.*, p. 101.

9 *All Are Called*, p. 33.

10 *Ibid.*, p. 33.

11 *The Message of 'A Course in Miracles,' Volume Two: Few Choose to Listen,* p. 88.

12 *Ibid.*, p. 124.

13 *Ibid.*, p. 108.

14 *Few Choose to Listen*, p. 108.

15 *All Are Called,* p. 25.

16 *Ibid.*, p. 67.

17 *Ibid.*, p. 66.

18 *Few Choose to Listen*, p. 95.

19 *All Are Called*, p. 101.

20 *Few Choose to Listen*, p. 114.

21 *All Are Called*, p. 251.

22 *Commonly Asked Question*, p. 20.

23 *Ibid.*, p. 20.

24 *Few Choose to Listen.*, p. 33.

25 *Commonly Asked Questions*, p. 8-79.

26 *All Are Called*, p. 102.

27 *Ibid.*, p. 84.

28 *Commonly Asked Questions*, p. 101.

29 *Ibid.*, p. 101.

30 I realize that this passage has not stated that the Holy Spirit was created by God, yet I feel safe in inserting this here, since the Course's only (and repeated) account of the origin of the Holy Spirit is that He was created by God. Further, this passage does talk about the Holy Spirit as a real Someone with Whom we have a real relationship. And if the Holy Spirit really is that, where else could He have come from but God's creation?

31 As I said in the previous note, this notion of God creating the Holy Spirit isn't alluded to in this passage, but I think it is fair to bring in here because a) it is something the Course mentions so frequently and b) it is the Course's only account of the Holy Spirit's origin.

32 *All Are Called*, p. 35.

33 *Glossary-Index for 'A Course in Miracles,'* 4th ed., p. 198.

How Metaphoric Is the Language of the Course?

by Robert Perry

Whenever I am asked how the Circle's views differ from those of Ken Wapnick, I always say the same thing: all of our differences come down to two very different ways of interpreting the Course. Wapnick interprets the Course more metaphorically and we interpret it more literally. That answer is probably not very satisfying; it doesn't say anything about how we see God or Jesus or forgiveness. In the end, however, it says *everything* about how we see those issues, and all the other issues in the Course as well.

A Course in Miracles, on the level of form, is just a very long string of words. It is just markings on paper. How one interprets those markings makes all the difference. For example, the words "Holy Spirit" could mean all sorts of things. The Circle sees those words as signifying an actual (though unbounded) Person, Who was created by God in response to the separation, and Who actively and lovingly works in our minds and in our lives to guide us home. Wapnick sees those words as signifying "an illusion,"[1] "a symbol,"[2] that was not created by God, but is merely a "projected split-off part of our self."[3] This symbol "does not really do anything,"[4] either in our minds or in our lives, for symbols do not act; only real beings do. Obviously, one's whole orientation toward the Holy Spirit would be dramatically different depending on which one of these interpretations one adopted.

How could the same term in the same book be interpreted in two such widely divergent ways? The answer, in this case, is the distinction between literal and metaphoric. Wapnick concedes that the Course, on the level of language, says the things that we at the Circle believe it says (he does not name the Circle; instead, he addresses these ideas as views commonly held by students). He just says that those statements in the Course should not be read literally.

61

This issue is pivotal in Wapnick's view. He says that not understanding the metaphoric nature of the Course's language is "perhaps the greatest source of confusion to students of *A Course in Miracles*."[5] This confusion has dramatic consequences. He says that "the misunderstandings of its students have led to conclusions, both theoretical and practical, directly opposite to what *A Course in Miracles* actually teaches,"[6] "misinterpretations that will seriously impede their progress on the journey Home,"[7] that "will ensure that students of *A Course in Miracles* never move beyond the lower rungs of the ladder."[8] Finally, "For all intents and purposes, these students are then pursuing a *different* spiritual path from *A Course in Miracles*."[9]

In this essay I will explore this issue of literal versus metaphoric in the Course. I will first present the Circle's approach to interpreting the language of the Course. I will then present my understanding of Wapnick's approach to the Course's language and will also give my reasons for believing it does not work. I will spend the bulk of my time on Wapnick's approach simply because the Circle approaches the Course's language in a more conventional way, in a way more similar to how people would normally approach the issue of metaphor. Along the way, I will identify how these different approaches yield different visions of *A Course in Miracles*.

THE CIRCLE'S APPROACH TO THE LANGUAGE OF THE COURSE

The Circle's approach to interpreting the Course is all about trying to discover what the author of the Course really meant when he said the things he did. In seeking this, we pay very careful attention to the context in which a statement occurs. Over time we have realized that we treat this context as a series of four concentric circles, going from the narrowest and most immediate to the broadest and most distant. I'll begin with the inner circle and move toward the outer.

1. The surrounding sentences and paragraphs

The most important context for a particular statement in the Course consists of the sentences and paragraphs right around it. These will usually provide dozens of clues—in the form of words and ideas that appear in the statement in question—as to how that statement should be interpreted. As we will see later, this is what people usually mean by the word "context."

2. Related discussion in surrounding pages

Most statements in the Course, especially the Text, will be part of one or more threads of discussion that weave in and out of perhaps several sections before fading out. For instance, the theme of "temptation" weaves in and out of the final sections of the Text, appearing in six of the final twelve sections. To fully understand any of the references to temptation in those sections, one should read them in light of the entire thread.

3. Related discussions elsewhere in the Course

There will often be strikingly similar discussions of a particular idea separated by hundreds of pages. For instance, the idea that healing must stand aside when the patient would be too frightened by it is discussed both early in the Text (T-2.IV.4-5) and in the Manual (M-6.1-2). To fully understand each passage, one should read it with the help of the other.

4. The Course's overall teaching

It is natural and helpful to bring into our interpretation of each statement in the Course our understanding of the Course's overall teaching. For instance, when you read "forgiveness" in the Course, you should read that word as the Course defines it (except where the Course is talking about conventional forgiveness). This macro-context, however, should be used cautiously. For our understanding of the Course's overall teaching will always be imperfect. The danger is that we might compromise the meaning of a given passage by assuming that "it has to mean *this*" since "I know that the Course teaches *this*." I see that happen all the time with Course students.

In the Circle's interpretive approach, these four contexts are all important, but they diminish in authority as you go down the list. The first is the most authoritative and the fourth is the least. In my experience, however, Course students generally turn that upside-down. The fourth context becomes virtually the only context, which means that students often just project onto each passage what they assume it *has* to mean in light of what they *think* the Course teaches. When I teach I will often quiz the class about what a particular passage means. One of the most difficult things is to teach students not to pick their head up from the book. If they do, it means they are ignoring the immediate context and asking themselves "What must this mean given what I know about the Course?" Instead I encourage them to keep their head down, looking for clues *on the page.*

What is the Circle's approach to the issue of literal versus metaphoric language in the Course? Frankly, I think we approach it much like a conventional reader would. People are generally quite able to discern a speaker or writer's intent in this regard. We all just do it naturally. In the last forty years, philosophers of language have tried and tried to understand *how* we do it, but no one questions the fact that we *do* do it. In *Philosophical Perspectives on Metaphor*, Mark Johnson writes:

> But although native speakers can easily identify figurative [metaphoric] utterances and understand them, explaining how this is possible has proved to be one of the more intractable problems of metaphor.[10]

I think the first part is true with the Course—that we "easily identify figurative utterances." We all know that when we read about God's Arms or about giving our brother the gift of lilies that the Course is speaking metaphorically. I doubt there has been a single Course student who went out and bought actual lilies for someone in the thought that the Course was literally requesting this. I doubt that any student has felt accused by the Course of physically nailing his brother to a cross. As native speakers of English we quite readily understand that the Arms and lilies and crosses are symbolic images. We notice the metaphor naturally. There are places in the Course where it requires more detective work, but by and large it is an effortless process.

Except when we come upon clearly metaphoric images, we at the Circle tend to take the Course at its word. We believe this is appropriate given how it claims it is written. The Course seems to place a great value on meaning what it says. We can see this value in the quotes below. Notice that the first two contain subtle but logical implications: the fact that it means what it says makes the Course more trustable (because it's not misdirecting us) and more practical.

You may believe from time to time that I am misdirecting

you. I have made every effort to use words that are almost impossible to distort, but it is always possible to twist symbols around if you wish. (T-3.I.3:10-11)

You have surely begun to realize that this is a very practical course, and one that means exactly what it says. (T-8.IX.8:1)

This course is perfectly clear. (T-11.VI.3:1)

Like the text for which this workbook was written, the ideas used for the exercises are very simple, very clear and totally unambiguous. (W-pI.39.1:2)

Along the same lines, the Course seems to intentionally avoid expressing itself in the highly symbolic way the Bible does. This shows up in at least three instances in which the Course is discussing a biblical symbol (the three symbols are the lamb of God, eating the forbidden fruit, and the new Heaven and new earth). In these cases, it mentions that the symbol either has been largely misinterpreted (T-3.I.5:2), that "the symbolism here has been given many interpretations" (T-3.VII.3:9), or that the symbol should not be taken literally (T-11.VII.1:4). These comments clearly signal a reticence about symbolism on the Course's part. The reason for this reticence is stated openly when the Course points out that symbolism is "difficult to understand, because symbolism is open to different interpretations" (T-5.I.4:5). The Course doesn't want to get too symbolic—too metaphoric—because its priority is on being "perfectly clear."

This is not to say that the Course doesn't use metaphors; the Course is full of them. It has a penchant for vivid imagery. There are hundreds of images in the Course. Many of these images repeat over and over,[11] carrying roughly the same meaning each time they do. They are, in a sense, part of the Course's vocabulary. However, the Course uses its metaphors in a very strict and rigorous way, in a way that does not leave them "open to different interpretations." Its images are not open-ended, meant to vaguely suggest an inexhaustible variety of potential meanings. Rather, each one is meant to point to a single, clear meaning. That meaning may be very rich and emotionally evocative, yet it is still single.

The Course accomplishes this by surrounding its images with literal teaching. Each vivid image is like a thin slice of metaphor sandwiched

65

between thick rolls of straight teaching. This makes it abundantly clear what the metaphor is intended to mean. For example,

> Brother, you need forgiveness of your brother [the first edition of the Course read "of each other"], for you will share in madness or in Heaven together. And you and he will raise your eyes in faith together, or not at all....Beside you is one who offers you **the chalice of Atonement**, for the Holy Spirit is in him. Would you hold his sins against him, or accept his gift to you? Is this giver of salvation your friend or enemy? Choose which he is, remembering that you will receive of him according to your choice. He has in him the power to forgive your sin, as you for him.   (T-19.IV(D).12:7-13:5, emphasis mine)

I have put in bold the phrase "the chalice of Atonement" because that is the metaphor I want to focus on. It is a vivid image that is obviously a reference to the chalice used at the Last Supper. By itself this chalice could mean anything—it could even mean what it means in a traditional Christian context—but it is not by itself. It is surrounded by straightforward teaching that guides how we should interpret it. The key is that this chalice is offered to us by our brother, and there are several passages right around the chalice reference which clarify just what our brother is offering us. He offers us "forgiveness" ("you need forgiveness of each other"). He gives us salvation ("Is this giver of salvation your friend or enemy?"). And he has "the power to forgive your sin." Clearly, our brother physically handing us the chalice is a metaphor for our brother giving us the saving gift of forgiveness.

In keeping with this desire for symbols that point to a single, clear meaning, the Course will often decode its longer metaphors for us. Rather than giving us the metaphor and leaving us to figure out that it was a metaphor and what it meant, the Course will often explain its meaning in plain, literal language. For instance, in "The Two Worlds" (T-18.IX) there is an extended metaphor involving a cloudbank. The metaphor points out things we all know about clouds: how insubstantial they are, how objects can pass easily through them, and how children make believe that they see recognizable shapes in them. After presenting this metaphor, the Course unlocks it for us, saying:

> So should it be with the dark clouds of guilt, no more impenetrable and no more substantial. You will not bruise

yourself against them in traveling through. (T-18.IX.8:1-2)

In other words, just as physical clouds are insubstantial and easily passed through (metaphor), "so should it be with the dark clouds of guilt" (metaphor decoded). This same pattern can be observed in "The Forgotten Song" (T-21.I), which talks about the blind. The section says that because the blind "must infer what could be seen from evidence forever indirect...they stumble and fall because of what they did not recognize, or walk unharmed through open doorways that they thought were closed" (T-21.I.1:2). It then openly decodes the metaphor for us:

> And so it is with you. You do not see. Your cues for inference are wrong, and so you stumble and fall down upon the stones you did not recognize, but fail to be aware you can go through the doors you thought were closed, but which stand open before unseeing eyes. (T-21.I.1:3-5)

Because of this value on plain, straightforward language, the Course often reminds us to take what it says *literally*. The words "literal" or "literally" occur over forty times in the Course. If you scroll through the references you can discern a motive behind their use. Jesus is expressing radical, extreme ideas and he doesn't want us to discount them as mere metaphor or hyperbole. Here are a few examples, in which I have italicized the words "literal" or "literally":

> It is hard to recognize that thought and belief combine into a power surge that can *literally* move mountains.
>
> (T-2.VI. 9:8)

> When I said "I am with you always," I meant it *literally*. I am not absent to anyone in any situation. (T-7.III.1:7-8)

> You have learning handicaps in a very *literal* sense.
>
> (T-12.V.5:1)

In these examples we can easily guess the thoughts the author is trying to guard against. He expects that we might unconsciously take the edge off of his words by thinking: "Certainly he can't mean that our thoughts can move actual mountains." "Surely he wasn't saying that he is with everyone all the time." "Obviously he doesn't mean that I really am mentally handicapped." In each case he wants us to know: "That is *exactly* what I mean." After all, this is a course "that means exactly what it says," and that is how we at the Circle read it.

WAPNICK'S ARGUMENT #1

Wapnick's approach, of course, is quite different than ours. He emphatically stresses that this is "a simple, clear, and direct course,"[12] but then he says that the Course is either mostly or entirely metaphoric, and the act of interpreting it is analogous to Freudian dream interpretation in which you reach to "the latent content…that lay beyond the dream's manifest symbolism,"[13] a process in which two different analysts can "ascribe totally different meaning to what the dream is saying."[14] In my mind, you can't have it both ways. *Either* the Course is perfectly clear *or* it is like a Freudian dream, in which the real meaning is hidden deep within deceptive symbols that can be variably interpreted. Wapnick's emphasis seems clearly to be on the second side—that the Course is highly metaphoric—and thus his views on that are what we will examine.

It seems to me that Wapnick presents at least two distinct arguments about the Course's metaphoric language, so I will address them separately, starting with the one he appears to stress the most. This first view (what I am calling "argument #1" here) comes down to a simple idea: Reality is beyond words, it cannot be literally described, and therefore the Course has no choice but to speak about it metaphorically. "Truth…cannot really be expressed in words, but only pointed to."[15] Words, as the old Buddhist saying goes, are merely fingers pointing at the moon. They are, at best, just distant symbols, just metaphors, directing our minds toward a reality where words cannot go.

Therefore, because of "the inherent limitation of language in not being able to express truth directly,"[16] the Course has to speak *indirectly*, symbolically, metaphorically. Wapnick says, "Jesus' actual words in *A Course in Miracles* cannot be taken literally."[17] "His words by their very nature will be inconsistent and *not* the literal truth."[18] As one can see from these quotes, this is not a *stylistic choice* on the part of the Course. It is an inevitable product of the "very nature" of words, of "the inherent limitation of language."

Perhaps an example is in order. In speaking about Heaven, the Course talks about God *and* Christ *and* the Holy Spirit. It uses these three different terms, which implies that there are three different beings occupying Heaven. This is a result of the nature of language, which is composed of a multiplicity of distinct words. As soon as you use language to describe Heaven, then, your words imply that Heaven is composed of a multiplicity of distinct *beings*. Wapnick remarks on this:

> We have already discussed that the language of *A Course in Miracles*—which is certainly dualistic and seems to reflect the existence of a differentiated Heaven where the three aspects of the Trinity are clearly separate from each other—is merely metaphoric.[19]

At first this principle seems rather innocent. After all, the Course repeatedly points out—just as Wapnick says it does[20]—that reality cannot really be described in words. And what Course student could argue with the idea that God and Christ and the Holy Spirit are not really three separate, distinct beings? Yet in the end, this principle—that Jesus' words by their very nature cannot be taken literally—has profound and sweeping consequences.

For instance, the Course's language says that God is aware that His Sons fell asleep and that He responded by creating the Holy Spirit in order to wake them up. It says that God has a plan for His Sons' awakening and (through the Holy Spirit) hears their prayers and always answers. Wapnick admits that the Course's words say all these things; that is not in question. However, he sees all of this talk as metaphoric. In his view, "God does not even know about the separation...and thus does not and cannot respond to it."[21] He therefore does *not* create the Holy Spirit, "does not truly 'give' an Answer—the Holy Spirit—to the birth of the thought of separation."[22] Further, He *cannot* design a plan for awakening,[23] and quite plainly "does not hear prayers."[24] Wapnick acknowledges that the Course speaks differently than he does in such cases, but says,

> These are all metaphoric expressions that Jesus (*himself a symbol*) uses in *A Course in Miracles* to express the Love of God that cannot be expressed except through such literary and quite obvious anthropomorphic devices.[25]

Wapnick is thus saying that the Course *has* to talk the way it does. It has to use these "metaphoric expressions," because "the Love of God...cannot be expressed *except* through such literary...devices" (italics mine). In other words: yes, the Course says things that we shouldn't take literally. It says, for instance, that God created a real Holy Spirit, even though He did no such thing (in Wapnick's view).

Yet, Wapnick explains, the Course *has* to speak metaphorically, because it is talking about a reality that words simply cannot literally describe.

As reasonable as this perspective may sound, it has, I believe, a fatal flaw: After explaining that the Course cannot say what it means in words (because of their inherent limitations), Wapnick, as we saw above, explains what the Course *really* means—*in words*. He is constantly translating the Course's so-called metaphors into a more literal set of words. For example, Wapnick quotes a series of passages from the Course about the Holy Spirit, and then says:

> On a more sophisticated level [than the passages he just quoted], however, and one consistent with the inherent non-dualistic thought system of *A Course in Miracles*, we can better understand the Holy Spirit to be the memory of God's perfect Love that "came" with the Son when he fell asleep. In this sense then the Holy Spirit is not really a Person Who was specifically and intentionally created by God, but…a distant memory of our Source.[26]

Here we see exactly what I am talking about. Wapnick is explaining in words the real meaning of the Course's "metaphorical" speech about the Holy Spirit, the very meaning that Wapnick claimed could *not* be expressed in words. In this light, his actual argument runs something like this:

> We cannot take the Course literally; there is a great distance between what the words say and what they really mean. This is because they point to a truth that is beyond all words. It is thus impossible for the Course to say in words what it really means because *no one* could say it in words. I will now tell you what it really means—in words.

For Wapnick to explain in words what he said the Course *couldn't* explain in words effectively nullifies his own argument. It demonstrates that the Course *could have just told us what it really meant*. It was not forced by the "inherent limitation of language" to use the misleading metaphors it (supposedly) did. It *could* have spoken more plainly. We know this with certainty, because Wapnick himself speaks more plainly. He has no problem in explaining what he claims is the Course's actual meaning in plainer, clearer, more straightforward language.

Let me explain this from another angle. I think that Wapnick is talking about two different senses of the word "metaphor" without delineating between them:

1. The first kind of metaphor speaks of things indirectly because those things simply cannot be described in words; they are beyond words. This is *not* the normal use of the word "metaphor." Normally, *metaphoric* language is contrasted with *literal* language, but in this definition, there is no such thing as literal language; all language is metaphor. This, then, is a different sense of the word "metaphor," but as long as its difference is carefully clarified, I have no problem with this definition.

2. The second kind of metaphor speaks indirectly about things that could be described directly, literally, but instead metaphor is used. This, of course, is the normal use of "metaphor." When we say that a statement is metaphoric, we assume that the meaning of that statement could have been put more or less literally (though perhaps lacking the same impact, richness and nuance).

These two definitions are quite different. For example, let's take two statements and see how they fare under each definition. The first statement is "God is formless, timeless spirit." This sounds quite literal, and under the second definition it *would* be considered literal. It would *not* be classed as a metaphor. However, under the first definition it *would* be a metaphor, because in that definition *anything* you say in words about God is metaphoric, because God is beyond words.

The second statement is "God's Arms are open wide to embrace you." This statement is metaphoric under both definitions, but for different reasons. It is a metaphor under the first definition simply because it uses words. Under that definition, anything expressed in words—no matter how literal it sounds to our ears—is a metaphor because words themselves are inherently metaphoric. It is a metaphor under the second definition because it uses words that literally denote physical objects ("Arms") and physical actions ("embrace") to speak about a nonphysical God.

Wapnick needs both definitions to make his argument appear to work. What he is really interested in proving is that the Course's language is metaphoric in the usual sense—metaphor #2. He wants to establish that the Course speaks in highly figurative and symbolic language, language for which he can give us a literal translation. How does he prove this? By designing a *new* definition of metaphor—metaphor #1—in which *all* language is metaphor; there is no literal. This definition automatically establishes that all of the Course's language is metaphoric. But it only establishes that the Course's language is metaphoric in its unconventional sense of the word. It does *not* prove that the Course's language is metaphoric in the usual sense (metaphor #2). Wapnick, however, seems to believe that it does. He seems to think that by establishing that all of the Course's language is metaphor #1 he has *also* established that all of it is metaphor #2. But this is not the case.

To make this completely clear, let me give an analogy. Let's say I claim that, in order to travel into town (I live a few miles out), I have to use a horse. This sounds strange. Why would I have to use a horse? But then I explain that, in my definition of "horse," *any* vehicle is called a horse. Cars and bicycles are all "horses." So here is my argument: Since all vehicles are horses (my special meaning of "horse"), to go into town I *have* to ride a horse. I *have* to ride a large, four-hooved, herbivorous mammal." You would probably object, saying that somewhere in there I switched my definition of "horse" from my *special* meaning to the *usual* meaning. You would point out that my argument only proves that I have to use a horse in *my* unconventional sense of the word. It does not prove that I have to use what *the rest of us* call a horse. In the same way, Wapnick's argument only proves that the Course's language is metaphoric in his unconventional sense of the word. It does not prove that all of the Course's language is metaphoric in the *usual* sense of the word.

Why is all this so important? Because Wapnick's teachings, to a large degree, rest on this argument about metaphor. Much of the Course's language says things that appear to be in direct contradiction to Wapnick's teachings. If that language means what it seems to mean, many of his teachings are automatically invalidated. He therefore needs a reason why that language means something else. Why does the Course say so many things it (in Wapnick's view) doesn't really mean? Why does it speak in such a misleading way? His answer is that it has no choice. The Course could not have simply said what it really meant because what it is talking about cannot be put in words. The Course therefore must use words that only indirectly point at what they refer to. It has to use highly metaphoric, misleading words. Yet Wapnick disproves his own argument by easily and constantly using words that more directly, more literally express what the Course "really" means. This shows that the Course could have just come out and said what it meant. It wasn't forced to use highly figurative language. It could have spoken more plainly. And we at the Circle believe that *that is exactly what it did*.

Even though at times Wapnick asks the reader not to treat his own words as literal, this does not rescue his argument, for his words are clearly *more* literal than the Course's. This still means that the Course could easily have expressed itself *more* literally. It was not forced to use misleading metaphors by the inherent limitation of language, for those same limits do not keep Wapnick from expressing the same thing far more literally.

Wapnick's first argument just does not work. This leaves him with no grounds for saying that the Course's language doesn't mean what it seems to mean—at least no grounds under this argument. However, as I said, Wapnick has another argument about the Course's metaphoric language.

WAPNICK'S ARGUMENT #2

Wapnick advances a second argument about metaphor, one which, it seems to me, receives less attention, and is not identified as a different argument. However, it *is* a different argument, so different, in fact, that it seems to be completely incompatible with the first:

> Only those statements that reflect the unified reality of Heaven and God and Christ should be understood as true and *should* be taken literally. To make the point one more time, Jesus' teachings come largely within a dualistic framework, since on the lower rungs of the ladder— where almost all of the Sonship typically are found—that framework is all that can be understood. However, Jesus also holds out to his students where the ladder is leading. And it is the non-dualistic statements, interspersed through the three books, that point the way we are to go when we are ready.[27]

In this new argument, the Course is written on two levels, which Wapnick labels Level One and Level Two:

Level One. A minority of the Course's language—"interspersed through the three books"—describes the unified, non-dual reality of Heaven. This language "*should* be taken literally." It is designed for the relatively few who are more advanced—"those on the higher reaches of the ladder"[28]—and who can therefore handle the straight stuff.

Level Two. Most of the Course's language is nonliteral, metaphoric: "Jesus' teachings come *largely* within a dualistic framework" (italics mine). This language is designed to speak to students "on the lower rungs of the ladder." These students, whom Wapnick sees as the definite majority, would be too frightened by the literal truth:

> You do not tell little children…that they do not have to be afraid since Daddy does not even know that they exist….Rather, you comfort them by letting them know that Daddy is not upset with them, will not punish them, and moreover, that he weeps over his loss and yearns for the children's return.[29]

In short, to the more advanced students, Jesus gives the straight stuff. To the beginning students, however, he gives a watered-down version that comforts them rather than scares them, as the real truth surely would.

It is important to note that these two levels, at least on their surface, say extremely different things. Wapnick is clear, in fact, that they often say *opposite* things: "Taking the words of *A Course in Miracles* literally [can have] the result…that conclusions are drawn that are the exact opposite of what Jesus is actually teaching in his Course."[30] Therefore, in deciding what the Level Two passages really mean, we must use the "interspersed" Level One statements as our decoder. We must reinterpret the vast bulk of the Course's language in light of those comparatively few literal statements. I'll discuss this element later.

As you can see, this is a very different argument from the first one. There, the Course in principle could *not* speak literally, due to the limited nature of words. Here, the Course is fully *able* to speak literally and in fact does so on occasion. When it does not speak literally, this is not an unavoidable result of the limitation of words, but a strategy it voluntarily chooses in order to reach students who can't handle the straight stuff.

Notice that this second argument contradicts the first. The first one says, "Jesus' actual words in *A Course in Miracles* cannot be taken literally."[31] The second one says, "Only those statements that reflect the unified reality of Heaven and God and Christ should be understood as true and *should* be taken literally."[32] In the first, Jesus does not speak literally because he *cannot*, due to "the inherent limitation of language."[33] In the second, Jesus *can* speak literally, but usually chooses not to because his younger students cannot handle the literal truth. The Course's words should *never* be taken literally; the Course's words should *sometimes* be taken literally. Jesus *cannot* speak literally; Jesus *generally chooses* not to speak literally. The two arguments are so directly contradictory that it seems that if one is true the other is false. It looks as if Wapnick's own arguments cancel each other out, so that neither one is left. Strangely, he never tries to explain the conflict between the two arguments. He does not even appear to notice it, even though statements of the two occur very close together, so that on one page he talks about when "Jesus' words...*should* be taken literally,"[34] and on the very next page he refers to his idea that they should never be taken literally, talking about "the inherent limitation of language in not being able to express truth directly [literally]."[35]

That being said, let me try to evaluate Wapnick's second argument on its own merits. That argument, put simply, is: the Course's occasional non-dualistic statements are literal and the rest of the Course is metaphoric. I will focus on six problems I see with this.

First problem: The key "denials of duality" cannot be found in the Course.

I have a problem with this whole two-level theory of the Course's language. I do think the Course at times speaks more from the absolute perspective of Heaven and at times speaks more from the perspective of earth. That would be hard to deny. What I do not see is the *conflict* between these two levels that Wapnick sees. In his view, the two levels are so far apart, in such extreme tension, that, in order to relieve this tension, we are forced to radically reinterpret the second level in light of the first. It is this distance, this extreme tension between the two levels that I do not see in the Course.

What Wapnick needs is evidence that the Course itself sees the same tension that he does. He needs places where the Course's

75

supposed literal language refutes an idea expressed by its supposed metaphoric language, places where the Course openly denies that one of its apparent "dualistic" teachings is literally true. I will call such hypothetical passages "denials of duality." Examples of these denials of duality would be the Course saying such things as: God does not respond to the separation, God did not create the Holy Spirit, the Holy Spirit is just a memory of God's Love, the Holy Spirit is only an illusion Who cannot work in this world, etc.

Wapnick certainly seems to be saying that these denials of duality actually appear in the Course—in those interspersed literal passages. For instance, he says, "Teaching those on the higher reaches of the ladder, Jesus states that God is not involved in the illusory dualistic world of specifics at all."[36] This suggests that there are actual places in the Course where Jesus explains that God is not involved in the world in any way, which is a cornerstone of Wapnick's teaching.

The problem is that these denials of duality cannot be found in the Course, and this is an extremely significant fact. There are places where the Course speaks, to use Wapnick's language, non-dualistically. In these places it says that reality is formless and changeless and that the world does not exist. I totally agree with that. What cannot be found are the denials of duality, where the Course states that God was *not* aware of His Son falling asleep, that He did *not* respond to the separation by creating the Holy Spirit, that the Holy Spirit is *not* a Person but only a projection of a split-off part of our mind, that He is *not* real but just a symbol, an illusion. These are all important teachings of Wapnick that are found nowhere in the Course. In fact, there is a long list of key Wapnick teachings that simply *cannot be found anywhere in the Course.*

Wapnick does not act as if this is the case. He will offer certain passages as examples of what I am calling denials of duality. But in each case, the passage, in my opinion, fails to be what Wapnick claims. As an example of this, I will explore Wapnick's support for the idea that the Holy Spirit is an illusion. (Later on, I will look at his support for the idea that God does not hear our prayers, and in the essay on metaphysics I examine his support for the idea that God is not aware of the separation. In each case, we will see the same thing.)

According to Wapnick, the section on the Holy Spirit in the Clarification of Terms denies that the Holy Spirit is real. He says that this section clearly teaches that the Holy Spirit is "a symbol and not reality."[37] Here is what he quotes:

> His [the Holy Spirit's] is the Voice for God, and has therefore taken form. This form is not His reality, which God alone knows along with Christ....And then the Voice is gone, no longer to take form, but to return to the eternal formlessness of God. (C-6.1:4-5, 5:8)

At first glance, these few sentences look like they might be exactly what Wapnick is saying: a denial of the Holy Spirit's reality. Even a cursory reading, however, reveals a reference to "His *reality*, which God alone knows"—a serious problem for Wapnick's point of view. In fact, such problematic references are found all over this section, which, it turns out, affirms all those "dualistic" things which Wapnick says are the stuff of metaphor. The section teaches that the Holy Spirit is "a creation of the One Creator, creating with Him" (C-6.1:2). Created by God and creating in turn—in the Course's system you don't get any more real than that. Hence, according to this section, the Holy Spirit is a real Being. The rest of the section talks about the Holy Spirit intentionally acting in the dream: "giving," "bringing," "establishing," and "showing" (2:1—to give just a few examples).

What, however, do we make of the section's clear statement that the Holy Spirit has a *real* side and an *illusory* side, a side that is eternal and a side that will pass away? This can be read in different ways. Wapnick reads it in light of what I call his metaphysical context, which includes his theory that the Holy Spirit is only a symbol, a projection of our memory of God's Love. Not only does this approach seem to simply discard the references to the Holy Spirit's real, eternal side, it also ignores what should really guide our interpretation: *the immediate context*. The section itself gives us direct indications of how to read its remarks about the Holy Spirit's two sides:

> In order to fulfill this special function the Holy Spirit has assumed a dual function. He knows because He is part of God; He perceives because He was sent to save humanity.
> (3:2-3)

This passage talks about both of those sides of the Holy Spirit and puts them in perspective. It portrays the Holy Spirit as a real Being Who has entered into the illusory realm of perception in order to fulfill a high purpose. In light of this passage, we can see how to view those other passages about the Holy Spirit's two sides: He is a *real, eternal*

Person Who has taken on an *illusory, temporary guise* in order to do His work in an illusory world. This guise is almost like a mask He wears over His true "face" (His eternal reality), a mask that allows Him to be seen and understood in a world where everyone wears masks. This interpretation is the very view of the Holy Spirit that Wapnick is arguing against, yet this interpretation is what the immediate context dictates. What's more, it is the interpretation that Wapnick himself used to teach. In *The Fifty Miracle Principles of 'A Course in Miracles,'* he said, "The idea is that the Holy Spirit has a foot in reality, in Heaven, and He has a foot in the dream….He's within the dream, but yet He's not part of the dream….He's like a go-between, an intermediary."[38] This is the exact position Wapnick argues against now. This doesn't necessarily mean that he is wrong now, it just means that this interpretation of this passage is such a natural one that even someone who now argues against it used to believe in it.

What we find with this passage is an example of what I find repeatedly: Wapnick's examples of denials of duality in the Course evaporate under close scrutiny. The Course does at times clarify that its language on a particular topic does not imply what it seems to. It says that even though its language about the ego suggests that the ego is an independent being, it is really just a belief (T-4.VI.1:3-7). It says that we should not take the language about increase in Heaven to imply real change (T-7.I.7:10) or simple addition (W-pI.105.4:4-5). It says that we should not take the language about extension in Heaven to imply an actual outward motion (T-18.VI.8:4-8). But it never says so many of the key things that Wapnick needs it to say, many of which are cornerstones of Wapnick's teaching. It never says, for instance, "We have spoken about the Holy Spirit as an actual Person, but do not take that language literally. He is really just your own memory of God's Love." It never says that, not once, even though it would have been very easy to do. And that is just one example of so many key Wapnick teachings the Course never states. If the Course never states them, how can they be pillars of the Course's teaching?

I agree that the Course at times clarifies that certain implications in its language should not be taken literally. I agree that the Course speaks at times more literally and at times more metaphorically. What I do not see in the Course are the key denials of duality that Wapnick needs. What I do not see is the evidence that the Course itself sees an extreme tension between two levels of language within it, a tension so great that we are forced to radically reinterpret one level—which makes up most of the language of the Course—to make it fit the other.

Second problem: The Course's so-called literal passages are seamlessly interwoven with its so-called metaphoric passages, showing that in Jesus' mind there is no conflict between the two.

This is another indication of a lack of tension between the two levels. If you take almost any example that Wapnick gives of the Course's literal, non-dualistic language, you can find very near it an example of what Wapnick considers metaphoric language, without any indication that there is a tension between the two, without any indication that the Course means one but not the other. It looks as if the Course means them both, and sees them as connected to each other, part of each other.

For example, in "The Link to Truth" (T-25.I.5-7), there is what Wapnick sees as perhaps the most important place where the Course comes out and tells us why it has to speak metaphorically. This, then, for Wapnick, is a bastion of the literal language in the Course. It makes statements that Wapnick considers very important to his whole case, such as:

> Since you believe that you are separate, Heaven presents itself to you as separate, too. Not that it is in truth, but that the link that has been given you to join the truth may reach to you through what you understand….[The Holy Spirit] must…use the language that this mind [your mind] can understand, in the condition in which it thinks it is.   (T-25.I.5:1-2, 7:4)

This, in Wapnick's view, is the Course at its literal best. However, throughout this discussion the Holy Spirit is described as an active, intentional agent Who is purposefully teaching you in a language you can understand, and actively using the things you believe in to do so, including the physical elements of "time and place" (7:1):

> It is the Holy Spirit's function to teach you how this oneness is experienced, what you must do that it can be experienced, and where you should go [in space] to do it.
>
> (6:4)

If you look over the passages I've quoted above, you can see for yourself that the Holy Spirit (or "Heaven" in the language of the first passage above) is described as *presenting* Himself to you as separate and *using* the language you relate to in order that He "may reach to you through what you understand." In short, He is *doing things for a purpose*, the very hallmark of an intelligent, active agent. That is how the language of this section presents the Holy Spirit, and that, in Wapnick's terms, is pure metaphor, since (in his view) the Holy Spirit is not a being and hence doesn't do anything, especially not in the physical world of "time and place" (one of Wapnick's primary dictums is that the Holy Spirit doesn't work in the world). So even this section, which for Wapnick lies at the heart of the Course's literal language, is interlaced with what Wapnick considers metaphor. It's not even the case that one sentence is "literal" while the next is "metaphor" (in Wapnick's schema). At times both levels exist in the same sentence. The very same sentences that tell us that Heaven must reach us in the language of separation (Wapnick's literal level) also depict the Holy Spirit actively using our language for the purpose of reaching us (Wapnick's metaphoric level).

In other words, what Wapnick sees as two different levels saying "the exact opposite"[39] of each other exist here side by side and are seamlessly interwoven. And this is the state of affairs that one finds again and again in the Course. If this is so, what justification is there for seeing them as two divergent levels?

Third problem: The Course does not indicate that it sees itself switching back and forth between two different audiences to whom it speaks in different ways.

I cannot find any indications that the Course sees itself as speaking to two different classes of students—advanced and beginner—in two different ways. If the Course's whole presentation is one of constantly shuttling back and forth between two audiences and two modes of discourse, you would think there would be indications of it. You would think there would be places where the Course says something like, "Earlier you were not ready to hear that your Father is not aware of the separation, but now you have come farther on the path and so I can tell you the truth plainly." That sort of statement would clearly identify that Jesus sees himself as speaking to two audiences in two different ways. But there is nothing in the Course like that, at least nothing that I can find. I doubt that Wapnick has been able to find such places, either, or he would have offered them as support for his point of view. Yet I have not come across Wapnick himself offering any Course passages to show that Jesus sees himself as switching back and forth between two different audiences to whom he speaks in two different ways. Wapnick assures us that this is so, but on what basis he assures us is unclear.

The Manual for Teachers *is* an example of the Course speaking to a different audience than it does elsewhere. One can see it right in the titles of the volumes. We have a Workbook *for Students* and a Manual *for Teachers*. The Manual is thus openly addressed to more mature students on this path. Therefore, if Wapnick's theory of two levels of language is right, we would expect the Manual to be full of places where Jesus says things like, "When you were younger on the path I told you a fairy tale, but now I tell you the plain truth." Yet there is nothing like that in the Manual. The Manual, in fact, sounds just like the rest of the Course, just as devoid of that sort of statement and just as packed with what Wapnick considers metaphor. Where is the evidence that Jesus is speaking in different ways to different audiences?

Fourth problem: Metaphor is not the right term for what Wapnick is talking about.

The fourth problem with argument #2 (that the Course's occasional non-dualistic statements are literal and the rest of the Course is metaphoric) is that I do not believe that metaphor is the right word to describe what Wapnick is talking about. What he is talking about is not how metaphor functions. When you call something a metaphor, you are saying that the literal state of affairs is *like* the metaphor, *comparable* to the metaphor. It's all about a similarity between the metaphor and what it refers to. For instance, when I say, "That soccer player is a tiger," what do I mean? I don't, of course, mean that he is a literal tiger. We all get that. What I mean is that, even though he is not an actual tiger, there is a similarity; I mean that he behaves like a tiger. He is aggressive. He is constantly on the offensive, not being content to simply defend. He is daring. He pursues his goal heedless of obstacles or danger. He does not play it safe, nor wait for the action to come to him. He reacts with lightning speed. He pounces on opportunities. He is fiercely competitive.

As you can see, even though the soccer player is not a literal tiger, there is a whole web of similarities between the soccer player and the word "tiger." A metaphor works only when these similarities exist. This characteristic of metaphor is at the heart of what metaphor is. Here is how Merriam-Webster's Dictionary defines "metaphor":

> a figure of speech in which a word or phrase literally denoting one kind of object or idea is used in place of another to suggest a likeness or analogy between them.

In metaphor, everything hinges on the "likeness or analogy." This, however, is not how Wapnick's approach appears to work. As an example let's look at what is perhaps his favorite example of metaphor in the Course: "God weeps at the 'sacrifice' of His children who believe they are lost to Him" (T-5.VII.4:5). This is a very problematic statement, given the rest of the Course's teaching about God. For that reason, this is where Wapnick's argument looks its best. He says that this is clearly a metaphor, and we would probably all agree. A formless, timeless God does not actually weep. So this *is* a metaphor. But a metaphor for *what*? Remember, to be a metaphor, it has to refer to something, something which it is *like* or *analogous* to. To unlock this metaphor, just as we looked at the essence of "tiger," so we need to look closely at the essence of this metaphor, which in this case is an entire situation captured in this brief line from the Course.

What is the situation portrayed in the line "God weeps at the 'sacrifice' of His children who believe they are lost to Him"? It appears to me to be this: a father (in this case, God) has children who experience themselves as exiled, ostracized, as no longer belonging to him ("lost to," according to Webster's Dictionary, means "no longer belonging to"). As a result, they feel a deep sense of *loss* (the word "sacrifice" tells us that). They probably think he has disowned them, but the fact is that they have excluded *themselves* (the sentence says they merely *believe* they are lost to him, and this belief seems to be the distancing factor). Consequently, they have *voluntarily* sacrificed the joy and peace of being where they belong: at home with their father. The father sees this whole situation; he sees that his children are feeling profound loss over their own choice to banish themselves from his presence. He sees that they are in needless pain. And seeing this, he weeps, because he deeply loves his children and wants only their happiness. Far from having cast them out, he loves them with all his heart.

What does this metaphor mean in more literal terms? To treat it as an actual metaphor, we have to preserve the essence of it—we have to say that God is experiencing something *like* or *analogous to* weeping. If we preserve that essence and apply it to God, I think "God weeps" means something like the following three points, which are arranged so that they go from the specific thrust of God weeps (first point) to the general premise underlying that specific thrust (third point):

1. God feels something analogous to human weeping...

2. because He is aware that we are in needless pain, that we feel profound loss after voluntarily exiling ourselves from Him...

3. and because He loves us and wants us to be happy.

The really difficult issue raised by this passage is: What is this emotion on God's part that is analogous to weeping? Whatever it is, I am sure we cannot comprehend it. I cannot imagine that it bears more than the most remote likeness to human emotion. Elsewhere, the Course likens this response of God's to incomplete joy (T-4.VII.6:4, W-pI.100.3:2) and a little sigh (W-pI.136.12:5). The images are flexible, but the basic idea remains: God feels something less than supremely happy in response to our dream of being exiled from Him. Anything else would make God's "weeping" not a metaphor but a simple falsehood.

Now let's turn to Wapnick's interpretation of the metaphor. He says, "God's weeping...represents the *reality* that God loves us."[40] In Wapnick's perspective, God is not aware that we are asleep and dreaming about separation ("[The Course's] basic metaphysical premise is that God does not even know about the dream"),[41] and so God feels nothing about this separated condition of ours. So, to use my three-point schema, Wapnick's literal interpretation of the passage about God weeping would look something like this:

1. God feels nothing even remotely analogous to human weeping...

2. because He is not aware that we are in any sort of pain...

3. but He does love us.

In my mind, calling this sort of thing "metaphor" stretches the meaning of metaphor to the breaking point and beyond. To say that "God weeps" is a metaphor means, as I said, that God feels something *analogous* to weeping, something *like* weeping. But that is certainly not true in Wapnick's interpretation (see point #1 in his interpretation above). This removes things from the realm of metaphor. True, Wapnick does keep some of the meaning of weeping (see point #3 in his interpretation), but not enough. He strips out most of its meaning, including its main thrust—some sort of negative feeling—keeping only the general underlying premise—God loves us. That does not much resemble what we mean by metaphor. Imagine that I say to you, "That soccer player is a tiger." Then you respond, "Oh, you mean he is aggressive, daring, always on the offensive, heedless of obstacles, unafraid of danger, fiercely competitive, and has quick reflexes." And I say, "Actually, I didn't mean any of that. He is fairly passive, stresses defense, tends to play it safe, and is somewhat slow. You see, by calling him a tiger I was speaking *metaphorically*. I meant that he really hopes his team will win." You would be perfectly justified in responding: "I don't think metaphor is the right word for that. Yes, tigers want to prevail over their opponents; they, in a sense, want to win. But if that is the only quality he shares with a tiger, that is not enough to make 'tiger' an appropriate metaphor for him. He has to be more tiger-like for the metaphor to *be* a metaphor."

From what I can see, a general version of the above three-point summary can be used to summarize Wapnick's view of all Course passages that speak of God's response to the separation. Whether the Course is talking about God creating the Holy Spirit, God having a plan for our awakening, God taking care of our future, God (or the Holy Spirit) planning the events of our lives, or other similar statements, in Wapnick's view they are all metaphors, the literal truth of which is something like the following formula:

1. God does not respond to your painful condition in any way…

2. because God is not aware of it in any sense…

3. but He does love you.

This, however, simply doesn't fit what we mean by metaphor. With metaphor, some essential meaning within the metaphor is pointing to an actual state of affairs. As I said, if you say that "God weeps" is a metaphor, you mean that God is experiencing something *analogous* to weeping. If you say that God "created the Holy Spirit" (W-pI.43.1:3) is a metaphor, you mean that God did something *like* creating the Holy Spirit. This is not what Wapnick is talking about. He is saying that God is experiencing nothing even remotely analogous to weeping, that He did nothing even somewhat comparable to creating a Holy Spirit. Thus, as Wapnick views them, the statements "God weeps" and God "created the Holy Spirit" are neither literally true *nor metaphorically true*. They are just plain false. They (in this view) contain a germ of truth—that God loves us—but that germ is not enough to rescue them from being essentially false statements.

Metaphor, then, does not seem to be the right term for what Wapnick is talking about. Almost in recognition of this, Wapnick himself offers a more appropriate term: *fairy tale*.

> Rather than our believing in the God of the ego's fairy tale Who is angry and vengeful, Jesus would have us believe instead, in these early stages of our journey of awakening, in the God of his corrected fairy tale Who truly loves us, independent of what we believe we have done to Him. And all of this is presented in a way we can relate to and understand. But if these words are taken literally, we would find ourselves back in our childhood world of fairy godmothers, Santa Claus, and a Sugar Daddy for a God.[42]

In other words, when Jesus tells us about this loving God Who is aware of our fitful sleep and actually responds to it, he is telling us a fairy tale. I like this term better than "metaphor" for what Wapnick is talking about because fairy tales are not true, being filled with fantastic elements (like unicorns and goblins) that are simply impossible. The Course remarks on this characteristic of them: "Fairy tales [which it describes a few sentences earlier as 'symbols of fantasy...of the ego'] can be pleasant or fearful, but no one calls them true" (T-9.IV.11:6). That is what Wapnick is saying about these statements in the Course: Jesus is telling us things that are not true, that are in fact impossible, because we are children who can't handle the truth. In this view, when Jesus says, "God weeps," he is simply telling us a falsehood that will make us feel better and will prepare us to someday accept the real truth, which is that God does not even know there is anything to weep about.

Fifth problem: Wapnick's Jesus looks misleading, even dishonest.

This leads to my fifth problem with Wapnick's argument #2: in my opinion, it portrays a Jesus who is either deliberately misleading or even arguably dishonest. This Jesus is, in essence, telling me, "Yes, my child, God really cares about the nightmare you are having, and so He created the Holy Spirit to help you out of it. God hears all your prayers and answers them all. Through His Holy Spirit He plans out your journey to ensure the most painless awakening possible." This Jesus tells me these sorts of things repeatedly, in the clearest possible language, while acting as if they are the truth. However, I find out later that he didn't mean any of it. He was just telling me fairy tales because that would make me feel better. He didn't *present* them as fairy tales, but as important spiritual teachings. As it turns out, though, the truth is almost the opposite of what he told me: God does *not* care about my nightmare (since He isn't aware of it), He did *not* create the Holy Spirit, does *not* hear my prayers and does not answer *any* of them.

Wapnick's Jesus is not just speaking metaphorically, he is intentionally telling me falsehoods and presenting them as the truth. At best this Jesus is misleading. At worst, he has crossed the line into dishonesty.

Sixth problem: Wapnick does not adhere to the metaphoric speech he claims we need.

My sixth problem with Wapnick's second argument is that Wapnick himself steps outside it. He explains that most Course students, indeed most human beings, are on the lower rungs. He then tells us that such people need to hear a fairy tale, for they cannot handle the straight truth. "Since we are still very much children in the spiritual life…the Course's gentle and loving use of language at this level is more than appropriate."[43] He even tells us that Jesus' fairy tale approach is "certainly the highest level [of communication] that they [his students] can tolerate in their fearful state."[44] After telling us so emphatically that we can only handle a fairy tale and not the real truth, he then proceeds to tell us what he considers the real truth.

If we are the spiritual children he says we are, then by his own theory this is the last thing he should tell us. After all, this is the sort of fairy tale that only quiets your fears when you believe it is the truth. Imagine that you are told, "There is this loving, caring Holy Spirit, Who only wants your happiness and Who is there to help and guide you in every moment. This is just a story, though; none of it is really true. In actual fact, the Holy Spirit is an illusion that doesn't do anything. He is just a metaphor." There is not much comfort in that, is there? To be effective, this fairy tale needs to be believed.

Yet Wapnick is constantly telling us all—the vast majority of whom he considers to be on the lower rungs—that it is only a fairy tale. This seems to fly directly in the face of his own theory. He is speaking to the same crowd Jesus was. If Jesus telling us fairy tales "is more than appropriate," why does Wapnick not follow suit and tell those fairy tales with the same straight face that Jesus did? If this is the highest level of communication that Jesus' students "can tolerate in their fearful state," why does Wapnick speak to them on a higher level? If this fairy tale approach was good enough for Jesus, then why doesn't Wapnick dutifully adhere to it?

Summary of problems with argument #2

In summary, I think Wapnick's second argument about the Course's metaphorical language—that the Course's occasional non-dualistic statements are literal and the rest of the Course is metaphoric—is riddled with insurmountable problems. The first three problems I list above add up to a single idea: there is a startling lack of evidence for Wapnick's claim that there are two levels of language in the Course (dualistic and non-dualistic) that often say the "exact opposite"[45] things. If Wapnick's theory is right, we would naturally expect to find places where the Course openly says that its dualistic statements are not actually true. We would expect to find a clear switching back and forth between dualistic and non-dualistic language, showing that they are two distinctly different levels of language that should be treated quite differently by the reader. And we would expect to find places where Jesus makes clear that he occasionally speaks to more advanced students and tells them the literal truth and otherwise speaks to beginners and gives them metaphor. But instead, we find a striking absence of all three of these things. We don't find the denials of duality that Wapnick needs (first problem). We find his two levels of language—supposedly so different—seamlessly interwoven with each other (second problem). And we cannot find Jesus indicating that he is giving a different story to different students (third problem). Instead, it looks like Jesus is giving the *same* story to *all* his students, a story he fully expects them to believe.

Whereas the first three problems were about lack of evidence for Wapnick's theory, the final three show the difficulties that result from his theory. In the fourth problem, we see that Wapnick isn't really treating the dualistic language as metaphor. Metaphor means that the literal state of affairs is like the metaphor, analogous to the metaphor. Yet Wapnick sees the literal truth as so unlike what the Course's words say that it is more accurate to call those words a *fairy tale*. Thus, instead of giving us a metaphor which is *like* the truth, the Course (in this view) is telling us a fairy tale which is simply *untrue*. That is a troubling picture of the Course, and leads directly to the fifth problem, for it makes Jesus look at best misleading and at worst dishonest. What kind of Jesus would tell us a fairy tale while acting as if he is imparting profound spiritual teaching? This Jesus, in fact, is so misleading that Wapnick cannot seem to bring himself to emulate him—my sixth problem. Rather than follow in his teacher's footsteps and simply repeat the "fairy tale," Wapnick (to his credit) prefers a more direct and honest approach. He breaks with what he sees as Jesus' approach and continually tells his students what he considers the literal truth. Hence, Wapnick's own actions implicitly acknowledge that there is something wrong with a Jesus who tells us fairy tales as if they are true.

We have now seen that neither of Wapnick's two arguments do what they are intended to do: prove that the Course is filled with highly metaphorical language which must be radically reinterpreted to find the underlying literal truth. We have also seen that the two arguments contradict each other and so cancel each other out. This entire state of affairs leaves Wapnick without any basis for claiming that the Course says one thing but means something else altogether. And this leaves him subject to what the Course actually says, a condition in which many of his key teachings simply do not hold up.

WAPNICK'S APPROACH TO INTERPRETING THE LANGUAGE OF THE COURSE

Wapnick's view that most (or all) of the Course's language is metaphor has major implications for how one should interpret that language. In short, it suggests an entire interpretive approach. At the foundation of this interpretive approach is a simple idea: there are certain things that, given its metaphysical foundation, the Course simply cannot teach. Here are some quotes from Wapnick which express this idea:

Therefore, the clear conclusion of this non-dualistic metaphysics is that God cannot be present in the illusory world, since this would compromise the absolute nature of God's Oneness by implying that there could actually exist a state that is *outside* of perfect unity, an evident and logical impossibility.[46]

And just as nonsensical [as our guilt and fear] is the thought that God—our perfect Creator and undifferentiated and unified Source—could weep, suffer loneliness, or even believe that He were incomplete.[47]

The Holy Spirit (or Jesus) would have to be as insane as we, if He were truly to address these illusory problems [in the world].[48]

In each case the reasoning sounds similar. God cannot be present in the illusory world because that would compromise His Oneness. God cannot weep or suffer loneliness because that would violate His perfect, undifferentiated nature. The Holy Spirit cannot address our earthly problems because that would make Him insane (because it would mean that He believes in a world that is not there). At this point I am not interested in the particular points Wapnick makes here (I actually agree that God does not literally weep and that God is not physically present in this world); I am interested in the basic interpretive approach that is revealed. In each case Wapnick assumes that our own logic, based on our own understanding of the Course's metaphysics, can tell us what the Course *can* and *cannot* teach. In the following passage, Wapnick more fully captures the essence of his interpretive approach:

> The uncompromising principle of not accepting as true any form that duality takes can serve as the criterion by which to know where the meaning of Jesus' words in *A Course in Miracles* should be taken literally and where metaphorically.[49]

We can translate this statement into the following rule for interpretation: "The Course simply cannot mean many of the things it says because that would violate its metaphysical foundation. We therefore must radically reinterpret those passages in light of our understanding of the metaphysics." For the sake of examining this interpretive approach, let me flesh it out in the form of the following six points, all of which, I believe, are at least implicitly reflected in the above quote:

1. We know that the Course's metaphysical foundation is non-dualistic—it teaches that reality is totally unified, undifferentiated and changeless, and that there is no world.

2. We know, through the sheer force of our logic, which ideas are *inconsistent* with the Course's metaphysics; namely, those ideas which are dualistic.

3. We know that the Course is totally consistent, that it never contradicts itself.

4. There are a great many passages in the Course that *seem* to contradict the Course's non-dualistic metaphysics, passages that seem to teach dualism.

5. These passages cannot mean what they seem to mean. They must be metaphoric. Otherwise, the Course would be inconsistent.

6. We can discern what these passages really mean by using the Course's metaphysics as our guide for interpreting them. We interpret them in light of the metaphysics (as we understand it). We reach below the form of the words to find an underlying meaning which *is* in harmony with the Course's metaphysics.

This interpretive approach can appear quite rational, but we need to look at it extremely carefully, for it has numerous results that are both dramatic and, in my view, highly problematic. To get a sense of this, I would like to go through those results one by one, while following a single, simple example: Wapnick's teaching that "God does not hear our prayers."[50]

First result: Multiple direct statements from the Course can be treated as irrelevant.

This is one of the truly dramatic results of Wapnick's interpretive approach. With this approach in hand, it doesn't matter how often or how clearly the Course says something. If that something seems to be inconsistent with the Course's non-dualism, you simply overrule those passages. You just conclude, "They can't mean that." In effect, you discard them as just so much metaphor.

This is the case with the example of Wapnick's teaching that God does not hear prayers. There are a number of places where the Course says just the opposite, that God *does* hear prayers. Below, I list eleven passages, from the Text, the Workbook, *Psychotherapy* and *The Song of Prayer*, that are all specifically about God hearing our prayers. In these passages, all mentions of "He" or "You" (capitalized) refer to God the Father.

> He has never failed to answer this request....Those who call truly are always answered. (T-4.III.6:4-5)

> Have confidence in your Father today, and be certain that He has heard you and answered you. (W-pI.69.8:1)

> I come to hear Your Voice...sure You will hear my call and answer me. (W-pII.221.1:5)

> You have remained with me, and always will be there to hear my call to You and answer me. (W-pII.232.1:3)

> You cannot fail to hear me, Father. (W-pII.290.2:2)

> I need but call and You will answer me.
> (W-pII.327.Heading)

> God has promised He will hear my call and answer me Himself. (W-327.1:2)

> Father, You promised You would never fail to answer any call Your Son might make to You. (W-pII.356.1:1)

> No call to God can be unheard nor left unanswered.
> (W-pII.358.Heading)

> And He has guaranteed that He will hear and answer them in truth. (P-2.V.4:5)

> Your prayer has risen up and called to God, Who hears and answers. (S-3.IV.4:2)

Here we have a very strong theme, one which stretches from the earliest portions of the Course (Chapter 4 of the Text) to the two supplements (*Psychotherapy* and *The Song of Prayer*). It is found in two Workbook lesson titles, lines which the Course wants us to repeat to ourselves dozens of times during a day. It is very clear and straightforward; the language is unambiguous. It is characterized by a near absence of what we would normally consider metaphoric language (if "hear" referred only to physical hearing we could call it a metaphor in this case, but it doesn't—one of its literal meanings is "to receive communication"). And it is emphatic: we can have *confidence* and be *sure* that God will *always* hear, because He has *guaranteed*, even *promised*, that He *cannot fail* to hear and answer *Himself.*

None of this matters, however, in Wapnick's view. He has of course read these passages, but to my knowledge he never says one word about them when he presents his view that God does not hear prayers. Clearly, even though they seem to directly address the issue of God hearing prayers, they are irrelevant to the discussion. Why? Because they smack of dualism. Given that, it simply doesn't matter how often or how clearly or straightforwardly the Course states that God hears our prayers. Nothing the Course could possibly say could establish that the Course actually teaches this. As this example shows, with Wapnick's interpretive approach in hand, *multiple direct statements from the Course can be treated as irrelevant.* Isn't there something highly suspicious about an interpretation of the Course that, when faced with a multitude of passages that directly disagree with it, can simply dismiss them by saying, "They can't mean that"?

Second result: The immediate context of a passage can be discarded in favor of using Wapnick's metaphysics as the "real" context of that passage.

We all decipher written and spoken statements by viewing them in light of their context. Like the Circle, Wapnick stresses the importance of context. He often warns that "specific statements are not to be wrenched from their context and taken as literal truth."[51] However, I believe that what Wapnick means by "context" is different than what the rest of us mean. Normally, when we talk about context, that means the sentences and paragraphs immediately surrounding a particular passage (the first level of context I described at the beginning of this essay). Indeed, this is what the dictionary definition indicates, as you can see by the following two definitions, one from The Oxford English Dictionary and one from Merriam-Webster:

> The whole structure of a connected passage regarded in
> its bearing upon any of the parts which constitute it; the

parts which immediately precede or follow any particular passage or "text" and determine its meaning.

the parts of a discourse that surround a word or passage and can throw light on its meaning.

That is what "context" means. When Wapnick talks about context in regard to the Course, however, I think for him that primarily means something significantly different. I think he mainly means the *metaphysical* context, which is what we can glean of the Course's overall view of reality (this roughly corresponds to what I called the fourth level of context). This is derived from statements scattered all over the Course and may have nothing whatsoever to do with the immediate context. He states this notion of context in the following important quote:

> A student should always evaluate any particular statement in the Course in light of the Course's overall metaphysical teaching.[52]

If you compare this to the two dictionary definitions, you can readily see the contrast. Normally, reading a statement in context means interpreting it in light of "the parts which immediately precede or follow" it. For Wapnick, however, it means interpreting a statement "in light of the Course's overall metaphysical teaching."

It is natural to interpret someone's statements (in this case, the Course's) in light of what you know about that person's basic worldview. This is what Wapnick does with the Course. He has pieced together his picture of the Course's basic view of reality (which is what metaphysics is about, being the branch of philosophy that deals with the question of what is ultimately real). He then takes this picture and interprets everything in the Course in light of it, assuming, quite naturally, that the Course would not teach something that contradicts its own view of reality. This approach, however, is incredibly subjective, for two reasons:

1. One can easily be wrong about the metaphysics. After all, there is no section in the Course that thoroughly and systematically spells out the Course's metaphysics. One has to piece its view together from hundreds of scattered passages, and the result is likely to be at least partly inaccurate.

2. Even if you get the metaphysics more or less right, how do you know what it implies about the meaning of a specific passage? All sorts of errors can creep in here, because the author isn't there to tell you, "*This* is what my basic worldview implies about this particular passage." You have to decide that for yourself, and your conclusions may be quite different than the author's.

So, we have *immediate* context and *metaphysical* context. These are extremely different ways of looking at context and they can generate completely different ways of understanding a passage. Let's return to our example of God not hearing prayers. As far as I can see, Wapnick presents only one passage that he believes supports his teaching that God does not hear our prayers (compared to the eleven passages I listed above). He mentions this passage repeatedly and at least twice says that he considers it to be a "very clear statement…that God does not hear our prayers."[53] Here it is:

> Think not He hears the little prayers of those who call on Him with names of idols cherished by the world. They cannot reach Him thus.   (W-pI.183.7:3-4)

This is a "very clear statement" that God does not hear our prayers? The first thought that comes to my mind is: What if you *don't* call on Him with "names of idols"? What if you *don't* pray "little prayers"? Does He hear you then? The passage seems to say that God doesn't hear your prayers when you call on Him the *wrong* way. What happens when you call on Him the *right* way? These are important questions, but the picture gets even more interesting when you look at the context. So let's do that.

The passage comes from Lesson 183, "I call upon God's Name and on my own" (from which the following quotes will be drawn). Its whole focus is on the significance, and on the actual practice, of calling on God's Name. In the paragraph directly before the one Wapnick quotes, the lesson instructs us in this practice, which is a particular method of meditation. In this method, we simply "repeat God's Name slowly again and still again" (6:1), clearing our mind of all worldly thoughts and feeling that this Name represents "the only wish we have" (6:6). Then come these sentences:

> Thus [by repeating God's Name in this fashion] do we give an invitation which can never be refused. And God

will come, and answer it Himself. (7:1-2)

This quote is highly significant. It says that calling God's Name over and over amounts to giving an invitation, and that once we give this invitation, "God will come, and answer it Himself." Now, if you call God's Name *as* an invitation, and if God comes in *response* to the invitation, then exactly who is it that you are inviting by calling His Name? Obviously, *God*. Further, how could He possibly respond to our invitation if He didn't *hear* it? He couldn't. As a result, we can accurately rephrase the above passage in this way:

> When you repeat God's Name with all your attention and
> desire you are inviting Him to come to you. He will hear
> you, and He will come.

Thus, the lines I quoted above clearly and necessarily imply what so many other passages state: that God *does* hear prayers. What else would we expect from a lesson whose entire emphasis is on calling on God? Imagine what a strange lesson it would be if it said, "Spend your practice periods today calling God's Name over and over and over. And be sure that He will *never* hear you."

So we have established that the lines I last quoted necessarily imply that God hears our call. Can you guess what the very next lines in the lesson are? The exact ones that Wapnick quotes as a "very clear statement" that God does *not* hear prayers. I'll quote the entire paragraph, which begins with the implication that God does hear prayers and ends with the lines cited by Wapnick as "proof" that He does not:

> Thus do we give an invitation which can never be
> refused. And God will come, and answer it Himself.
> Think not He hears the little prayers of those who call on
> Him with names of idols cherished by the world. They
> cannot reach Him thus. He cannot hear requests that He
> be not Himself, or that His Son receive another name than
> His. (7:1-5)

The paragraph, as you probably can see, is a contrast, which says that God hears certain prayers and does not hear others. We have already explored the lines that speak of Him hearing prayers. What about the other lines? What does it mean to call on God "with names of idols cherished by the world"? What are these "idols"? Again we must look to the immediate context. The lesson is littered with references to them (I count sixteen), calling them, among other things, "the tiny, nameless things on earth" (5:2), "the little things of earth" (11:3), and "the names of all the gods you valued" (4:3). These "idols" are obviously the things of the world that we value, things that our desire has turned into false gods. We "pray" to them simply by thinking about and desiring them. Now we can see the real thrust of this paragraph, which I'll state in this way:

> When all that occupies your mind is God's Name, you invite Him to come to you, and He will hear and respond. On the other hand, when what occupies your mind are the names of the worldly things you desire, God will neither hear nor answer, for you are calling not on Him, but on false gods.

To put it even more concisely: Dwell on God's Name, and God will hear and will come; dwell on worldly things, and God will not even hear, for you are calling on other gods. The meaning dictated by the immediate context is that God does hear certain kinds of prayers. Ironically, Wapnick's only piece of support for the idea that God does not hear prayers, when read in context, turns into support for the idea that He does. How could this happen? How could Wapnick read this passage the way he does? The answer is simple: he ignores the context—the immediate context. He doesn't quote the crucial first two sentences of the paragraph, the ones that speak of God responding to (and therefore hearing) our invitation. And he doesn't interpret calling on God "with names of idols" according to the context, which shows that this sort of calling only covers some prayers, not all. Instead, he interprets the passage according to what he considers a more important context—what I am calling the metaphysical context. Read in that context, "Think not He hears the little prayers of those who call on Him with names of idols" apparently means, "Think not He hears any prayers." Oddly enough, interpreting this passage in light of Wapnick's metaphysical context wrenches it out of its immediate context. And since "immediate context" is what we mean by "context" (context being "the parts which immediately precede or follow any particular passage…and determine its meaning"), we can simply say that his interpretation wrenches it out of its context.

As I said in my remarks about the Circle's interpretive approach, I think both the immediate and the metaphysical context have value. However, as I also said there, the immediate context has to be considered far more authoritative. There is where we see the author signaling more or less directly what he means by a particular statement. The metaphysical context is a vastly more subjective and uncertain guide. Therefore, if the metaphysical context yields an interpretation that is the opposite of what the immediate context yields, you must go with the immediate context. And you must call into question either your idea of the metaphysics or your idea of what the metaphysics says about this particular passage.

Third result: We can teach things that the Course never says, and even present those teachings as pillars of the Course's thought system.

We have just seen that the only passage Wapnick cites in support of the idea that God does not hear prayers fails to support that idea, and in fact, when quoted in its context, supports the idea that God does hear prayers. This means that, in this case, Wapnick is teaching something which does not have a single passage supporting it in the Course. Rather, the Course clearly says the direct opposite in at least eleven passages.

This may seem like a problem for Wapnick, but within his interpretive approach I don't think it is at all. Based on this approach, even if the Course never comes out and says that God does not hear prayers, we still know that it *must* teach that. How could God hear prayers when the Course's "basic metaphysical premise is that God does not even know about the dream"[54]? Likewise, based on this approach, even if the Course repeatedly states that He does hear prayers, we know that it simply can't mean that. We can discount those passages as being metaphoric. In short, because the idea that God does not hear prayers follows so logically from Wapnick's metaphysics, apparently nothing that the Course says, or doesn't say, is able to disprove this teaching.

As I said earlier, in my opinion there are a number of key Wapnick teachings that fit this same pattern: no direct support in the Course and a series of clear and direct statements to the contrary. Many of these are not just incidental teachings of his, but ideas he presents as pillars of the Course's thought system. For example, "[The Course's] basic

97

metaphysical premise is that God does not even know about the dream."[55] This may sound surprising, but the interpretive approach I sketched above makes this sort of thing quite natural. If you read that approach carefully (particularly the six points that begin with the one that says, "We know that the Course's metaphysical foundation is non-dualistic…"), you see that the real power in them is not the actual words of the Course, but Wapnick's formulation of the metaphysics.

Fourth result: Our own logic becomes more authoritative than the Course's.

Above I claimed that the real support for the idea that God does not hear prayers is a combination of Wapnick's metaphysics and his logic. If there is no world, then logic seems to require that God has nothing to do with the world. And if God has nothing to do with the world, then logic demands that He obviously cannot hear the prayers we utter in this world. Nothing else appears to make sense. The question, however, is: can we rely so heavily on our own logic?

In my experience we cannot. There is no question that the Course constantly employs logic. I find, however, that it is very hard to guess where the Course will go with its logic. The Course's logic often takes off in unforeseen and unforeseeable directions. I believe, therefore, that rather than using our logic to decide what the Course *has* to say, we need to pay attention to *its* logic and see what it *does* say.

Returning to our example, there does seem to be a logical problem with the God of the Course actually hearing our prayers. After all, this God is formless and knows nothing about form (T-30.III.4:5). How can He hear our prayers? Rather than merely conclude that He cannot, I think the best move is to find out if the Course addresses this issue. Here is one place where it does:

> The guiltless and the guilty are totally incapable of understanding one another. Each perceives the other as like himself, making both unable to communicate, because each sees the other unlike the way he sees himself. God can communicate only to the Holy Spirit in your mind, because only He shares the knowledge of what you are with God. And only the Holy Spirit can answer God for you, for only He knows what God is.
>
> (T-14.IV.10:1-4)

It would take too much space to comment on this complex passage adequately. The gist of it is that, currently, we cannot communicate with God directly. Why? Because "the guiltless [God] and the guilty [us] are totally incapable of understanding one another." Feeling guilty ourselves, we view God as guilty. We address Him as an attacking, and hence guilty, God. However, since He is nothing of the sort, He cannot understand what we are saying. We are addressing Him as if He were someone else. To achieve real communication, this passage says, your message must portray the other person as he views himself. Yet we do not know God as He knows Himself. Therefore, we cannot communicate with Him.

Here, then, the Course is acknowledging roughly the same problem that Wapnick has acknowledged: It seems logically impossible for God to receive our communications. However, the Course then heads off in a different direction. It says there is a solution to this problem: the Holy Spirit. He speaks to God *for* us, "for only He knows what God is." Only the Holy Spirit's communications fit the principle that, to be understood, your message must portray the receiver as the receiver views himself. Apparently, the Holy Spirit relays our communications to God in a way that God can understand. Elsewhere, the Course says something similar: that the Holy Spirit hears beneath our words to the prayer of the heart, seeing this prayer as a call for help (M-29.6:1-8), and that this prayer of the heart, not our words, is what God hears (M-21.1:3-7). In hindsight, we could have guessed the Course would bring in the Holy Spirit to resolve our communication gap with God, for, after all, He is our Communication *Link* with God. The Course says that God "keeps this channel [the Holy Spirit] open to receive His communication to you, *and yours to Him*" (T-15.VIII.5:5; italics mine). The Holy Spirit is thus a two-way channel. God communicates to us and we communicate to God through Him.

In summary, then, Wapnick sees a difficulty: how can a non-dualistic God hear our prayers? Based on his logic, he concludes: He obviously cannot. The Course sees the same difficulty, but then offers its own logical conclusion, one which is quite different than Wapnick's: God can, *through the Holy Spirit*. The Holy Spirit translates our words into some kind of formless essence, and this is what God "hears." I believe we need to be constantly aware of the limitations of our logic and pay very close attention to the Course's. Its logic will often resolve conceptual difficulties that seem insoluble to us.

I see this as a major issue in Wapnick's teaching. Again and again he appears to assume, based on logic, that the Course simply *cannot* teach a certain thing. In some cases, he sees a problem where the Course, to all appearances, does not. This is true, for instance, with his assumption that God cannot be aware of the separation. The Course states clearly that He is (see T-4.VII.6:4-7 and T-6.V.1:3-8) and never acts like this presents any sort of problem. In other cases, Wapnick sees a potential problem where the Course sees one, too, but then Wapnick assumes the problem is insurmountable while the Course offers a resolution for it. For instance, that is what we saw with the question of how God can hear our prayers.

That is why I included point #2 in my six-point summary of Wapnick's interpretive approach: "We know, through the sheer force of our logic, which ideas are inconsistent with the Course's metaphysics." It seems to me that in Wapnick's case, his logic often ends up being more decisive than the Course's own teaching.

Overall result: Wapnick's metaphysics and logic carry more authority than the Course and thus have the apparent right to reshape the Course.

This is the sum total of the preceding four results and what makes Wapnick's interpretive approach of such concern to me and to us at the Circle. It has the apparent power to reshape the Course. It has this power for a very simple reason: in this approach, Wapnick's metaphysics and Wapnick's logic carry more authority than the words of the Course. This metaphysics can come in and dictate what the Course's words *really* mean, regardless of what they *seem* to mean. Yet those words cannot turn around and correct Wapnick's metaphysics, even where it seems that they should. The words have been disempowered. The real power lies in Wapnick's metaphysics and logic.

The results, as we saw above, are dramatic. The metaphysics is so powerful that it can create core teachings out of thin air, teachings that do not have a single passage in the Course to directly support them (which is what we saw with the example of God not hearing prayers). The support for these teachings appears to lie solely in the fact that they seem to logically follow from Wapnick's metaphysics. The metaphysics then goes into the Course and manufactures support for these teachings there. It takes certain passages, wrenches them from their context, projects its meaning onto them, and then claims them as decisive support. Further, it doesn't matter how many times the Course says something contrary to these teachings. Those passages are irrelevant. The metaphysics dictates that they simply can't mean what they seem to mean. In sum, the power is in Wapnick's metaphysics more than in the words of the Course. When the two clash, the metaphysics wins. It has power to redefine the Course's words but they have no power to turn around and redefine it.

Do all of Wapnick's teachings fit the description in the above paragraph? Not at all. Saying that would be a gross overstatement. Much of what he teaches does come from the Course, in my opinion. Even many of the things he teaches with which I disagree have at least some arguable basis in the Course. However, as I have said above, there are a number of key Wapnick teachings that fit the description I just gave: they have no overt support in the Course and they fly in the face of repeated statements from the Course.

I am especially concerned because Wapnick's approach is not framed as what it is, as a rather daring, risky, creative interpretation. Instead, it is framed as "pure Course." In the eyes of many students and perhaps the world at large, Wapnick is the official representative of the Course. He is seen as the ultimate Course purist, the one who is standing up for the Course's purity against all those who would distort it. This is what concerns me: that Wapnick's approach has the self-granted right to create its *own* Course while being perceived as the authority on the *pure, unadulterated* Course.

CONCLUSION

What I have attempted to show in this essay is that approaching the Course's language as largely metaphoric entails massive, insurmountable problems. We saw that Wapnick's first argument amounts to something like this: "Since reality cannot be described literally, the Course could not have expressed itself literally. I will now tell you what it really meant—literally." If Wapnick can put the Course's teaching in more literal terms, there was clearly nothing preventing the Course from doing the same thing.

We then came to his second argument—that the Course's

occasional non-dualistic statements are literal and the rest of the Course is metaphoric. This not only contradicts the first, but has a number of problems of its own. To begin with, there is a dramatic lack of evidence for the idea that the Course sees itself speaking on two levels that often say the exact opposite things. Second, in this theory, the Course is not really speaking in metaphor, but rather telling us fairy tales, comforting falsehoods. In this view, Jesus is so misleading that Wapnick himself refuses to emulate his teaching method, opting instead for telling the literal truth as he sees it.

Finally, we looked at the interpretive approach that stems from treating most of the Course as metaphor. In this approach, we first form our view of the metaphysics based on the Course's comparatively few non-dualistic statements. We then take our metaphysics and read everything else in the Course in its light. No matter what the words say on a literal level, no matter how contrary they are to our view, we claim that underneath the obscuring metaphor of their outer skin beats the pure heart of our metaphysics. As a result, the words of the Course are disempowered—and why not? After all, they're just metaphor. We have every right to disregard them and instead stamp our view of the metaphysics indiscriminately onto every passage.

Perhaps most significantly, treating most (or all) of the Course as metaphor simply doesn't accord with the Course's own attitude toward its language. In Wapnick's view, the metaphor is really there to obscure the meaning, to veil the truth so that students on the lower rungs are not brought face to face with what could only frighten them. The metaphor's purpose is to put distance between symbol and meaning, so that the comforting surface-level of the Course safely conceals the radical, unsettling truths that are really being taught there. This cover protects the student from those truths, presumably until he is ready to face them.

This idea of language-as-veil runs head-on into how the Course itself regards its language. As I said near the beginning of this essay, the Course claims that it "is perfectly clear" (T-11.VI.3:1), that it uses "words that are almost impossible to distort" (T-3.I.3:10). It indicates that it wants to avoid symbolic images that are "open to different interpretations" (T-5.I.4:5), and so it surrounds its metaphors with straight teaching and even has a habit of interpreting them for us. And it urges us to take its statements literally, to resist our temptation to scale them down to fit our expectations.

In all of this we can see a single value: the Course wants to speak plainly, to use words and symbols that are not inherently open to a wide array of divergent interpretations. Whenever we encounter any symbol we have to undertake a journey, from the symbol to what it means. This may take a mere fraction of a second, but it is a journey nonetheless. The Course wants to safeguard this journey by making sure there is a short, straight, clearly marked path leading from the symbols it uses to their meaning. The Course sees us as particularly prone to wandering off due to our resistance to the ego-dispelling meaning at the other end of the path. And so it makes every effort to make that path smooth and straight. The last thing it wants is to give us a symbol that is so distant from its meaning that we don't know which path to take, which way to go. The Course therefore uses metaphor, but in a special way, in a way that makes sure that we can successfully make that journey from metaphor to meaning.

The Course's attitude toward its language stands in marked contrast to Wapnick's approach. As I mentioned earlier, Wapnick likens the levels on which the Course is written to Freud's distinction between the *manifest* content of a dream (its symbols) and the *latent* content (its meaning). This is a perfect analogy, because in Freud's system—as in Wapnick's—there can be an enormous distance between the manifest content and the latent, and for the exact same reason: because the conscious mind cannot handle the latent content. It therefore must appear in highly symbolic form. The result, as Wapnick points out, is that unraveling the symbol and getting to its meaning is a difficult, precarious and uncertain process:

> Thus, two analysts of differing persuasions could obviously agree on the dream's manifest content, but could ascribe totally different meanings to what the dream is saying. To use a simple example, a Freudian would tend to interpret a church steeple in a person's dream as a phallic symbol, possibly reflecting sexual conflict, while a Jungian might see instead a symbol of the dreamer's spiritual strivings.[56]

This is exactly the situation the Course is trying to avoid. Enigmatic symbols with multiple meanings may kindle our fascination, but they can also leave us forever frustrated in our quest to find their meaning. The Course says that its words are not like that. It claims that it "is perfectly clear" (T-11.VI.3:1), that it "means exactly what it says" (T-8.IX.8:1). And in this, as in other matters, we at the Circle take it at its word.

Notes

[1] *The Message of 'A Course in Miracles,' Volume Two: Few Choose to Listen*, p. 88.

[2] *Ibid.*, p. 124.

[3] *Ibid.*, p. 108.

[4] *The Message of 'A Course in Miracles,' Volume One: All Are Called*, p. 339.

[5] *Few Choose to Listen*, p. 43.

[6] *Ibid.*, p. 1.

[7] *Ibid.*, p. 58.

[8] *Ibid.*, p. 96.

[9] *Ibid.*, p. 35.

[10] Mark Johnson, ed., *Philosophical Perspectives on Metaphor* (Minneapolis, Minnesota, University of Minnesota Press, 1981), pp. 20-21.

[11] I have been making a list of repeating terms in the Course and have so far catalogued over fifty.

[12] *Few Choose to Listen*, p. 211.

[13] *Ibid.*, p. 71. In this discussion, Wapnick doesn't say that this is how the Course is written, but he clearly implies it. After explaining Freud's distinction between manifest and latent dream content, he then applies this to Workbook Lesson 194, saying that "what Jesus is teaching is not the manifest content that we should literally place our future in God's Hands, but rather the latent content that we should abandon the ego's insane yet vicious notion that our guilt demands punishment at the *hands* of a vengeful deity."

[14] *Ibid.*, p. 71.

[15] *Ibid.*, p. 70.

[16] *Ibid.*, p. 96.

[17] *Ibid.*, p. 92.

[18] *Ibid.*, p. 55.

[19] *Ibid.*, p. 107.

[20] *Ibid.*, pp. 49, 96.

[21] *The Most Commonly Asked Questions about 'A Course in Miracles'* (co-written with Gloria Wapnick), p. 4.

[22] *All Are Called*, p. 35.

[23] *Commonly Asked Questions*, p. 7.

[24] *Few Choose to Listen*, p. 63.

[25] *All Are Called*, p. 35.

[26] *Ibid.*, p. 33.

[27] *Few Choose to Listen*, pp. 95-96.

[28] *Ibid.*, p. 65.

[29] *Ibid.*, p. 72.

[30] *Commonly Asked Questions*, p. 85.

[31] *Few Choose to Listen*, p. 92.

[32] *Ibid.*, p. 95.

[33] *Ibid.*, p. 96.

[34] *Ibid.*, p. 95.

[35] *Ibid.*, p. 96.

[36] *Ibid.*, p. 65.

[37] *Ibid.*, p. 124.
[38] *The Fifty Miracle Principles of 'A Course in Miracles,'* (1985), pp. 130-131.
[39] *Commonly Asked Questions*, p. 85.
[40] *Few Choose to Listen*, p. 69.
[41] *All Are Called*, p. 314.
[42] *Few Choose to Listen*, p. 69.
[43] *Ibid.*, pp. 72-73.
[44] *Ibid.*, p. 115.
[45] *Commonly Asked Questions*, p. 85.
[46] *Few Choose to Listen,* pp. 49-50.
[47] *Ibid.*, p. 46.
[48] *Ibid.*, p. 159.
[49] *Ibid.*, p. 95.
[50] *Commonly Asked Questions*, p. 120.
[51] *Few Choose to Listen*, p. 45.
[52] *Ibid.*, p. 67.
[53] *Commonly Asked Questions*, 120, *Few Choose to Listen*, p. 63.
[54] *All Are Called*, p. 314.
[55] *Ibid.*, p. 314.
[56] *Few Choose to Listen*, p. 71.

Does the Holy Spirit Actually *Do* Things in the World?

by Greg Mackie

Note: This is a revised and expanded version of a "Course Q & A" article that appears on the Circle of Atonement's website (www.circleofa.com) and in the book How Can We Forgive Murderers? And Other Answers to Questions about *A Course in Miracles.*

The question of whether the Holy Spirit acts in the world is a crucial one, because it has a direct impact on our understanding of God's relationship with the world, and our relationship with God. Did God actively respond to the separation by creating the Holy Spirit, a loving Being Who literally has a plan for the world's salvation and helps us bring that plan to fruition by actively guiding our thoughts, words, and actions if we will let Him? Or does God not even know about the separation, in which case the Holy Spirit is just an illusory split-off part of our own minds, a metaphorical symbol for the memory of God that we brought into our dream of separation, a memory that does not have a plan or actively help us in any way, but is simply a stationary lighthouse that passively illuminates the way back to our true home?

Clearly, these are two dramatically different views of God and the Holy Spirit. The first is the view of the Circle; the second is the view of Ken Wapnick. (This, at any rate, is our opinion, based on Wapnick's body of work.) In the Circle's view, then, the Holy Spirit definitely *does* act in the world; in Wapnick's view, He definitely does *not*. This is probably one of the most significant differences between our vision of the Course and Wapnick's.

Since Wapnick's views are so influential in the Course community, we thought it would be helpful to compare his view on this question with the Circle's. In this article, I will first present the Circle's position on this question and our reasons for holding it, and then present Wapnick's position (including quotations from his works) and our reasons for disagreeing with it. Some of the endnotes contain additional information, so please read those as well. It is my hope that this article will be helpful to Course students in their own efforts to discern where *A Course in Miracles* stands on this crucial issue.

THE CIRCLE'S VIEW: THE HOLY SPIRIT DOES DO THINGS IN THE WORLD

Wapnick and we would probably agree that the resolution of this issue comes down to one very simple question: What does the *Course* say about it? We simply differ on how to interpret what the Course says about it. In a nutshell, the Circle's reasons for believing that the Holy Spirit *does* act in the world can be boiled down to the following two points: 1) The Course very clearly states that the Holy Spirit does things in the world, and 2) The Course offers no reason to believe that it doesn't mean these statements literally. In my presentation of the Circle's view, then, I will simply be presenting Course material describing how the Holy Spirit acts in the world, material that we take quite literally.

Before I do this, however, I want to clarify how I understand the question being posed here, and what I mean by the answer I'm presenting. As I am understanding it, the question basically means this: "Does the Holy Spirit actively do things in the world in the same sense that we, the members of the Sonship, actively do things in the world?" This is what I think most people mean when they ask whether the Holy Spirit does things in the world. So, while I know the Course teaches that the world is an illusion and therefore no *real* acts occur in the world, the question I'm addressing here is whether or not the Holy Spirit acts *within the illusion*. In the Circle's view of the Course's teachings, He *does* act within the illusion, in the same sense that everyone in the Sonship does. This is what we mean when we say that the Holy Spirit does things in the world.

With that clarification out of the way, I would now like to present some reasons for the Circle's view.

Our reasons for believing that the Holy Spirit does things in the world

While the Course tells us that the Holy Spirit's primary function is to teach us true perception—in other words, to help us change our minds, not our external world—it also tells us clearly that one means the Holy Spirit uses for changing minds is working within the world of form. The Holy Spirit Himself has taken form to teach us in this world (see C-6.1:4), and He uses the forms of the world for His teaching purpose. Indeed, there is literally no form in this world He *cannot* use for this purpose:

> All that you made can serve salvation easily and well. The Son of God can make no choice the Holy Spirit cannot employ on his behalf. (T-25.VI.7:4-5)

And so, again and again, the Course depicts the Holy Spirit using things like time, bodies, relationships, situations, words, etc., as means to teach the lessons of salvation. Indeed, the Course itself—a form brought into the world by the Holy Spirit through Jesus—is a prime example of the Holy Spirit using form as a teaching tool.

Why does He use form as a teaching tool? Because we who are committed to the ego have a heavy investment in the world of form that the ego made. Form is what we believe in; it is a language we can understand. Therefore, in order to be an effective Teacher, the Holy Spirit needs "to use what the ego has made, to teach the opposite of what the ego has 'learned'" (T-7.IV.3:3). He needs to *use* the world of form as a means to teach us how to *transcend* the world of form.

Not only does the Holy Spirit use form to teach *us*, but He also uses it to enable us to teach *others*. This is an important emphasis in the Course. If we are to fulfill our function of extending healed perception to others, we must do so in a language *they* can understand. In order to get the message, they need "a body they can see. A voice they understand and listen to, without the fear that truth would encounter in them" (M-12.3:5-6). And so, the Holy Spirit guides us in using forms, like the body, to communicate with those who need to receive the message of salvation in a concrete, tangible way.

If the Holy Spirit does indeed work within the world of form, what exactly does He do? The following points are a list of some of the things the Course explicitly says the Holy Spirit does (or has done) in the world:

He has given us God's plan for salvation, which includes a script for our entire journey through the world.

The plan for salvation (also called the plan of the Atonement) is God's response to the separation, and we are told that the Holy Spirit has the function of "bringing the plan of the Atonement to us" (C-6.2:1). The content of that plan is forgiveness, the earthly reflection of the formless Love of God. Yet because we believe in a world of form, the plan has also taken form. In fact, we are told that the Holy Spirit has written the script (see W-pI.169.9:3) for every single thing that happens in the world.[1] Absolutely nothing is left to chance (M-9.1:3). While this may seem painfully restrictive at first glance, ultimately it is deeply reassuring, as the following passage invites us to recognize:

> What could you not accept, if you but knew that everything that happens, all events, past, present and to come, are gently planned by One Whose only purpose is your good? (W-pI.135.18:1)

He gives each of us a function in His plan for salvation: both the general function of forgiveness, and a special function in the world.

In addition to giving us God's plan for salvation, the Holy Spirit has the function of "establishing our particular part in it and showing us exactly what it is" (C-6.2:1). Since the content of the plan is forgiveness, our general function in that plan is also forgiveness—primarily, extending forgiveness to others. Yet because each of us is different on the level of form, the Holy Spirit has given each of us a particular form in which we are to fulfill our function of forgiveness:

> Such is the Holy Spirit's kind perception of specialness; His use of what you made, to heal instead of harm. To each He gives a special function in salvation he alone can fill; a part for only him. (T-25.VI.4:2)

Our special function is the specific form our forgiveness takes in the world, a form that is uniquely suited to our individual personalities, talents, and life circumstances (see T-25.VII.7:1-3 and W-pI.154.2:1-2). In short, it is the particular part each of us has been assigned in God's plan for salvation.

Our special function could take a wide variety of forms. For example, Helen and Bill had the special function of taking down the Course. A part of Bill's special function was to be a classroom teacher.[2] In the Course material, the Manual discusses the functions of teacher of pupils and healer of patients, and the *Psychotherapy* supplement discusses the function of psychotherapist. All of these are examples of forms our special function could take, though of course there are countless more. The key point is that each and every one of us has a special function assigned by the Holy Spirit, whatever it may be.

He chooses the people we are to help as part of our special function in the world, and puts us in contact with them.

The Course is clear that literally every encounter with another person is pre-arranged by the Holy Spirit. For instance, here is a description of how the teacher of God meets up with those he is to teach:

> The plan includes very specific contacts to be made for each teacher of God. There are no accidents in salvation. Those who are to meet will meet. (M-3.1:5-7)

A later reference in the Manual says that even the specific purpose for each contact is pre-arranged: "Not one is sent without a learning goal already set, and one which can be learned that very day" (M-16.1:7). The bottom line is that our special function is always a way to help other people, and the Holy Spirit brings us together with those who will benefit the most from our particular form of help.

He gives us all the physical things and circumstances we need to fulfill our special function in the world.

To some Course students, it may seem almost sacrilegious to suggest that the Holy Spirit literally gives us *things*. Yet the Course unequivocally states that He supplies us with material possessions (see T-13.VII.12-13) and money (see P-3.III.1,4-6). In addition, He takes care of the circumstances of our lives, including bringing about meetings with specific people (as we saw above) and arranging our life situations (see T-20.IV.8:1-8).

I want to say a little more about T-13.VII.12-13, because I have heard some Course students claim that this passage isn't referring to *material* things, but to *spiritual* things like peace, forgiveness, etc.

However, if we examine the passage and the paragraphs immediately preceding it, we can see that this simply isn't the case. The "things" referred to here (all references in this paragraph are from T-13.VII) are described as things we buy in stores (1:3), things we need on earth (10:4), things that can be owned or possessed (10:10-12), things the ego wants for salvation (10:11), things that we need in time and need to be renewed (12:4), things that meet temporary needs (12:6), things the Holy Spirit has no investment in and doesn't emphasize (12:7, 13:2), and things that *could* be used by us "on behalf of lingering in time," but needn't be because the Holy Spirit can prevent this from happening (12:7). Given these descriptions, how could these things possibly be spiritual things like peace and forgiveness? There is only one class of things that fits all of these descriptions: *material* things.

Of course, the Holy Spirit does not give us things to serve our ego needs; He is not a divine butler at our beck and call, Who delivers worldly goodies to keep our egos fat and happy. Rather, He gives us things only to enable us to fulfill our special function in God's plan for salvation. Thus, the surprising answer to the often-asked question of whether the Holy Spirit manifests parking spaces is "Yes, He does, *if* doing so serves God's plan."

He gives us detailed guidance for all of our decisions and all of our actions in the world.

In the Course's view, we are utterly incapable of making sound decisions on our own. Our limited human judgment is simply not adequate to the task. Therefore, we need a Guide Whose judgment is *unlimited*, a Guide Who can make decisions *for* us. That Guide, of course, is the Holy Spirit.

Again and again, we are told to let go of our judgment and allow the Holy Spirit's judgment to replace it. An entire section of the *Manual for Teachers* (M-10) is devoted to this topic. And while the Holy Spirit's most important role is to guide our *perception* of the world, the Course is clear that He is to specifically guide our *actions* in the world as well. In fact, the Course goes so far as to say that Jesus—through whom the Holy Spirit works—will *control* all of our actions automatically if we allow him to guide our thoughts (see T-2.VI.2:8-9). Throughout the Course, we are told very explicitly that if we turn to the Holy Spirit, He will tell us "what to do and where to go; to whom to speak and what to say to him, what thoughts to think, what words to give the world" (W-pII.275.2:3; see also T-2.V(A).18:4-5, W-pI.71.9:3-5, and W-pI.rVI.In.7:2). Not only will He tell us what to do, but He will even "do it for [us]" (T-14.IV.6:6). It can't get any clearer than that. There is simply no doubt that the Course depicts the Holy Spirit doing things in the world.

KEN WAPNICK'S VIEW: THE HOLY SPIRIT DOES NOT DO THINGS IN THE WORLD

In spite of all of the evidence presented above for the Holy Spirit's activity in the world, Wapnick has a very different view of the Holy Spirit[3]: "He does not actively do anything."[4] Not only does He not actively do anything in the world, but He doesn't even actively do anything in our *minds*; as we will see below, He is not a real Being, and thus cannot act in any way.

Given the evidence, why does Wapnick hold the view he does? It certainly isn't because he is unaware of the evidence. He does not deny that the Course depicts the Holy Spirit doing things in the world. What he does deny is that those depictions are to be taken *literally*. He offers various reasons for why the Course doesn't literally mean the things it says about the Holy Spirit, reasons that are based on the underlying assumption that the Course can't possibly mean these things, given its overall thought system. (We will explore that assumption in more detail below.)

As I've already made clear, we disagree with Wapnick's view. We can find no evidence whatsoever in the Course to support it. We can find nothing in its overall thought system that precludes the possibility of the Holy Spirit acting in the world. In fact, the thought system we see in the Course makes the Holy Spirit's activity in the world absolutely indispensable to our salvation.

Wapnick's reasons for believing that the Holy Spirit does not do things in the world, and our reasons for disagreeing with him

Before beginning this exploration of Wapnick's view, I would like to briefly address a couple of issues that came up in my recent reading of Wapnick's work: First, Wapnick does occasionally make statements that suggest the Holy Spirit *does* act in the world, at least in the role of guiding behavior. Here is one example: "Our *function* in the world is therefore not to feed the hungry, free the oppressed, nor to serve any other social or benevolent cause, although certainly *our behavior may be so guided by the Holy Spirit*"[5] (emphasis in final phrase mine).

I do not know what to make of such statements. It seems to me that Wapnick is contradicting himself. Wapnick may argue that he doesn't intend these statements to be taken literally, but that instead they should be interpreted in the context of his overall teaching that the Holy Spirit does not act in the world. This is actually the same way that he says we should interpret the *Course's* statements about the Holy Spirit acting in the world.

However, this strikes me as a very confusing way to proceed. Why state in such plain, literal language that the Holy Spirit guides behavior, when you actually believe He *doesn't* guide behavior? Such an approach seems bound to lead to misunderstandings. At any rate, Wapnick's references to the Holy Spirit guiding behavior are very rare. His overall position on the Holy Spirit is abundantly clear, and it doesn't include the Holy Spirit guiding behavior.

Second, it should be said that Wapnick seems to have changed his mind on this issue. In his early works, up until about the mid-1980's, he clearly taught that the Holy Spirit *does* act in the world. For instance, in the very first piece Wapnick wrote about the Course, *Christian Psychology in 'A Course in Miracles,'* he says that we should find out from the Holy Spirit "the particular function He has reserved for us in His plan for salvation"[6] and "turn over to the Holy Spirit all our problems regardless of their form, and…refer to His wisdom all questions for which we need answers."[7] Then he adds, "Perhaps it seems at first to be the height of arrogance to believe that the Holy Spirit is so intimately involved with the minutia of our daily lives."[8] In *The Fifty Miracle Principles of 'A Course in Miracles'* (1985), he says that the Holy Spirit is a Being Who "can function in a world of symbols [this world],"[9] and "can use all situations and relationships to teach us the single lesson that the separation is unreal."[10]

Wapnick's earlier works certainly seem to present a view of the Holy Spirit that has much more in common with Circle's view. But as I've said, he really seems to have changed his mind since the early days of his writing about the Course. All of his current works heavily stress that the Holy Spirit does *not* do things in the world in any way, and it is his current position that I will focus on here.

With these issues out of the way, the following italicized points present some of Wapnick's main arguments for the idea that the Holy Spirit does not do things in the world. I will also present our response to those arguments.

The Holy Spirit doesn't do things in the world because the world is an illusion.

This argument runs basically as follows: The Holy Spirit can't *really* act in the world, because there is no world to act *in*. The world is just an illusion in our minds. If the world is an illusion, then the Holy Spirit's seeming "acts" in the world must be illusions as well. Wapnick puts it this way:

> In fact, the Holy Spirit or Jesus do nothing in the world, because all correction and healing occur at the level of the mind. "There is no world!"[11]

This point is perfectly logical, and we have no argument with it as far as it goes. From the Course's standpoint, the world is indeed an illusion in our minds. Therefore, all acts in the illusory world, whether they are ours or the Holy Spirit's, are illusions. Given this, we wholeheartedly agree with Wapnick that the Holy Spirit doesn't do real things in the world, just as we don't do real things in the world.

But this valid point doesn't really address the question I think most people have in mind when they ask if the Holy Spirit does things in the world. The question isn't whether or not the Holy Spirit's acts within the illusion are real, but whether or not He *does* act within the illusion. In other words, to repeat the version of the question I presented above: Does the Holy Spirit actively do things in the world in the same sense that we, the members of the Sonship, actively do things in the world? The ultimate reality-status of those things and of that world is not really relevant to this question. Therefore, the world's illusory nature can't be used to refute the idea that the Holy Spirit does things in the world.

The Holy Spirit doesn't do things in the world, because His role is to help us change our minds, not to guide us in the world.

This is closely related to the first point. Wapnick is emphatic that the Holy Spirit's "activity" takes place *only* within our minds, not the world: "We are taught in the text that it is *not* the role of the Holy Spirit to guide us in the world of *effects*—the material world of specifics—but rather to help us change our minds about the *cause* of our problems: our belief in the reality of sin and guilt."[12] He often cites the following passage from the Text as evidence for this:

> In gentle laughter does the Holy Spirit perceive the cause, and looks not to effects. How else could He correct your error, who have overlooked the cause entirely?....*You* judge effects, but *He* has judged their cause. And by His judgment are effects removed.
>
> (T-27.VIII.9:1-2,4-5)

Of course it is true, as I said above, that the Holy Spirit's function is to teach us true perception—to help us change our minds. That is what this passage is getting at. We think the *cause* of our pain is an outside world independent of our own minds, but in fact the outside world is only an *effect* generated by the *real* cause of our pain: the guilt in our own minds. The Holy Spirit knows this, and has already undone the guilt in our minds through His judgment that we did nothing meriting guilt. This passage is encouraging us to acknowledge the real cause of our pain (the guilt in our minds) *and* the Holy Spirit's undoing of that cause, so that we can change our minds, let go of guilt, and relieve our pain.

But it simply doesn't follow that because the Holy Spirit sees the cause of our pain as in our minds instead of out in the world, He therefore does not do anything in the world. When this passage says He "looks not to effects," it doesn't mean that He has nothing to do with effects; it simply means that He does not erroneously ascribe the cause of our pain *to* those effects, as we do. This doesn't in any way overrule all the evidence already presented that He does things in this world. And, as we will see in the next point, His activity in the world of effects actually plays a role in *facilitating* the change of mind that is the Holy Spirit's goal.

The Holy Spirit doesn't do things in the world because if He did, that would make the error real.

This is a major argument of Wapnick's; he says that if God or His agents were to act in the world, they "would be violating the Course's 'prime directive' (to borrow a term from *Star Trek*), which is not to make the error real."[13]

My first response to this argument is that Wapnick seems to have radically redefined the Course idea of making error real. I am aware of six Course passages that refer more or less directly to this idea.[14] In every one of these passages (read in light of its immediate context), making error real means making the errors of *other people* into real sins through focusing on and magnifying those errors in our minds. This, the Course says, makes forgiveness impossible because seeing our brothers as sinners blinds us to the Christ in them.

But in Wapnick's view, making error real—which he has rephrased in his writings as "making *the* error real"—seems to mean the act of accepting as true any idea that (in Wapnick's view) implies the *physical world* is real. In this reinterpretation, the word "error" no longer refers to the mistakes of another person, but instead to "*the* error" of the separation, and the universe of time and space that stems from it. What ideas make the error real, according to Wapnick? For the most part, they seem to boil down to this: *any idea that suggests that activity in the world—such as the activity of God or His agents—has an important role in salvation.*

As you can see, the Course's idea of making error real and Wapnick's version of it are quite different. The Course's idea addresses the *practical* concern of our dwelling on other people's mistakes. But Wapnick's version addresses his *theological* concern of avoiding anything that seems to imply that the world of time and space is real. The two are quite far apart. However, by grafting *his* meaning onto the *Course's* phrase—by using "making error real" to refer to his concept—he makes it appear that the Course is holding the same theological concern he is. He makes it appear that the Course's "prime directive" is concerned not with focusing on the errors of others, but with believing in ideas that seem to imply that the physical world is real.

"Not to make the error real," as Wapnick uses the phrase, is thus not the "prime directive" of the Course at all. Wapnick's theological concern does not really seem to be shared by the Course. Certainly the Course doesn't share Wapnick's theological concern about the Holy Spirit; I cannot think of anyplace in the Course where it says anything like, "Don't you realize that seeing the Holy Spirit as active in the world would imply that the physical world is real?" On the contrary, we have already seen that His activity has a prominent role in salvation. The Course never says that such activity inevitably makes the physical world real.

In fact, there are passages in the Course that indicate the Holy Spirit acts in the physical world to prove that it is *unreal*. One example is in Chapter 30, Section VIII of the Text. The second paragraph of that section discusses a miracle that brings about a positive external change in a brother's life situation. According to that paragraph, one powerful effect of that miracle and the external change it brings about is the following:

> The miracle attests salvation from appearances by showing they can change....The miracle is proof [your brother] is not bound by loss or suffering in any form, because it can so easily be changed. This demonstrates that it was never real, and could not stem from his reality.
>
> (T-30.VIII.2:2,6-7)

In other words, the miracle changes external situations, and in so doing proves that those external situations are only illusory appearances, not reality. We are thus saved from those appearances.

Think about the implications of that. Miracles come from the Holy Spirit, "Who gives all miracles" (T-30.VIII.4:7). Their primary result is a change of mind, but they also produce positive external effects. And these external effects are not simply pleasant by-products of miracles, but actually perform a vital role in reinforcing that change of mind: They prove the unreality of appearances. Therefore, the result of the Holy Spirit's intervention in the world (through the external effects of the miracles He gives) is that the physical world is shown to be *unreal*. This is reason enough to dismiss the idea that the Holy Spirit cannot do things in the world because that would automatically make the error real.

The Holy Spirit doesn't do things in the world; if we believe He does, we are falling into the trap of "spiritual specialness."

According to Wapnick, the belief that the Holy Spirit does things in the world is not only incorrect, but is actually a sneaky ego ploy to get us to engage in what he calls "spiritual specialness."[15] In his view, the belief that the Holy Spirit does things in the world is simply the ego's insatiable drive for specialness masquerading in a "spiritualized" form. In particular, seeing the Holy Spirit as a personal Being Who has "specially chosen [us] to do *holy, special, and very important work* in this world"[16] is nothing more than the ego's last-ditch effort to make the error real, to defend its specialness against the threat posed by the ego-undoing message of *A Course in Miracles*. Therefore, Wapnick concludes, we really shouldn't seek guidance concerning our function at all: "Focusing on hearing Jesus or the Holy Spirit is clearly setting oneself up for a painful fall, for such a practice grossly underestimates the unconscious investment in the reality of the ego's thought system of specialness."[17]

Certainly, the idea that we have a special function in the world can be a fertile ground for ego-based specialness. But to say that this idea is *inherently* ego-based is a classic case of throwing out the baby with the bathwater. As we saw above, the Course clearly says that the Holy Spirit *has* given us a special function in the world. Rather than being an ego trap, this special function is, in the words previously quoted, "the Holy Spirit's kind perception of specialness; His use of what you made, to heal instead of harm" (T-25.VI.4:2). It is the Holy Spirit's reinterpretation of our desire for specialness, in which He converts it from an ego trap to a means to serve God's plan.

Far from discouraging the idea, then, Jesus really wants us to know that we *do* have a special function, because "[our] part is essential to God's plan for salvation" (W-pI.100.Heading). If we totally reject the idea that the Holy Spirit has given us a special function and does things in the world to help us fulfill that function, it will have the devastating effect of causing us to reject our part in God's plan. Ironically, in trying to escape "spiritual specialness," we will end up playing right into the ego's hands.

The Holy Spirit doesn't do things in the world because only our own minds really do things; the Holy Spirit only seems to do things.

This is Wapnick's explanation for the many passages in the Course that depict the Holy Spirit doing things in our lives. Such passages, in his view, aren't meant to be taken literally, but simply "reflect…the *experience* within our split minds of the abstract Presence of God's Love."[18] In truth, Wapnick says, only our own minds actually do anything; it only *seems* that the Holy Spirit does things for us.[19]

Wapnick uses the following analogy to make his point: Just as our experience is that the sun moves when in fact the earth is moving around a (relatively) stationary sun, so our experience is that the Holy Spirit "moves" and does things for us when in fact our *minds* are "moving" in relation to the "stationary" Presence of God's Love.[20] Thus, what seems to be the Holy Spirit's activity in the world is actually a deception of our ego-driven minds, which "interpret *our* change of mind as being done for us by the Holy Spirit."[21]

The problem with this theory is that it finds absolutely no support in the Course. Of course, our minds do "move," but so does the Holy Spirit. Recall the line from the Text I quoted above, which said that not only will the Holy Spirit tell us what to do, but He will even "do it for [us]" (T-14.IV.6:6). Wapnick's idea that the Holy Spirit does nothing seems to be based not on evidence from the Course, but on his own logic, rooted in the idea I will discuss in the next point.

The Holy Spirit doesn't do things in the world because God does not even know about the separation.

According to Wapnick, the Holy Spirit does nothing because the Course's "basic metaphysical premise is that God does not even know about the dream."[22] This idea is central to Wapnick's view of the Course: "This God [the God of the Course] does not even know about the separation...and thus does not and cannot respond to it."[23] Therefore, God could not possibly have literally created a Being like the Holy Spirit in response to the separation. Given this, it goes without saying that He didn't create a Being Who could actually *act* within the illusory world of separation.

But the Course never actually says that God doesn't know about the separation. In fact, there are two passages that directly say otherwise. One is T-6.V.1:5-8; the other is the following:

> Unless you take your part in the creation, [God's] joy is not complete because yours is incomplete. *And this He does know. He knows it in His Own Being and its experience of His Son's experience.* The constant going out of His Love is blocked when His channels are closed, and He is lonely when the minds He created do not communicate fully with Him.
>
> (T-4.VII.6:4-7, emphasis mine)

Clearly, this passage tells us that God knows we have somehow cut off our minds from Him—or at least cut off our *awareness* of Him. Wapnick may dismiss this passage as metaphor, but we at the Circle find that very hard to do. A metaphor usually brings to mind a specific concrete image, an image that represents or symbolizes a more abstract idea. A Course example would be the metaphor of giving your brother lilies, which represents forgiveness. But this passage doesn't contain such language; instead, it speaks in abstract terms about things like God's Being, knowledge, and experience—language that is more philosophical, theological, and metaphysical in nature. The two sentences I emphasized in particular look a lot more like the technical language of abstract theology than the colorful language of concrete imagery; they are more metaphysics than metaphor. Therefore, we have every reason to believe that this passage represents Jesus' literal teaching about the nature of God, a teaching that he wants us to take seriously as a statement of the Course's theology.

In our opinion, this passage (along with T-6.V.1:5-8) is strong evidence that God knows about the separation, and could therefore respond to it by creating a Being capable of acting within the illusion of separation. Indeed, T-6.V.1:5-8 concludes with a statement that God *did* respond to it: "So He thought, 'My children sleep and must be awakened'" (T-6.V.1:8).[24]

The Holy Spirit doesn't do things in the world because He is only an illusion.

This point follows from the previous one. For if the Holy Spirit is not a Being created by God in response to the separation, then just what is He? Clearly, He can't really be anything substantial. Wapnick, in fact, says point-blank that "the Holy Spirit is an illusion."[25] One of the Course passages he offers as evidence for this rather startling claim that the Holy Spirit is only "a symbol and not reality"[26] is this one from the Manual:

> His [the Holy Spirit's] is the Voice for God, and has therefore taken form. This form is not His reality, which God alone knows along with Christ....
> ...And then the Voice is gone, no longer to take form, but to return to the eternal formlessness of God.
> (C-6.1:4-5,5:8)

Wapnick's claim apparently rests on the lines in this passage referring to the unreality of the Holy Spirit's form, and the fact that His form will disappear once the dream is over. But while these lines do say that the *forms* He takes are unreal (as all forms are), they certainly

121

don't say that *He* is unreal. On the contrary, we see in this passage a direct reference to "His reality, which God alone knows along with Christ."

Moreover, the section from which these lines are drawn (C-6) says that the Holy Spirit is "a creation of the One Creator, creating with Him and in His likeness or spirit," a creation that "is eternal" (1:2). An eternal creation of God is real by definition. Throughout this section, the Holy Spirit is described as a real Being Who works in the world (see especially 2:1). He does this in order to accomplish His "dual function" (3:2) of serving as a bridge between Heaven's knowledge and the world's perception: "He knows because He is part of God; He perceives because He was sent to save humanity" (3:3). And even though His *form* will disappear when the dream is over, the Course assures us elsewhere that *He* will remain with us forever in Heaven when the dream is done (see T-5.I.5:5-7).

Therefore, the passage Wapnick quotes here does not depict the Holy Spirit as an illusion; rather, it depicts Him as a *real, eternal Being* Who takes on *illusory, temporary forms* in order to serve His function of mediating between the reality of Heaven and our illusory world.[27]

The Holy Spirit doesn't do things in the world because He is only the memory of God.

What is the nature of the illusion described in the previous point? According to Wapnick, the Holy Spirit is simply "the memory of God's Love and the Son's true Identity as Christ that he carried with him into his dream."[28] He is "a distant memory of our Source,"[29] a memory that comforts us within the dream of separation just as the memory of a human loved one comforts us when we feel lonely and cut off from our earthly home. We experience this memory as a personal Being external to ourselves only because we have projected this ego-threatening memory outside of our minds: "The figures of Jesus or the Holy Spirit are really the projections (reflections) of the memory of a non-dualistic God within our dualistic minds."[30] The Holy Spirit is thus nothing more than a "projected split-off part of our self,"[31] the part that remembers God.

But there are at least two problems with this definition of the Holy Spirit as the memory of God. First, the Course itself never uses anything like this definition. The closest it ever comes is to say that the Holy Spirit *reminds* us of God (see, for instance, T-5.II.7:1-5), but saying that He reminds us of God is quite different than saying that He is actually the *memory* of God. That would be like saying that when my wife reminds me of the trip to San Francisco we took ten years ago, she herself *is* my memory of that trip.

Second, the term "memory of God" has a specific, technical meaning in the Course, and it is not synonymous with the Holy Spirit. Rather, the term "memory of God" refers to our final awakening in Heaven, accomplished by God in His last step (see, for instance, W-pII.8.5 and C-3.4). One passage, in fact, spells out the relationship *between* the memory of God and the Holy Spirit: "I have within me both the memory of You [God], *and* One [the Holy Spirit] Who leads me to it" (W-pII.352.1:7, emphasis mine). Here, the memory of God and the Holy Spirit are clearly depicted as different things. Thus, rather than defining the Holy Spirit as the memory of God, I think we are wiser to adhere to the definition of the Holy Spirit that the Course itself gives us: a Being Whom God created in response to the separation, a Being Who can and does do things in the world to carry out God's plan of salvation.

The Holy Spirit doesn't do things in the world because pure, non-dualistic spirit simply cannot interact with a dualistic world without compromising spirit's non-dualistic nature.

This is the heart of the matter. This is the fundamental assumption underlying all of the arguments presented above against the idea of the Holy Spirit doing things in the world—the assumption at the core of Ken Wapnick's entire view of the Course's thought system. He explains his basic interpretive stance toward the Course in a section of *Few Choose to Listen* entitled "An Uncompromising Non-Dualism."[32] In that section, one way in which he expresses his basic rule of Course interpretation is to paraphrase M-27.7:1, replacing the word "death" with "duality," as follows: "*Accept no compromise in which **duality** plays a part.*"[33]

In this view, God's Heaven is so purely non-dualistic, so absolutely One, that nothing within it can possibly reach down and interact with a dualistic, separated world in any way, shape, or form. If anything in this realm of pure spirit were to do so, its purity and Oneness would be impossibly compromised. Therefore, whenever the Course talks about spirit interacting with the world (as when it describes the Holy Spirit doing things in the world), it simply can't be taken literally.

Why, then, does the Course talk this way? According to Wapnick, Jesus' purpose for this "metaphorical" language is to comfort beginners on the path by "couch[ing] his teachings in words that his students—always referred to as children (or sometimes even younger)—can understand without fear."[34] Taking this language literally is fine for beginners, but once we have progressed beyond the beginning stage, we should give up childish notions like the idea of spirit interacting with the world, or we will "find ourselves back in our childhood world of fairy godmothers, Santa Claus, and a Sugar Daddy for a God."[35]

But how do we know that Wapnick's assumption that spirit cannot interact with the world is correct? The Course itself never states this once; it is only a logical inference based on a particular interpretation of certain passages. Not only does the Course not state this, but it states the opposite—that spirit can and does interact with the world—countless times. How do we know that it does not mean what it says? If the choice is between a questionable logical inference never stated in the Course and a teaching stated again and again in the Course, which should we choose?

In the Circle's view, the clear choice is the latter. Whenever we are trying to determine what the Course teaches, I think we are on much firmer ground when we stick to what the Course itself actually says, rather than taking unwarranted logical leaps. And besides, we actually have a very obvious, irrefutable example of non-dualistic spirit interacting with a dualistic world without compromising spirit's non-dualistic nature. That example is us: the Sonship.

Think about the current situation of the Sonship as the Course describes it. Our true nature is spirit. Our home is the absolute Oneness of Heaven. Yet somehow, in a way that the Course says is unexplainable, we managed to convince ourselves that we are something other than spirit. Out of this mental error, we managed to project a dualistic, illusory world with which we interact. But in spite of this, we are told, we have not really compromised our spiritual nature. We remain in the Oneness of Heaven, which we never really left.

Clearly, then, it is possible for a non-dualistic Sonship to somehow mentally separate from God, make an illusory, dualistic world, and interact with that world without compromising the Sonship's non-dualistic nature. Now, here's the punch line: If this is so, then why can't a non-dualistic God respond to the separation by sending a Teacher and Comforter Who can and does interact with the illusory, dualistic world without compromising God's non-dualistic nature? Personally, I see no reason why He cannot.

CONCLUSION

We at the Circle have every reason to believe that the Course literally "means exactly what it says" (T-8.IX.8:1) when it tells us that the Holy Spirit does things in the world. We see no reason to believe otherwise. Personally, I am immensely comforted by this, because it means that we are not cut off from God, all alone in a nightmare world that our remote Father can't help us out of because He does not even know about it. Instead, He knows in His Own Being that we are suffering in seeming exile. And so, out of His Love for us, He created the Holy Spirit, a Guide Who leads us home using every means at His disposal. Nothing is too "impure" for our Guide to use; He even uses the illusory world that we made to imprison ourselves as a means to set us free. In the pages of the Course, Jesus assures us that we have Help in this world. Why not take him at his word?

Notes

[1] For more about the Holy Spirit's script and how it relates to the Course's idea that *we* are responsible for everything that happens to us in our lives, see my "Course Q & A" article on the Circle's website, entitled "Are all the events and circumstances in our lives predetermined, or do we have free choice?"

[2] See the section entitled "Bill's Class" in Ken Wapnick's *Absence from Felicity*, pp. 269-280.

[3] All of the works cited below as sources of Ken Wapnick's views are published by the Foundation for *A Course in Miracles*, located in Temecula, California. All of the works were written by Wapnick; one work, *The Most Commonly Asked Questions about 'A Course in Miracles,'* was co-written with his wife Gloria.

[4] *The Message of 'A Course in Miracles,' Volume One: All Are Called* (1997), p. 247.

[5] *Ibid.*, p. 341.

[6] *Christian Psychology in 'A Course in Miracles,'* 2nd ed. (1st ed. 1978; 2nd ed. 1992), p. 38.

[7] *Ibid.*, p. 40.

[8] *Ibid.*, p. 41.

[9] *The Fifty Miracle Principles of 'A Course in Miracles,'* 2nd ed. (1st ed. 1985; 2nd ed. 1990), p. 93.

[10] *Ibid.*, p. 95.

[11] *The Most Commonly Asked Questions about 'A Course in Miracles'* (1995), p. 86. The Course quotation is from W-pl.132.6:2.

[12] *Ibid.*, p. 119.

[13] *Ibid.*, p. 90.

[14] T-9.III.6; T-9.IV.4-5; T-11.V.14; T-12.I.1; T-12.III.2; and S-2.I.3.

[15] See the discussion on pp. 137-142 of *The Message of 'A Course in Miracles,' Volume Two: Few Choose to Listen* (1997).

[16] *Ibid.*, p. 137.

[17] *Ibid.*, p. 142.

[18] *All Are Called*, p. 314.

[19] One ramification of this is that Wapnick disagrees with the Circle's view that the Holy Spirit has written the script for our journey through the world. Instead, *"We—the decision maker in our minds—are the ones who write and choose our scripts"* (*Commonly Asked Questions*, p. 88).

[20] See *Few Choose to Listen*, pp. 125-126.

[21] *All Are Called*, p. 314.

[22] *Ibid.*, p. 314.

[23] *Commonly Asked Questions*, p. 4.

[24] For more on the topic of whether God knows about the separation, see Robert Perry's article entitled "Does God Know We Are Here?" This article is available in Issue #21 of the Circle's newsletter *A Better Way*, or on the Circle's website.

[25] *Duality as Metaphor in 'A Course in Miracles'* (tape set of Ken Wapnick workshop). See also *Few Choose to Listen*, p. 88, where Wapnick says, "Just as forgiveness remains an illusion because it corrects the sin that never was, so too must the Holy Spirit be an illusion as well, because he corrects (or translates) what is useless and meaningless."

[26] *Few Choose to Listen*, p. 124.

[27] This is another instance in which Wapnick has changed his mind compared to his stance in earlier works. In *Fifty Miracle Principles* (p. 93), a work that is a combined transcript of two taped workshops done in 1985, a questioner asks Wapnick: "If the separation is an illusion, and the Holy Spirit came into existence to solve that, is not the Holy Spirit an illusion?" Wapnick's answer: "No, because God created Him. It is a good question though. The Course's answer is that when the separation is totally healed and the Holy Spirit is no longer needed, He still exists because God created Him. And then the Course says that He returns to Heaven and blesses our creations (text, p. 68) [Second Edition: text, p. 74; T-5.I.5:5-7]."

[28] *Commonly Asked Questions*, p. 103.

[29] *All Are Called*, p. 33.

[30] *Few Choose to Listen*, p. 108.

[31] *Ibid.*, p. 108.

[32] *Ibid.*, pp. 94-99.

[33] *Ibid.*, p. 94.

[34] *Commonly Asked Questions*, pp. 85-86.

[35] *Few Choose to Listen*, p. 69.

Is the Bible Compatible with the Course?

A Comparison of the Views of Ken Wapnick and the Circle of Atonement

by Allen Watson

Note: In Bible quotations, I quote from the New American Standard Version; I abbreviate its name in references as "NASB."

I found it somewhat difficult to write this essay, because there is not a lot of quotable material on the subject in Ken Wapnick's writings. Although Wapnick's general attitude towards the Bible is quite evident, specific statements about it are few in number, and generally are lacking in detailed explanation for his stance. In a sense, this could be a very short essay. My findings could be summarized in a few sentences, as follows:

Wapnick's view of the Bible in relation to A Course in Miracles: The spiritual paths taught by the Bible and the Course are "totally incompatible."[1] Wapnick views the Bible as so thoroughly corrupted by the egos of its authors[2] that it is of no use to a student of the Course; its teaching and that of the Course "ultimately do not mix."[3]

The Circle's view of the Bible in relation to A Course in Miracles: The Course sees itself as a continuation of the same stream of inspiration that produced the Bible, continuing and expanding on the themes that are true in it, while correcting themes that are in error. The Bible must therefore be read with discernment, but it does contain a great deal of truth, and read properly it can significantly enhance and enrich the journey of students of the Course.

WAPNICK'S ATTITUDE TOWARDS THE BIBLE

During a two-year period (approximately 1990-1991), I attended a dozen or more workshops taught by Ken Wapnick, a few lasting only

127

an afternoon, many filling an entire weekend, and one that lasted five days. I read nearly all of the books he had published up until that time, several books that were published later, and I listened to dozens of audiotapes of his lectures. Based on that large sample of his teaching, I would say that Wapnick likes to stress the uniqueness of the Course and the ways in which it differs from other spiritual paths. He therefore downplays any similarities between the Course and other paths, even the Bible. He seems to feel that marking similarities between the Course and other spiritual teachings such as the Bible "blurs…its distinctive contribution to the world's spiritualities."[4]

Wapnick's early publications seem to embrace the Bible and to expand on the parallels between it and the Course. For instance, his *Glossary-Index* documents the hundreds of scriptural quotations and allusions in the Course, clearly showing how the Course draws heavily on the Bible. This section was retained and even expanded in later editions, so apparently Wapnick continues to see some value in cross-referencing the two books, but the emphasis seems out of character with his later writings. Part II of his *Forgiveness and Jesus* is titled "New Testament Teachings." In its Introduction, Wapnick speaks of the teachings of Jesus recorded in the gospels concerning the two great commandments, loving God and loving our neighbor, and says, "These two commandments can be translated into…the key principles of *A Course in Miracles.*"[5] The entire second half of the forgiveness book is devoted to showing how the teachings of the Course are not simply foreshadowed by but in large measure are actually part of the teaching of Jesus and his apostles as recorded in the New Testament.

From my personal exposure to his teaching in the early nineties and from his later publications, it seems evident that Wapnick no longer sees such a close connection between the Bible and the Course. There can be no question that his later teachings actively discourage students from attempting to blend the Course with the Bible in any way, and try to brand the Bible as untrustworthy, hopelessly corrupt, and even dangerous. Wapnick says, "It [the Bible] is the ego's story, with the character of God being the ego's self-portrait,"[6] an allegation that for a teacher of the Course is akin to a Catholic priest attributing a book to Satan.

POINTS OF COMPARISON

In the paragraphs that follow I will present three particular points related to the Bible on which Wapnick has expressed a point of view that, to us, seems discordant with the Course. I will follow each point

128

with the Circle's response, expressing what we believe is a point of view more consistent with that of the Course.

Is the God of the Bible the God of the Course?

Wapnick: No

In *Commonly Asked Questions,* Wapnick answers a question about God in the Bible contrasted to God in the Course by pointing out differences in how the Bible and the Course portray God. He cites examples such as these:

- The Bible reports that God created the physical universe, whereas the Course "unequivocally states...that God did not create this world."[7]
- As pictured in the Bible, God sees sin as real and responds to it, while the Course teaches that sin does not exist.
- The God of the Bible takes vengeance on sinners and punishes them; the God of the Course repudiates attack entirely.

Based upon these differences in how the two books describe God, Wapnick concludes, "The God of the Course is not the God of formal religion, and certainly not the God of the Bible."[8]

The Circle's response

To me, this seems to be poor logic. There are not two "Gods" involved here, just two descriptions of the same God. If two people give different descriptions of an automobile accident, do we conclude they must be speaking of different accidents? Would we say, "The accident of Mr. Smith is certainly not the accident of Mr. Jones"? Of course not! When there are many points of similarity along with the differences, we realize that, although one or both of the descriptions must contain some errors, the two descriptions are speaking of the same accident.

Likewise, while the Course and the Bible describe God differently, they are clearly talking about the same God. It is up to us to decide which description is the most accurate: the Bible's, or the Course's.

We at the Circle agree with Wapnick about what the Course teaches on these points: that God did not create the world, that God sees no sin, and that God is not vengeful. We also agree that some parts of the Bible conflict with the Course on these points. We do not, however, accept

Wapnick's conclusion that this completely invalidates all that the Bible has to say about God, nor do we agree that the Bible is in total disagreement with the Course on all of these points. Although I know of no biblical support for the ideas that God did not create the world, or that God does not see us as sinners separated from Himself, there are at least a few places where the Bible seems to convey a gentler picture of God, a God Who does not seek to punish us. For instance:

> "As I live!" declares the Lord GOD, "I take no pleasure in the death of the wicked, but rather that the wicked turn from his way and live."   (Ezekiel 33:11, NASB)

> But You are a God of forgiveness, gracious and compassionate, slow to anger and abounding in lovingkindness; and You did not forsake them.
> (Nehemiah 9:17, NASB)

> The Lord is not slow about His promise, as some count slowness, but is patient toward you, not wishing for any to perish but for all to come to repentance.
> (2 Peter 3:9, NASB)

Even among fundamentalists, there are some (counted heretics by most) who teach that, in the end, every living being will be saved—even the devil! One passage often quoted by them is this one, which speaks of Jesus in heaven:

> For this reason also, God highly exalted Him, and bestowed on Him the name which is above every name,

> so that at the name of Jesus every knee will bow, of those who are in heaven and on earth and under the earth,

> and that every tongue will confess that Jesus Christ is Lord, to the glory of God the Father.
> (Philippians 3:9-11, NASB)

In the usual interpretation of "those who are…under the earth" the phrase refers to demonic forces. Further, to confess Jesus Christ as Lord is, in most evangelical systems, the phrase that describes what one does to be saved. Thus, even the demons will be saved. Every knee will bow, every tongue will confess, and thus, these interpreters say, every being will be saved. How could it be otherwise? With this universality of salvation the Course quite agrees, although it does not

130

teach the existence of the devil or of demons.

In fact, there are many points on which the Bible and the Course are in total *agreement* about God. Here are just a few (the references are representative, not comprehensive):

God is Love (I John 4:8; T-9.I.9:7)

This is a central tenet of the Course in regard to God. It makes a great deal of the fact that God is Love and that we, who are His creations, must therefore be love also. God as Love is also a central teaching of Christianity, and therefore a strong meeting point of the two.

Certainly, one can find many passages in the Bible that speak of a God Who is vengeful and wrathful, although these are mostly in the Old Testament, but they do not negate the picture of a loving God that runs all through the Bible, especially in the New Testament. The Course itself declares: "The New Testament...gospel is really only the message of love" (T-6.I.15:1).

God is a Trinity of Father, Son, and Holy Spirit (Matthew 28:19; T-5.I.4:1-3)

The doctrine of the Trinity has long been recognized as a distinguishing mark of the Bible and Christian teaching. No other religion that I know of speaks of a triune God (though some other religions do have threefold images of the Absolute that seem to parallel the Trinity in certain respects). The Course unmistakably and firmly grounds itself on Christian New Testament theology when it speaks of God in these same terms, and even uses the word "Trinity" to describe God.

The frequent references in the Course to God as "Father" are distinctively biblical, and forge a strong link between the Bible and the Course.

The central role given to the Holy Spirit is also a distinctive emphasis of the Bible (specifically, the New Testament) that the Course shares.

God is a loving Father just waiting for His Son to return home (Luke 15:11-32; T-8.VI.4:1-5:1)

In its references to the Parable of the Prodigal Son, the Course does not simply *agree* with the teaching of the Bible, it *bases* its own teaching on the Bible and refers to the parable as an authoritative

131

account of Jesus' teaching about God. It even appeals to us, "Listen to the story of the prodigal son, and learn" (T-8.VI.4:1). It directs us to pay attention to the story in the Bible.

To say, as Wapnick does, that the God of the Course is "certainly not the God of the Bible" simply does not fit the facts, in my view. Yes, there are numerous differences between the two pictures of God. Yes, many of those differences are of major significance. Nevertheless, there are also many similarities in the two views, and many of those similarities are as significant as the differences. In my opinion, there are enough similarities that we can easily conclude that the God of the Course is the same God as the God of the Bible, but seen with a clearer vision. In the Bible, the picture of God is heavily distorted by the egos of its writers; in the Course, the picture of God is (or seems to be) undistorted.

To me, the same God who spoke through the Holy Spirit to Helen Schucman, as recorded in *A Course in Miracles,* was also speaking through the biblical authors, and very likely in much the same way. They, too, were inspired by God as Helen was inspired by God. The difference—and it is a huge difference—is that in Helen Schucman, God found someone who was supremely capable of detaching herself from her ego, enabling her to record what she heard with matchless clarity.

God has been speaking to humankind for thousands of years. The drastic differences in the messages that have been written down, from the Old Testament to the New Testament and then to the Course, are due, not to a different God speaking, but to differing degrees of clarity in the scribes.

How does the spiritual path taught by the Bible compare with that taught by the Course?

Wapnick: The spiritual path of the Bible is incompatible with the Course

In contrasting the Course with other spiritual paths, Wapnick focuses his attention on the dangers of diluting the Course with foreign elements drawn from other spiritual paths, hoping to avoid what he characterizes as "serious distortion of what *A Course in Miracles* actually teaches and how it is meant to be practiced."[9] He admits that other spiritual paths such as the Bible share the goal of returning to God, but stresses the extent to which the Course's "theology and practice are different."[10]

In responding to those with points of view that differ with his, Wapnick has a tendency to ascribe the disagreement to the other person's ego. For instance, if you point out similarities between the Course and another spiritual path, Wapnick sees it as the ego's resistance to the true message of the Course. He calls such comparison "a subtle ploy of the ego for changing *A Course in Miracles* so that its teaching will be less threatening."[11] He says it stems from students "attempting to scale it [the Course] down to their own level of understanding."[12] In effect, Wapnick seems to be saying, "If you disagree with me, if you see the Course and the Bible as similar in any way, you are listening to your ego, and are operating from ignorance." He *assumes* that the Bible and the Course are incompatible, and brands any opinion to the contrary as ego-based or immature thinking.

The Circle's response: The two paths as a whole are incompatible but many of the details are transferable

We at the Circle agree that the Course has many unique elements and that it can easily stand on its own as a spiritual path. We agree, also, that there is reason to guard against diluting the Course with elements from other paths. If elements from other traditions are allowed to obscure or supercede similar elements in the Course, the clear curriculum of the Course can become muddled. The big difference here is one of degree. Wapnick overstresses the uniqueness of the Course, to the point where he can't acknowledge the genuine similarities between it and other paths. The Circle agrees with him on its uniqueness and completeness, but also believes that the Course displays numerous similarities to other paths, particularly the Bible, similarities that can illuminate the path of the Course if we compare them to these other paths with skill and discernment.

To say, as Wapnick does, that the spiritual truths taught by the Bible and by the Course are "totally incompatible"[13] is an over-generalization. *Partly* incompatible, certainly; *largely* incompatible, maybe; but definitely not *totally* incompatible. In reading Wapnick's book *'A Course in Miracles' and Christianity: A Dialogue*, in which Wapnick and Fr. W. Norris Clarke compare and contrast the Course with Christianity, it is clear that both Wapnick and Clarke sometimes make the rather incredible assumption that Christianity and Catholicism are identical, and that Catholic teaching is representative of all Christian teaching. Also, Clarke seems to accept that Wapnick's interpretation of the Course accurately represents the Course; he never asks if alternative interpretations exist. (Wapnick, of course, does not view his own pronouncements about the Course as interpretation. In an interview with Ian Patrick,[14] Wapnick stated that what he says is what the Course says, which is a particularly absurd claim for anyone to make, since it is *impossible* to teach about the contents of a book without interpreting its words.)

Wapnick holds up the teaching of a particular segment of Christendom and claims it is the whole. He then concludes that since the Course differs from the teaching of that *segment* of Christianity, it is totally incompatible with *all* of Christianity. The truth is that the Course does not entirely disagree with Catholicism and that Catholicism is not the whole of Christianity.

For instance, at one point Wapnick contrasts the teaching of the Course concerning Atonement with the view presented in the New Testament. The more conservative branches of both Catholicism and Protestantism teach that man is sinful and separated from God by his sin, but that Jesus, through his sacrificial death, has taken our punishment upon himself, and reconciled us to God. That teaching can be summed up in the words "Jesus died for our sins." In the Course, Jesus refutes this teaching when he says, "I was not 'punished' because *you* were bad" (T-3.I.2:10). Two entire sections of the Course (Section I of both Chapter 3 and Chapter 6) are devoted to a radical reinterpretation of the meaning of Jesus' crucifixion, one that strips it of any possible connection to the idea of sacrifice.

There is no question that the teaching of the Course on this point is entirely incompatible with *traditional, theologically conservative* Christianity, including Protestant fundamentalists and strictly orthodox Catholics. A significant percentage of Christian churches and leaders, however, do not hold these conservative views. A vast number of Christians hold views about the crucifixion that are much more closely aligned with the Course than they are with that traditional teaching. Many liberal Protestant churches no longer teach that atonement was purchased by the sacrificial death of Jesus.

These nontraditional Christian groups do not entirely repudiate the Bible, as Wapnick seems to do. Instead, they reinterpret it. The scholars of the Jesus Seminar (a nonsectarian group of scholars consisting mostly of liberal Christians, with some Jews as well), for instance, have devoted years to the study of the gospels in an attempt to determine what the original teaching of Jesus was, and what parts of the gospels were later added by men who mixed their imperfect understanding with the pure teaching of Jesus. (Interestingly, this picture of the gospels is quite in accord with the Course.) While these scholars reject large portions of the gospels as suspect, they also retain a central core, which they believe represents the true teaching of Jesus. As Robert Perry has pointed out in some of his articles, that central core contains remarkable parallels with the teaching of *A Course in Miracles*.

A second group of Christians who maintain respect for the Bible while rejecting traditional theology consists of the churches that could be categorized as "New Thought" (Unity, Religious Science, and Christian Science, for instance). They hold views on some points nearly identical to what the Course teaches. Some of these churches have embraced the Course and sponsor Course study groups. This has happened, not because the Course is being misinterpreted and corrupted by the admixture of Christian teachings that are "totally incompatible" according to Wapnick, but because—at least in many points—the Course and these Christian churches teach similar things. They find the Course a welcome addition to their curriculum.

In my book *Seeing the Bible Differently* (published by the Circle), I dealt with this question at some length. I would like to quote extensively from that book at this point:

> I see the Course standing in relationship to the New Testament almost exactly as the New Testament stands in relationship to the Old. It is a higher, more complete understanding of God's unchanging revelation. It is presenting the same content (the same original revelation from God) in a purer manifestation. In some ways, the new form presented in the Course seems to be a radical change from what the New Testament teaches; it seems to completely contradict that teaching. But in reality, it does not contradict; it fulfills, it uplifts, it augments. It is a more perfect reception of the same truths God has always been trying to impart to us.
>
> When the New Testament teachers declared that Jesus'

single sacrifice had rendered any lesser sacrifices unnecessary, completely loosing mankind from all penalty for sin for all time, it was a change no less radical than the one the Course now makes in declaring that no sacrifice at all is needed, because no sin has actually occurred. The discerning reader can see a definite continuity in this progression of teaching, a movement from a lesser understanding to a greater. The new teaching does not make the old teaching wrong; it is simply more complete.

There is a story of four blind monks who encounter an elephant. Each approaches the elephant and grasps a particular part: one the trunk, one a leg, one the tail, and one the elephant's huge abdomen. And each reports on what an elephant feels like:

"An elephant is like a snake." "An elephant is like a tree." "An elephant is like a rope." "An elephant is like a wall."

Were any of the monks "wrong?" No; according to what they had experienced of the elephant, they were all correct. But all of their understandings were incomplete.

The Bible is an imperfect reception of the revelation of God's nature, and the way He interacts with mankind. The revelation that inspired it was correct, but men's egos "mis-received" it and distorted it to some degree. If we accept what the Course is saying, *A Course in Miracles* is a more complete understanding, a purer expression of the same truth about the same God. Therefore, just as the Apostles did not need to totally invalidate the Old Testament in order to proclaim their new understanding, neither do we, as Course students, need to invalidate the Bible in order to hold to the higher understanding the Course presents. The Bible and its teachings are part of what got us here, part of what prepared us for the Course, just as the Law acted as a tutor, keeping mankind in custody until the later revelation could come through.[15]

The Course is thus a worthy successor to the Bible. It is quite capable of standing on its own, but it owes a lot to its heritage in the Bible. The best way to see the relationship between the Bible and the

Course is to understand the Course as the next major step in revelation after the Bible. It is grounded in the Bible, it takes up the truths the Bible was trying to impart to us, but it presents them in a higher form. Some have said the Course might be thought of as "the Third Testament," and that, in my mind, is a title the Course merits.

The spiritual path given to us in the Course is much clearer and better defined than anything in the Bible. The path the Bible recommends—repentance for our sins, and faith in the sacrificial death of Jesus as payment in full for those sins—is, indeed, incompatible on the whole with the Course's path; you cannot follow both paths at once. Yet there are common elements, and significant aspects of what the Bible says that can integrate comfortably with the Course's message.

Is the Jesus of the Bible the same as the Jesus of the Course?

Wapnick: No

Wapnick's stance on this issue is complex and, on the surface, often contradictory. To summarize his position in broad strokes, he teaches that the Jesus of the Bible is not the Jesus of the Course. Wapnick writes quite emphatically and clearly: "The Jesus of the Bible and the Course are mutually exclusive figures, with only the common name linking them together."[16] He claims that the Jesus of the Bible "represents the collective projections of the various authors of the gospels and epistles."[17] He explains that while the Jesus who wrote the Course is the same Jesus who lived two thousand years ago in Palestine, the Jesus depicted in the Bible is not the same as either. Thus:

> The Course's Jesus *is* the same as the earthly Jesus.
> The Bible's Jesus *is not* the same as the earthly Jesus.
> Therefore, the Course's Jesus is not the same as the Bible's Jesus.

Wapnick is not devaluing the Course's picture of Jesus. On the contrary, he is saying that the Bible's picture of Jesus is inaccurate, and therefore out of accord with the picture given by the Course.

The Circle's response: Yes, they are the same Jesus

I share with Robert and Greg a conviction that the Jesus who is speaking to us in the Course is the same Jesus who walked the streets of Nazareth two thousand years ago, and whose teachings are recorded in the gospels. I believe that large portions of the gospels accurately reflect his actual words, and that other parts are based on something he taught, but with distortions introduced by the writers, some minor and some major. This seems to be the way that Jesus himself treats the Bible in the Course. He often quotes the Bible approvingly (for example, T-2.II.1:9; T-3.VI.1:4; T-4.In.1:1; T-4.III.5:3; T-5.I.3:4-6; and many others), and often when he refers to some portion of the gospels he uses the words "I said" (for example, T-7.III.1:7 and T-8.IV.2:4), clearly claiming those words as his own and validating their authenticity.

Yet he also does not hesitate to correct the Bible and even to reject some of its sayings outright (see especially T-6.I.14:1-16:1). Therefore, we must recognize with Wapnick that some things said about (or by) Jesus in the Gospels are inaccurate pictures of the real Jesus.

Notice this line: "As you read the teachings of the Apostles..." (T-6.I.16:1). Obviously, Jesus *expects* us to read the New Testament! Would he be saying that if the Bible were "totally incompatible" with his teaching in the Course? In *Absence from Felicity*, Jesus reportedly told Helen: "You have every right to examine *my* credentials—in fact, I encourage you to do so. You haven't read the Bible in years."[18] This line not only encourages Helen (and by implication, everyone) to read the Bible, by pointing to his credentials there, but also the Jesus of the Course clearly shows that he and the Jesus of the Bible are one and the same.

In this context, it is worth noting that more than sixty percent of the biblical references in the Course are to material in the gospels. Barely twenty percent of the references are from the Old Testament. Clearly, to the Course, the life and teachings of Jesus are the most important part of the Bible. Jesus refers primarily to that material because it represents the story of the work he started two thousand years ago and is now continuing by bringing the Course into the world.

Throwing out the baby with the bathwater

In my opinion, in his attitude towards the Bible, Wapnick rejects the good with the bad. He zeros in on the many ways the Course disagrees with the Bible, and on that basis, makes the mistake of rejecting the entire thing.

There can be no question that the Course drastically disagrees with the Bible on many points. Some of those points of disagreement are pillars of conservative Christian theology. For instance, all of the following beliefs can be found in the Bible, and the Course disagrees with all of them:

- God created the physical world.
- Humanity corrupted itself with sin so that its nature became sinful.
- Humankind has been separated from God by its sin.
- Sin is real and justice demands it be punished.
- Jesus was God the Son, the only Son of God, equally God and man, born without sin, and divine in a unique sense. (The Course teaches that Jesus was a man like any of us who was the first to complete his part in the Atonement and to completely identify with the Christ; we are all his equals.)
- Jesus died on the cross in our place as a sacrifice to pay for our sins.
- Jesus now sits in Heaven as a king on a throne, and will rule over the world in some future incarnation.
- The devil is a real and extremely powerful being that opposes God.
- Only a select few will be saved in the end; the Last Judgment will separate the righteous from the unrighteous, rewarding the former with Heaven and banishing the latter to hell and eternal suffering. (The Course teaches that it is not Jesus who will carry out the Last Judgment, but the Sonship as a whole. The traditional teaching about the Last Judgment is totally reinterpreted, everyone will return to God, and there is no hell.)

Thus, Wapnick's assertion that the thought system presented in the Bible is totally incompatible with the Course *is* correct, if by that he means that the basic theological teachings of the two books are profoundly different. They are based on different premises, utilize different (and irreconcilable) means, and arrive at different conclusions. To the biblical system, the separation between man and God is terribly real and is the core problem that must be resolved; to the Course, the separation never happened, and the core problem is the illusion that it did.

The Course, however, does not reject the Bible because of these profound differences, as Wapnick seems to do. Instead, it teaches that even the most profound disagreement in the Bible can be reinterpreted in a positive light. Jesus goes to the trouble of showing how four very difficult biblical passages (even Old Testament verses), which seem to lend support to traditional views of God's vengeance on sin, can be reinterpreted to teach God's love instead (T-5.VI.5-9). One such example is the biblical saying, "Vengeance is mine, saith the Lord" (Romans 12:19). He reinterprets this to mean that vengeance cannot be shared, and should therefore be given to the Holy Spirit to be undone. To me, this shows that nothing in the Bible is so awful that it cannot be translated into a loving statement. He gives such reinterpretations in more than one place (for example, T-3.I.3:1-8, 5:1-6:7). He even tells us that he is giving these examples "to show how the Holy Spirit can reinterpret them in His Own Light" (T-5.VI.5:1). To me, this seems to imply that they are given as examples of how we can reinterpret all the "fearful" passages of the Bible with the help of the Holy Spirit. We need not reject the Bible, but we do need to ask the help of the Holy Spirit to reinterpret it in His Own Light.

HOW THE COURSE SEES THE BIBLE

Before drawing things to a conclusion, let me briefly summarize how we at the Circle understand the Course's stance toward the Bible. I feel it will be helpful to present this in a positive framework, rather than as a response to Wapnick's views.

One continuing stream

The Course sees itself as a continuation of the same stream of inspiration that produced the Bible. It sees the Bible as written by men inspired by the Holy Spirit and sees itself as written almost directly by the Holy Spirit. The inspiration breaking through into the world is the identical inspiration that was breaking through in the Bible and during the ministry of Jesus on earth. That revelation has become progressively clearer and clearer, with the Old Testament beginning the process, with truth greatly blocked and imperfectly perceived; the New Testament becoming clearer; and the Course, in our time, giving the purest representation of truth to date.

The Bible is the Divine truth filtered through human egos

The Course sees the Bible as the product of inspiration from the Holy Spirit filtered through, muddied, and distorted by, human egos. Jesus says that his apostles misunderstood and misinterpreted the crucifixion, for example, because of their own anger and guilt, which are manifestations of the ego (T-6.I.14).

The Course is the Divine truth without filters

The Course sees itself as the product of the same inspiration, but with little or no distortion produced by a human ego. As such, it has the job of continuing the truth that came through in the Bible and correcting the distortion. We believe the Course to be the purest revelation of spiritual truth so far, bar none. I am not really qualified to make that statement categorically regarding all spiritual traditions, but it is evident to anyone reading it that the Course at least presents itself as the purest revelation within the Judeo-Christian stream of revelation.

There are entire sections of the Text dedicated to correcting the Bible's misunderstanding of the crucifixion (T-3.I; T-6.I). Jesus openly, and frequently, corrects or reinterprets the meaning of biblical passages. Clearly, the Course sets its own authority above that of the Bible.

Given this understanding of the relative authority of the Bible and the Course, it is easy to see how one can take the Course as one's primary spiritual path yet still value and benefit from the Bible, while it is very difficult, if not impossible, to take the Bible as one's primary authority and still derive value and benefit from the Course. To do so would be to undercut and ignore one of the Course's major goals, which is to correct the errors of the Bible.

The Gospels are of primary importance

In particular, the Course sees the gospels as the most important part of the Bible. This is evidenced by the heavy preponderance of quotations from the gospels, as compared to quotes from other parts of the Bible. It particularly sees itself continuing the work recorded in the gospels, as well as clarifying the real nature of that work and correcting misunderstandings of it. In that sense, the Course is the most recent chapter in the story of the ministry of Jesus. Familiarity with the four gospels—and perhaps also with the Gospel of Thomas—is therefore expected (although not required, as I explain later) of serious students of the Course. Familiarity with the rest of the Bible is of lesser value and importance, though not without benefit.

The heart of the Biblical message is love

The Course continues and expands on a whole set of biblical themes, all of which come under the heading of the idea that "God is Love." Any teaching thread in the Bible that lends itself to support of this central idea is echoed and amplified by the Course.

The central error of the Bible is fear

The Course corrects a whole set of biblical themes, all of which come under the heading of "God is fear." Any teaching thread in the Bible that is based upon fear of God, fear of judgment and hell, or punishment for sin, is rejected and denounced by the Course (for example, see T-3.I.2:8-4:2 and T-6.I.16).

Familiarity with the Bible is assumed

The Course assumes that we will be familiar with the Bible and read it. As I pointed out previously, Jesus recommended to Helen that she read the gospels to gain a deeper familiarity with him and his life. This is a great snapshot of the Course's whole approach to the Bible: Use it to become familiar with Jesus, with his life, his works, and his teaching. Doing so can help you realize that he has the authority to tell you what he tells you in the Course.

In the Manual for Teachers, Jesus speaks of our relationship with himself. Speaking of himself in the third person, he says:

> It is possible to read his words and benefit from them without accepting him into your life. Yet he would help you yet a little more if you will share your pains and joys with him, and leave them both to find the peace of God.
>
> (C-5.6:6-7)

He tells us that we do not need to utilize his personal presence as our teacher in order to derive benefit from the Course, yet, if we are willing to do so, we will receive more help along our spiritual path. Traveling the path *with* Jesus is less difficult than traveling it *without* him.

142

I believe the exact same relationship exists between the Bible and students of the Course. Making the Bible a part of your spiritual program, although recommended, is not an immutable requirement; indeed, the Course refers to itself as "a unified thought system in which nothing is lacking that is needed, and nothing is included that is contradictory or irrelevant" (W-pI.42.7:2). Still, if you are willing to make the Bible a part of your spiritual program, I think that Jesus will be able to help you in ways that he cannot do if you omit it.

We must read the Bible with discernment

The Course wants us to read the Bible, especially the gospels, but with discernment. It wants us to read it in the purifying light of its own teachings. It is not pure truth. There are mistakes we must be aware of, and in particular, we should avoid any taint of fear (see T-6.I.16).

IN CONCLUSION

To the Course, the Bible is not the ultimate source of truth, as it is for many conservative Christians. The Course does not hesitate to contradict it and to identify parts of it as inaccurate. Nevertheless, there are large parts of the Bible that the Course quotes or refers to with obvious agreement and approval.

If the Bible were a relatively useless book that is totally incompatible with the thought system presented in the Course, as Wapnick states, why would the author of the Course have quoted it so frequently and approvingly? Why would he demonstrate how we can reinterpret it? Why would he assume we would be reading it? Would he not have avoided mixing the Bible's thoughts with his own in the Course, instead of lacing the Course liberally with biblical quotes and references? Would he not have warned us against mixing it with his teaching?

Rather than treating the Bible as the final authority, and rather than rejecting it outright, the Course treats it as a useful sourcebook and a valuable reference, which, because some parts of it express the ego's beliefs instead of God's truth, should be read with cautious discernment. Many of its ideas, its stories, and its lyrical expressions can be successfully integrated with the thought system of the Course in ways that support and clarify what the Course says. Any of its material that is based on fear, on the reality of sin, or on the notion of a punitive God, should either be rejected or reinterpreted in the light of love. Much as the Holy Spirit sorts through our thoughts to remove all but the loving thoughts, so too we need to sort through the Bible with His help to glean all its loving thoughts, while discarding anything else.

Notes

[1] *The Most Commonly Asked Questions about 'A Course in Miracles,'* (co-written with Gloria Wapnick), p. 112.

[2] *Ibid.*, p. 102.

[3] *Ibid.*, p. 113.

[4] *Ibid.*, p. 111.

[5] *Forgiveness and Jesus: The Meeting Place of 'A Course in Miracles' and Christianity*, p. 147.

[6] *The Message of 'A Course in Miracles,' Volume One: All Are Called*, p. 57.

[7] *Commonly Asked Questions*, p. 4.

[8] *Ibid.*, p. 4.

[9] *Ibid.*, p. 110.

[10] *Ibid.*, p.111.

[11] *Ibid.*, p.111.

[12] *Ibid.*, p. 111.

[13] *Ibid.*, p. 112.

[14] "In Conversation with Ken and Gloria Wapnick—Part 2," by Ian Patrick; *Miracle Worker: Magazine of the UK Miracle Network*, Issue 27, March/April 1999, p. 5.

[15] *Seeing the Bible Differently: How 'A Course in Miracles' Views the Bible*, pp. 56–57.

[16] *Commonly Asked Questions*, p. 103.

[17] *Ibid.*, p. 102.

[18] *Absence from Felicity: The Story of Helen Schucman and Her Scribing of 'A Course in Miracles,'* 1st ed., p. 229. Page numbers in later printings may be a lower number.

The Spiritual Program of
A Course in Miracles

The Circle's Vision and
Ken Wapnick's Vision Compared

by Greg Mackie

In the Course community, much has been said and written over the years about the Course's teachings, and its promise that fully accepting its teachings will awaken us to God. But comparatively little has been said and written about the aspect of the Course that enables its promise to be fulfilled: the Course's spiritual program. By "program," I mean the "organized, well-structured and carefully planned program" (T-12.II.10:1) the Course lays out for us in its three volumes, the curriculum we are asked to follow in order to "pass" this course and "graduate" to God. In short, the Course's program is the answer to the question: "If this is a course in miracles, how do we *take* this course?"

One of the Circle's major goals has been to pay more attention to this neglected aspect of the Course. We believe that the program Jesus gave us is his answer to the often-asked question of how to make the Course practical, and that a fuller understanding of the Course's program will do more than anything else to allow Course students to reap the benefits of the Course's path.

Given the vital importance of this topic, we thought it would be helpful to compare and contrast Ken Wapnick's vision of the Course's program with our own. That is the purpose of this essay. In it, I will first present the Circle's vision, and then present my understanding of Wapnick's vision, based on his various teaching materials. (I will include additional information in some of the endnotes as well.) I will note both agreements and disagreements between the respective visions, using my outline of the Circle's vision as a framework for ease in comparison. Finally, I will look at the "big picture" each vision

145

presents of the developmental progression of the Course's path, and share some thoughts on the question of which vision will better enable the Course's promises to be fulfilled in the lives of its students.

THE CIRCLE'S VISION

Before I share the Circle's vision, a few preliminary comments are in order. First, I want to give credit where credit is due. While many at the Circle have contributed to its vision of the Course's program, the person most responsible for developing the vision I present here is Robert Perry.[1] I am immensely grateful to him for his marvelous body of work on this topic.

Second, since we are working to actively implement this vision at the Circle, I thought that information about specific people at the Circle who are focused on a particular aspect of the vision might be of interest. Therefore, I will mention such people where appropriate.

Finally, I want to make clear that our vision is our interpretation of the Course, and we make no claim to certainty about it. We do believe that this vision comes from the pages of the Course itself, and that it is therefore a reasonably accurate picture of *Jesus'* vision for the Course. But we certainly acknowledge that this is our opinion. All we ask is that students measure our (and Wapnick's) views against the only standard that really matters: the Course itself. With that in mind, let's take a look at the Circle's vision.

The Circle's interpretive stance: For the most part, the Course is literal

In our opinion, virtually all of the differences between the Circle's vision of the program and Ken Wapnick's are rooted in our different interpretive stances toward the Course, specifically our different views of what in the Course is to be taken literally, and what metaphorically.[2] For this reason, I want to begin my description of each vision with a brief description of the interpretive stance behind it.

At the Circle, we believe that by and large, the Course should be taken literally. We acknowledge that the Course certainly contains many metaphorical and poetic elements; usually these elements are fairly easy to identify, and when we find them, we interpret them as metaphors. But for the most part, we take the Course at its word. Jesus tells us that the Course "means exactly what it says" (T-8.IX.8:1).

Therefore, when we read the Course's teachings or its descriptions of the program contained in its three volumes, we take what we read seriously as a literal account of what Jesus wants us to learn and how he wants us to take his Course. We see no reason why it should be taken any other way.

General overview of the program

The central idea around which the Circle's vision is built is that *A Course in Miracles* is a literal course in miracles, just as its title suggests. The word "course" denotes an educational program, and the word "miracles," in Course usage, denotes the acceptance of healed perception into our minds from the Holy Spirit or Jesus, *and* the extension of that healed perception to others (see, for instance, W-pI.159.Title-3:1).[3] This acceptance and extension of miracles is, in the Course's view, the way that we reawaken to God. Therefore, its very title tells us that *A Course in Miracles* is *an educational program in learning how to accept and extend the healed perception that reawakens us to God.*

While we fully acknowledge, in line with the Course's teachings, that there are many valid paths to God, our focus at the Circle is on the path laid out for us in the Course itself. In our view, there is no need to borrow from other teachings to make the Course practical, because the Course itself tells us in great detail how to do its own program. We believe that the Course is a unique, complete, and sufficient spiritual path, "in which nothing is lacking that is needed, and nothing is included that is contradictory or irrelevant" (W-pI.42.7:2). It contains everything we need to follow it all the way to God.

Finally, we see the program as an integrated process, in which the Course's thought system—what it aims to teach us—gradually penetrates deeper and deeper into our minds. Together, the three volumes of the Course comprise a single process of progressively internalizing the Course's thought system, a process that builds as one progresses through the volumes.

The role of the Course's three volumes

Now let's look at the role each of the Course's volumes plays in the program. In general terms, we believe that each volume has a distinct and essential role, which can be described as follows:

- Text = study
- Workbook for Students = practice
- Manual for Teachers = extension

All three volumes contain all three elements, of course, but each volume has its own particular focus. With that in mind, what follows is a brief summary of how we see each volume fitting into the overall curriculum of the Course.

Text = Study

The purpose of the Text is to introduce to us the thought system Jesus intends us to learn. It is the "theoretical foundation" (W-In.1:1) for everything that follows in the Course. The other volumes of the Course build upon the foundation of the Text.

The importance of study

In order to learn what Jesus wants us to learn from the Text, we must *study* it. Intellectual study of the Text—reading it straight through as it was given (as a general rule), and applying intellectual tools to its interpretation—is absolutely necessary if we want to understand its ideas. This understanding is the foundation and preparation for the practice and extension that follow in the other two volumes. Because such understanding is so important, intellectual study of the Course is at the heart of everything we do at the Circle. It is not the only thing we do, nor is it the most important. But everything we do flows from it.

Study is often dismissed in Course circles as an empty, impractical "head trip" that gets in the way of true spiritual experience. We have heard the criticism that our emphasis on study—in particular, our emphasis on taking the Course literally—improperly focuses on the letter of the Course at the expense of the spirit. It is true that study for its own sake can become an empty intellectual exercise. To us, however, study in its proper place is eminently practical, because rather than blocking experience, it is the gateway *to* experience.

I have already suggested one reason for this: study is the foundation for practice, which leads to experience. Another reason is that in the Course's view, learning and accepting new ideas on the deepest level— exchanging the ego's thought system for the Course's thought system—is salvation itself, the very thing that brings us the experience of God. Therefore, since study is a process of learning and accepting new ideas, and learning and accepting the Course's new ideas is salvation, study is more than practical; if done in the proper way, study is *itself* a practice that can lead to salvation. We have found again and again that our focus on the letter of the Course, rather than violating the spirit, actually *reveals* the spirit.

Another reason we regard study so highly is that Jesus himself clearly does. As he was dictating the Course, he constantly stressed the importance of study to his scribes, Helen Schucman and Bill Thetford. He emphasized "the need to study the notes,"[4] and reminded Helen and Bill that "good students assign study periods for themselves" (an assignment he ended up making for them himself).[5] The importance he placed on study is evident in this comment that he made to the two of them:

> Bill has very intelligently suggested that you both should set yourself the goal of really studying for this course. There can be no doubt of the wisdom of this decision, for any student who wants to pass it.[6]

Admonitions to study appear in the published Course as well (see, for instance, T-1.VII.4:5 and T-4.In.3:10-11).

How to study the Text

Given the importance of study, the question of *how* to study the Text (and the rest of the Course) has been a vital one for the Circle. Robert Perry and Allen Watson, in particular, have devoted a great deal of time and effort to it. One thing we have learned is that in order to study the Text profitably, one must study it in a way that is in harmony with the Course's unique writing style, a writing style we like to describe as *symphonic* (a term first applied to the Course by Ken Wapnick) and *holographic*. It is symphonic in that rather than presenting ideas in a linear fashion, it presents them in the manner of a symphony: various themes enter, develop, exit, re-enter, and interweave with one another in a constantly evolving and harmonious pattern. It is holographic in that the elements of the Course are like a hologram: each part contains the whole.

How to study this richly interwoven, interconnected, and ultimately transformative literary masterpiece is a topic that could fill a book; in fact, one of the Circle's books *is* devoted to this topic.[7] But speaking in very general terms, our method is a three-step process of *observation*, *interpretation*, and *application*. These three steps could be summed up as follows:

> *Observation:* After a quick inspectional reading, we try to *observe* everything on the page, reading slowly and attentively, remembering that Jesus once told Helen that "every word is meaningful."[8]

> *Interpretation:* We try to *interpret* what those words mean by placing them in their context—primarily (though not exclusively) their *immediate* context—reading them in light of that context, asking ourselves questions about what the words mean and searching for answers as we read, paying close attention to how the words are connected with one another.

> *Application:* We try to *apply* what we are reading to our own lives, reading everything as personally addressing us, mentally applying the message to ourselves, and following any injunctions Jesus gives us to apply what he is teaching.

Through all of these techniques, we slowly begin to see the whole in each part, and how each part fits into the whole. When we study the Text in this way, just reading the Text becomes a transformative experience.

We believe that the Text is an inexhaustible wellspring of wisdom that we have not even begun to tap, a mother lode from which we will be mining treasures for generations to come. For this reason, one aspect of my personal vision is to help lay the foundation for a tradition of Course scholarship—a community of Course scholars—based on the study techniques we are developing at the Circle, and rooted in a commitment to following the Course's program as Jesus instructed.

The place of the Text in the program

In conclusion, the Text represents the first step in the process of progressive internalization that I mentioned above. Through study of the Text, the ideas that will eventually become our new thought system enter our minds and are considered for the first time.

Workbook for Students = Practice

The purpose of the Workbook for Students is "to train your mind to think along the lines the text sets forth" (W-In.1:4). It enables us to practically apply the thought system presented to us in the Text—to *practice* the ideas that we *studied*. It is a training manual for the Course's form of spiritual practice.

The importance of practice

As important as study is to the realization of the Course's goals for us, practice is equally important. In the Workbook, Jesus says that "your practicing can offer everything to you" (W-pI.rIII.In.4:5). He tells us that "it is doing the exercises that will make the goal of the course possible" (W-In.1:2). The Course mentions "practice" and "practicing" a total of 350 times, and has devoted an entire volume to it. Because of the importance of practice, we at the Circle—again, Robert Perry and Allen Watson in particular—have striven to learn what we can about the purpose, process, and forms of Workbook practice, so we can practice more effectively and help others to do the same.[9]

Following the instructions—the importance of structure

In our view, perhaps the most basic rule for doing Workbook practice is simply this: Follow the instructions given in the Workbook itself. This rule is given in the Workbook's Introduction: "You are merely asked to apply the ideas as you are directed to do....Nothing more than that is required" (W-In.8:3, 9:5). Jesus is clear that we are to follow the Workbook's practice instructions "just as closely as [we] can" (W-pI.rIII.In.1:3). He fully understands and accepts that we will not follow them perfectly, but he always urges us to follow them as best we can. Not one line of the Workbook suggests otherwise. Again and again, we are told that its practices are "required" if we want to receive the benefits they offer. The Workbook's emphasis on following the instructions is so strong that the Circle once opened one of its Workbook workshops with a session entitled "He Really Means It."

We need to follow the practice instructions Jesus gives us because we need *structure* in order to train our minds: "Structure...is necessary for you at this time, planned to include frequent reminders of your goal and regular attempts to reach it" (W-pI.95.6:1). Of course, we are not

151

to pursue structure as an end in itself, but it is a vital and necessary means of mind training for those who lack mental discipline (which is virtually all of us). It is this mind training through structure that will enable us to find the happiness, peace, and salvation that we seek (see W-pI.20.2).

Therefore, Workbook practice is structured throughout. The structure builds gradually in the first half of the Workbook, and then recedes gradually in the second half, as our minds presumably become better trained. But the Workbook never removes structure entirely. Instead, it ends up settling on a basic pattern that we call the four-fold structure of Workbook practice:

- Morning and evening quiet times
- Hourly remembrance of the idea for the day
- Frequent reminders of the idea for the day (in between the hourly remembrances)
- Response to temptation (applying the idea for the day immediately to sources of upset)

The variety of Workbook practices

Workbook practice is, in Robert Perry's words, "an act of repeating, dwelling on, and applying *meaning*, primarily in the form of concentrated, psychologically impactful sentences." But though repeating psychologically impactful sentences is the primary practice, Workbook practice also takes a wide variety of specific forms. The Workbook is like an immense toolbox, with specific practice tools to suit every mind and every need. Through doing the Workbook, we develop a "problem-solving repertoire" (W-pI.194.6:2) that we can apply with "great specificity" (W-In.6:1) to every aspect of our lives, a specificity that the Workbook tells us is necessary in order for us to ultimately recognize the universal applicability of the Course's ideas (see W-In.6:2).

Here is a list of just a few of the rich and varied practices given in the Workbook:

- Repeating the idea for the day
- Setting a Course-based goal for the day
- Devoting oneself to spending the day with God

152

- Three types of meditation (though they are not expressly called "meditation")
- Prayer (especially the prayers in Part II)
- Exercises for forgiving specific people
- Mentally extending peace and light to specific people
- Exercises in thinking about the Course's logic
- Reading a teaching passage slowly and thinking about it
- Letting related thoughts come
- Giving thoughts to the Holy Spirit so He can give them back in "purified" form
- Asking the Holy Spirit to guide both our perception and our daily decisions
- Letting our mind relate the idea for the day to our needs, problems, and concerns
- Searching for and releasing ego thoughts, so they can be replaced with our real thoughts
- Looking at our external and/or internal world and declaring the truth about it
- Affirming our commitment to our function of saving the world

Should the Workbook be gone through more than once?

Our answer to this question is a pragmatic one, based on our understanding of what the Workbook aims to accomplish. We believe that the Workbook is ultimately meant to establish in us a lifelong habit of frequent and deep Course practice. Therefore, a person is done with the Workbook when the Workbook has accomplished this purpose in her: when she can successfully maintain a regular habit of daily (if imperfect) practice on her own, without the firm structure imposed by the Workbook. If this habit is not established, then it is probably a good idea to go through the Workbook again.

Allen Watson has a wonderful analogy for this: the Workbook is like the training wheels on a bicycle. We use training wheels as long as they are needed for training purposes, and set them aside once we've learned how to ride the bicycle without them. In like manner, we use the Workbook as long as it is needed for mind-training purposes, and set it aside once we can do our Course practice without it.

Post-Workbook practice

Based on the Workbook's Epilogue, one might conclude that once we are done with the Workbook, all structured practice is set aside, and all we do from then on is allow the Holy Spirit to direct our practice from within. But while it is theoretically possible to reach this advanced state just by doing the Workbook, we at the Circle don't think this is what Jesus expects of most of us.

We base this conclusion in part on Section 16 of the Manual, "How Should the Teacher of God Spend His Day?" This section outlines a practice structure for beginning teachers of God: those who, among other qualifications, have "gone through the workbook" (M-16.3:7), but are not yet advanced enough in their training to be ready for total "lack of structuring on their own part" (M-16.2:2). In other words, this section of the Manual provides a practice structure for those who are not yet ready for the unstructured kind of practice that the Epilogue of the Workbook is talking about.

The form of practice outlined in this section (starting with paragraph 2) is what we at the Circle call "post-Workbook practice." It is a more loosely structured form of practice in which the student does what he has found meets his needs, while still working within the basic structure of practice laid out in the Workbook. A person doing this form of practice can and often will continue to use practices from the Workbook's toolbox to meet his specific needs. The main difference is that there is no specifically assigned lesson for the day.[10]

The place of the Workbook in the program

Ultimately, Workbook practice is a *process*, a process of continually repeating and dwelling upon the Course's ideas so that they gradually sink deeper and deeper into our minds (for an excellent summary of that process, see W-pII.284.1:5-6). The Workbook is the second step in the process of progressively internalizing the Course's thought system. Through practice, the thought system that entered our awareness through study sinks into our minds more deeply and becomes more fully our own.

Manual for Teachers = Extension

The purpose of the Manual for Teachers is to serve as a manual for those who have devoted themselves to *extending* the healed perception gained through studying the Course's thought system in the Text and practicing it in the Workbook. More specifically, while the Manual can be of benefit to any Course student, it is primarily intended as an instruction manual for more experienced Course students who have become *teachers of God*: miracle workers who are now ready to take up their function of extending healed perception to others. Extending healed perception is how teachers of God teach others what they have learned.

This purpose of instructing teachers of God is given in the Manual's Introduction:

> This is a manual for the teachers of God....Who are they? How are they chosen? What do they do? How can they work out their own salvation and the salvation of the world? This manual attempts to answer these questions.
>
> (M-In.4:4, 8-12)

A secondary purpose of the Manual, not mentioned until its final section, is to serve as a clarifying summary of some of the Course's teachings (see M-29.1:1-3).

The meaning of "extension"

In order to understand the purpose of the Manual, it is crucial to understand what is meant by "extension." (I am referring here to what might be called "earthly extension," the earthly reflection of extension in Heaven.) Basically, extension is communicating to another person— by thought, word, or deed—our healed perception of that person. "To teach is to demonstrate" (M-In.2:1), and extension is the living demonstration to others of the healing that has taken place in our minds.

The "thought" part of the definition of extension is paramount, because the Course tells us that "only minds communicate" (T-7.V.2:1). All communication is ultimately mind-to-mind, not physical. But the "word or deed" part of that definition should not be overlooked or dismissed, because the Course also tells us that the Holy Spirit uses the body as "a means of communication" (T-8.VII.2:1), and thus as "a means of joining minds" (T-8.VII.2:5).

Communicating our healed perception behaviorally is a crucial part of the process, because words and actions are the only language that many people can understand. They need "a body they can see. A voice they understand and listen to, without the fear that truth would encounter in them" (M-12.3:5-6; see also M-21.4:3). Behavior is a way of "acting out" our thoughts, bearing witness to them and thus communicating them more clearly. And so, extension to others is more than just having loving thoughts about them; in many if not most cases, it includes loving words and loving acts as well.

The importance of extension

If study and practice are important steps in the Course's program, we at the Circle believe that extension is the most important step of all. It is the step that gets the most attention in the Course itself, and is the only step that is also a major part of the Course's *teaching*, not just the program. As an indicator of just how important extension is, there are seven occurrences in the Course material of the phrase "there is no other way" (plus one occurrence of "there is no other teacher and no other way"). Amazingly, *every single one* of these occurrences refers, in one form or another, to the idea that there is no other way to salvation except through extending salvation to others.[11]

The main reason extension is so important to our salvation is because it is the ultimate thought reinforcer: "What you teach is teaching you. And what you project or extend you believe" (T-6.III.2:8-9). The Course constantly stresses this idea: it is through *giving* the healing we have received that we truly come to *recognize* that we have received it (see, for example, W-pI.187.5:1-3; T-29.III.1:8; and T-6.III.4:9). The following lines from the Workbook express succinctly just how important this idea is to the Course's program:

> We will not recognize what we receive until we give it. You have heard this said a hundred ways, a hundred times, and yet belief is lacking still.   (W-pI.154.12:1-2)

It is only through extension to others that we truly and fully embrace the Course ideas that we have studied and practiced. Extension is thus the final step in the Course's program, the step that makes learning complete.

The meaning of the term "teacher of God"

Another term that is crucial to understand is the term "teacher of God." We have already learned about the teacher of God's function—extension of healing to others—but what makes a person a teacher of God? The general view in the Course community is that *everyone* is a teacher of God, but in our opinion, the Manual does not share this view. Instead, it mentions two qualifications: one that applies generally to teachers of God in *all* paths of awakening, and one that applies more specifically to teachers of God who are on the Course's path.

The general qualification is that to become a teacher of God, one must see truly common interests with another person (see M-1.1:2)—a recognition that the Course clearly does not regard as a common, everyday occurrence. The more specific additional qualification for those on the Course's path is that they must have completed the Workbook (see M-16.3:7), a qualification which assumes that they have completed the Text as well. This only makes sense: to teach a course, you have to have completed that course yourself. The main point I want to make here, though, is that a teacher of God in the Course's system isn't just anyone who picks up the Course, but a person who has reached the next *developmental stage* in the progression of her spiritual journey, a progression that goes from student to teacher of God to advanced teacher of God (M-4.2:2, et al.) to Teacher of teachers (M-26.2:2).

The forms the teacher of God's role takes

The teaching that a teacher of God does can take a wide variety of forms, many of which won't look like overt teaching at all. The key is to communicate the mental content of healed perception, which can be done just as easily by a garbage collector as it can by someone doing formal teaching. That being said, there are two teaching roles that the Manual focuses on: the *teacher of pupils* and the *healer of patients*. Interestingly, these are the very roles Jesus took on in his own earthly life, as he himself was a teacher who worked miracles of healing.

The first role, teacher of pupils, is that of a Course mentor, someone who becomes a personal teacher to newer Course students, shepherding them in the study and practice of *A Course in Miracles*. Most Course students are not aware that this role is described in the Manual, but in our view, it is very plainly there.[12] Indeed, the Manual seems to assume that becoming a pupil of a Course teacher will be the characteristic way to begin the Course: both Manual references to new students of the Course portray them as pupils of a teacher (M-24.3 and M-29.1-2). Even the well-known passage that says a student can begin with any of the three volumes (M-29.1-2) is actually directed at the Course *teacher*, who is called upon to advise his *pupils* concerning which volume to start with (or whether to study the Course at all). One major ramification of this is that, contrary to popular opinion, Jesus did *not* intend the Course to be a self-study Course. At the Circle, Mary Anne Buchowski has been working to implement the teacher-pupil aspect of the Course's program.

The second role, healer of patients, is that of a spiritual healer, someone who goes to people with healing needs (including physical illness) and extends miracles to them. As with the teacher-of-pupils role, most Course students are not aware that this healer role is described in the Manual, but we consider it to be plainly there.[13] At the Circle, Nicola Harvey has been instrumental in getting this aspect of the program started. She herself is a Course-based healer, and it is her goal to train others in this role.

The importance of helping and joining with others

Both of the roles described above—teacher of pupils and healer of patients—are *helping* roles, in which the teacher of God answers the call of another person who has come to her for help. And while the content of the help is always healed perception extended on the level of the mind, the form this will very often take is some form of service to others: extending behavioral help to those who need it.

This service to others is vitally important to the Course's path. In the context of discussing another form of helping relationship—that of psychotherapist and patient—the *Psychotherapy* supplement extols the salvific benefits of reaching out to help others in the world:

> Hear a brother call for help and answer him. It will be God to Whom you answer, for you called on Him. There is no other way to hear His Voice. There is no other way to seek His Son. There is no other way to find your Self. Holy is healing, for the Son of God returns to Heaven through its kind embrace. (P-2.V.8:4-9)

> Healing is holy. Nothing in the world is holier than

helping one who asks for help. And two come very close to God in this attempt, however limited, however lacking in sincerity. Where two have joined for healing, God is there. (P-2.V.4.1-4)

The last line of this second passage touches upon the key healing element in these helping relationships: whatever form the teacher of God's extension takes, the key is that extension is an act of *joining* with another person. In many cases, this joining will be nothing more than a brief interaction in which healing is exchanged—what the Course calls a "holy encounter" (T-8.III.4:1). But in some cases, this brief interaction will blossom into something more: a mutual, ongoing relationship dedicated to the common goal of healing—what the Course calls a *holy relationship*. The teacher-pupil relationship described by the Manual is a prime example of the holy relationship.

This joining of two (or more) people in a holy relationship dedicated to the common goal of healing is the real instrument of salvation. For this reason, we at the Circle believe that joining in groups dedicated to the common goal of walking the healing path of the Course together can be extremely helpful. While the Course does not mention groups per se, such groups are a logical extension of the mutual joining in holy relationships that the Course does mention and make central to its program. "Salvation is a collaborative venture" (T-4.VI.8:2). In keeping with the collaborative nature of salvation, we have developed a community of mutual support in Sedona that has proven to be immensely helpful to those who have been part of it. It is our hope that our community might serve as a model for similar communities elsewhere.

The importance of mutually joining with others in a common goal can hardly be overstated. The *Psychotherapy* supplement puts it this way:

What must the teacher do to ensure learning? What must the therapist do to bring healing about? Only one thing; the same requirement salvation asks of everyone. Each one must share one goal with someone else, and in so doing, lose all sense of separate interests. Only by doing this is it possible to transcend the narrow boundaries the ego would impose upon the self. Only by doing this can teacher and pupil, therapist and patient,

159

you and I, accept Atonement and learn to give it as it was
received.   (P-2.II.8:1-6)

The place of the Manual in the program

The Manual represents the final step in the process of progressively
internalizing the Course's thought system—the crowning phase of the
program. By fulfilling our function of extension as teachers of God, we
join others and thus let go of the ego's thought system of separation. In
this joining, the Course's thought system that entered our minds
through study and became reinforced through practice reaches the
deepest level of our minds, and is finally recognized as *fully* our own.
"And as [the teachers of God] teach His lessons of joy and hope, their
learning finally becomes complete" (M-In.4:8).

KEN WAPNICK'S VISION

A few brief comments before I begin this section:[14] First, it must be
said that Wapnick really doesn't seem to place much emphasis on the
Course's program in his writings. (He generally uses the term
"curriculum" instead of "program"; I regard these terms as basically
synonymous.) As an example, in his two-volume set *The Message of
'A Course in Miracles,'* his 608-page magnum opus on the Course, he
devotes only one 27-page section to a description of the program and
how to follow it.[15] I am not aware of any other writings of his that
discuss the entire program in any great detail.

Second, while I believe the picture of Wapnick's views I present
below is accurate in the essentials, I must confess that I have found it
difficult to firmly nail down his views on certain things. In my opinion,
the major reason for this is simply that there are self-contradictions in
his work. He may argue that the things I see as self-contradictions are
simply cases of him speaking on different levels, or responding to the
needs of different audiences. Perhaps this is sometimes the case, but
there are a number of cases in which the conclusion that he is
contradicting himself seems unavoidable. I will give some examples of
this throughout the rest of this essay.

I say this at the outset simply because I am aware that given the
apparent contradictions in Wapnick's work, any claim I make about his
views—even if I directly quote a statement from him in support of it—

is potentially open to refutation by a statement he makes elsewhere. I think this is unavoidable. Fortunately, however, Wapnick's *emphasis* is quite clear in his work, because he repeats his strongest convictions very frequently and forcefully. Therefore, in what I've written here, I've striven to accurately report what he emphasizes most strongly, even if I cannot report every single exception, qualification, or apparent contradiction. I have done my best to be fair, charitable, and accurate.

Finally, a note on capitalization conventions: Wapnick's convention is not to capitalize the names of the Course's volumes. However, I will go ahead and capitalize them except in direct Wapnick quotes, just for consistency within this essay.

Wapnick's interpretive stance: For the most part, the Course is metaphor

The Circle and Ken Wapnick have dramatically different interpretive stances toward the Course, and this is the central difference between them: while we at the Circle take most of the Course literally, Wapnick takes most of it metaphorically.[16]

Wapnick's central dictum for Course interpretation is *"Accept no compromise in which **duality** plays a part."*[17] What this means is that for Wapnick, only the rare passages that in his opinion reflect the Course's non-dualistic metaphysical foundation should be taken literally (what he calls "Level One" language). But anything in the Course that seems to suggest duality—such as references to God knowing about the separation, spirit interacting with the world, individual Sons of God having mutual relationships, and forms and behavior playing a role in salvation—is to be regarded as metaphor (what he calls "Level Two" language).[18] It is not meant to be regarded as a literal statement of the Course's teaching, but instead as a comforting "fairy tale"[19] directed to those on the lower rungs of the spiritual ladder.

This stance has a major impact on Wapnick's vision of the Course's program. In general, it leads to a tendency on his part to strip out anything in the program that he sees as duality—anything that suggests that form has an important role in salvation. It's not that he strips out form entirely; how could he? No spiritual path in this world can be totally without form—the Course itself is a form—and the Course's

161

program has so many form elements that they can't be overlooked entirely. But while Wapnick acknowledges the necessity of *some* dualistic form in the Course's program, such acknowledgement is rare, and generally buried amid strong warnings against taking the form of the program seriously. To take form seriously, in his view, is to fall into the ego trap of making the error real and seeing salvation in form. This is a major emphasis of his work.

Ultimately, Wapnick's stance (which for convenience I will refer to using the shorthand phrase "duality-as-metaphor stance")[20] causes him to reject or greatly minimize much of what the Course actually says about its program, including much of the Course evidence I presented above for the Circle's vision. In our view, Wapnick's stance leads to a vision of the program that is greatly stripped down and incomplete. I know this is a strong statement, but I hope my reasons for saying it will become clear as we examine his vision below.

General overview of the program

In general terms, Wapnick affirms as we do that the Course is an educational program in spiritual awakening. However, for him the miracles this course in miracles aims to help us bring about are strictly internal. The Course is thus, in his view, an educational program in learning how to accept healed perception into one's *own* mind, *and nothing else.*[21] This is all it takes to awaken to God; the element of *extending* healed perception to others, as the Circle understands it, is essentially missing from Wapnick's vision.

Wapnick also affirms that while the Course acknowledges the validity of other paths—it "is but one of 'many thousands' of the 'universal course'"[22]—it is a unique, sufficient, and complete spiritual path. Like us, he emphasizes fidelity to the Course as it is, though he is not always consistent on this point. On the one hand, he tells us that "there is no right or wrong in pursuing *A Course in Miracles* as a spiritual path."[23] But on the other hand, he says that to guard against the ego, it is a good idea "always to return to Jesus' own instructions for his curriculum,"[24] and even says that if students deviate from the Course in any way whatsoever, then "for all intents and purposes, these students are then pursuing a *different* spiritual path from *A Course in Miracles.*"[25]

I find it difficult to reconcile these statements, but the last quote certainly captures Wapnick's main emphasis, which is on doing the

Course exactly the way Jesus wanted it to be done. Like us, he cites the Course's line asserting that the Course "means exactly what it says" to support his views. Of course, Wapnick and we do not always see eye to eye concerning how to *interpret* what it says.

In general, Wapnick shares our view that the program is a *process* of learning. He uses the term "integrated curriculum"[26] to describe the Course. He says that "the process resembles the ascent up a spiral staircase,"[27] and speaks of the "cumulative impact of the Course's learning process."[28] However, in spite of this general agreement, I don't see much in Wapnick's vision that suggests a process of progressively internalizing the Course's thought system as we proceed through the volumes. My reasons for saying this will, I think, become clear as we proceed.

The role of the Course's three volumes

Before examining Wapnick's view of the three volumes in more detail, there is one apparent disagreement between his vision and the Circle's that I would like to mention at the outset, simply because it seems to be a crucial one. That disagreement is this: it really seems that in Wapnick's vision, unlike the Circle's, the three volumes do not truly have distinct roles in the program. Now, I should note that Wapnick does *claim* that they do:

> Clearly...Jesus conceived of his Course as an integrated work in which each book had its own particular place, making a unique contribution to the student's learning and growth, as well as being integrated with the other two books.[29]

However, in examining Wapnick's discussions of the three volumes, I find it difficult to discern a truly distinct role for each one. Yes, he does see each volume as having a somewhat different focus. But instead of each volume representing a different basic activity that builds on the previous ones—study (Text), practice (Workbook), and extension (Manual)—it seems that in Wapnick's system each volume presents us with the same basic activities, without any significant progressively building relationship between them.

Now, let's look at each volume in turn.

Text

We start out with an agreement between the Circle and Wapnick. Wapnick agrees that the purpose of the Text is to introduce us to the Course's thought system: it is "the basic theoretical foundation for *A Course in Miracles*."[30]

The importance of study

Given this agreement, Wapnick also shares with us the conviction that study of the Text (and the rest of the Course) is important. Like us, he believes that the Text "should in general be read and studied straight through, as it was given."[31] He sees such study as essential to learning the ideas that will ultimately lead us to spiritual experience. He also agrees that Jesus himself values study, often quoting the same *Absence from Felicity* and Course passages we do in support of it.

How to study the Text

As I have said, the major disagreements between Wapnick and the Circle concerning Text study have to do with the question of *how* to study it. Before addressing that issue, however, I need to mention one more thing that the Circle and Wapnick agree on: the uniqueness of the Course's writing style. Needless to say, Wapnick shares our view that the Course's writing style is symphonic, since he was the one who originally applied that term to the Course. He says that like a symphony, the Course's themes are "introduced, set aside, reintroduced, and developed."[32] And though he doesn't use the term "holographic," it is clear that he affirms the basic idea behind that term: "This [symphonic style] results in an interlocking matrix in which every part is integral and essential to the whole, while implicitly containing that whole within itself."[33]

Turning back to the question of how to study the Text, Wapnick doesn't generally talk much about study techniques, beyond saying that we should "pay very careful attention to what has been written."[34] But one place where he does advocate a particular approach to Course study is an article of his entitled "How to Approach *A Course in Miracles*: Transcending the *I*."[35] In this article, Wapnick describes his approach as follows:

> You cannot understand *A Course in Miracles* when you
> try to pick at it from your own brain, from your own

thinking. *It is not outside you.* Rather, you do with this Course what you do with any great work of art—a great poem, a great Shakespearean play, any great work of literature: *You let the words resonate inside you.* You don't pick them apart and analyze them. You just let them work within you, and they will inevitably lead you to that place inside that is beyond all words, all thoughts, all concepts.[36]

We see clearly here both what we should not do, and what we should do. What we should not do is analyze the Course intellectually: "If you try to analyze it and focus on the literal meaning of the words, you are going to miss its heart."[37] Yes, reading and study is necessary, especially for beginners on the lower rungs of the spiritual ladder, but careful analysis of the meaning of the Course's words is ultimately an ego-based approach. Why? Because it presumes that the body's brain is capable of learning, and that the Course is something outside of our own minds. Therefore, this entire approach supports the ego's goal of blocking the non-dual truth; trying "to understand and pull *A Course in Miracles* apart in terms of meaning…almost guarantees that we will never 'get it.'"[38]

If we really want to "get it," what we should do instead is simply "read these words and let them work within [us]."[39] This nonanalytical approach shifts the locus of learning from the body's brain to the nonphysical mind, where we "read [the Course] and automatically know what it means."[40] After all, "learning…does not occur as [we] look at this book or study it,"[41] but happens without our effort as we let the words soak into our minds, much as we experience a great work of art. This approach, in Wapnick's view, affirms the nondual truth that the Course is not really a separate thing outside us, but something that is inside our own minds.

Reading the Course, then, is not a process of studying and attempting to understand a teaching given to you by another, more enlightened mind (Jesus). Rather, "when you read *A Course in Miracles*…you are talking to yourself, the right-minded self within."[42] You don't try to discern its meaning, but instead give up the entire dualistic idea of *you* learning from *it*, and just let yourself "become one with it."[43]

While this approach may sound good on the surface, I see a number of reasons why Wapnick's rejection of intellectual analysis of the Course is not warranted:

Intellectual analysis of the Course doesn't cause us to miss the Course's heart; it reveals that heart.

This is another way of saying what I said earlier: focusing on the letter of the Course doesn't violate its spirit, but instead *reveals* that spirit.

Wapnick himself engages in intellectual analysis of the Course, thus implicitly acknowledging that such analysis is necessary.

In fact, in the very article of his that we have been examining, his contention that we shouldn't analyze the Course is based on his analysis of a passage from Workbook Lesson 188.

Intellectual analysis of the Course does not presume that the brain learns; it simply acknowledges that in this perceptual world, the nonphysical mind learns through the brain.

The brain is part of the body, and the Course says that "the body is a learning device for the mind" (T-2.IV.3:1). Therefore, the brain is a learning device for the mind. In applying our analytical skills to the Course, then, we are simply using our brains as tools to help our nonphysical minds learn the Course's ideas.

Intellectual analysis actually enhances our appreciation of works of art.

I think that the Course is indeed a great work of art, but it does not follow that the Course should therefore not be intellectually analyzed. Virtually all art experts affirm that analyzing works of art, when done in the right spirit, is vital to deepening our appreciation of those works.[44] I have found this to be true in my own experience of art, especially with the Course.

Intellectual analysis is necessary because, in an important sense, the Course is outside our minds.

Wapnick claims that to really learn from the Course, "you have to transcend the subject-object duality,"[45] and no longer "think that there is a *you* studying *this*."[46] —you have to see the Course as something inside your mind. But though the Course is "inside" our minds in the sense that there is a place deep in our minds that already understands it perfectly, the fact is that we currently don't have much access to this place. Indeed, in the Course's view we aren't even capable of transcending the subject-object duality. Such transcendence would put us in the realm of knowledge, which the Course says we can't experience at all in this world, except in brief moments of revelation.

That's why we need the Course: a book that is outside us in the inherently dualistic realm of perception, accessible via intellectual tools, written by an author whose mind is "outside" ours in the sense that it currently has much greater access to truth than ours does. The realm of perception, the "ego framework" (C-In.3:1), is the only place where learning is needed, or even possible. If we could just transcend duality entirely and become one with the Course, we wouldn't need the Course.

Rejecting intellectual analysis of the Course's meaning opens the door to subjectivity.

This, I think, is the central issue. Wapnick's idea that the Course is just something inside us that is not to be analyzed gives us license to interpret it however we like. There are no objective standards of truth to measure our interpretations against; the Course just means whatever we want it to mean. With this approach, ironically an approach that Wapnick himself argues strongly against elsewhere in his writings, we just end up projecting our own ideas onto the Course, and therefore our minds aren't really changed.

The way out of this subjectivity, I believe, is the very intellectual analysis that Wapnick discourages so strongly. To expand upon the previous point about the Course being outside our minds: It is extremely useful and valuable to assume that the Course is something objective, something independent of our conscious minds and thought systems, which can therefore teach us something new if we examine it carefully and thoughtfully. This assumption is essential to learning new ideas from the Course. How many of us would have ever come up with a shocking idea like "there is no order of difficulty in miracles" on our own? How many of us could grasp the saving power of the idea that "I am as God created me" without carefully studying this external book to learn about all that is implied in that idea?

It is very difficult to learn anything beyond ourselves if we think the Course is just part of ourselves. To really learn from the Course, we need to acknowledge that this book outside of us has something to teach us that is beyond what our minds currently grasp. By allowing the Course to speak to us with an independent voice, we don't just project our own ideas onto it, but allow new ideas to come into our conscious minds, bringing about maximal change.

Applying Wapnick's duality-as-metaphor stance to study: de-emphasizing the Course's literal words

It should be clear by now that while Wapnick and the Circle agree that study is valuable, the kind of study he has in mind is quite different from the rigorous analysis of literal meaning advocated by the Circle. His entire picture of study is rooted in what amounts to an all-determining "study technique": his duality-as-metaphor interpretive stance. It is this stance that causes him to be so leery of the "subject-object duality" inherent in the idea of intellectually analyzing a book outside of our own minds. This stance colors the whole study process, so let's now take a closer look at what Wapnick does with it.

In short, Wapnick uses his duality-as-metaphor stance to *deny* or *minimize* a great deal of what the Course's words literally say. Words are dualistic forms, and so in his view, what the Course's words seem to say on the surface should not be taken seriously as straight teaching, with very few exceptions. Indeed, he continually takes interpretive approaches like the Circle's to task for "almost slavishly holding to the literal meaning of the words, rather than using them as symbols to go beyond to their true meaning."[47] In his view, "such rigidity regarding *form* wreaks havoc with the Course's *content*."[48]

But the content Wapnick has in mind is not what is ordinarily meant by the "content" of words. Normally, when I say the word "cat" to denote an actual cat, the *form* is the word "cat," while the *content* is the idea of the actual cat, to which the word points. I'm using the word "cat" literally, so there is a more-or-less direct correspondence between form and content.

In Wapnick's view, however, the actual "content" of the Course's words is often far removed from the literal meaning the words convey. For example, Wapnick says that when the Course tells us the Holy Spirit does things for us in the world, it doesn't really mean what those words seem to say on the surface. Instead, what it *really* means is simply that the Holy Spirit is our Friend—a Friend Who does nothing in the world—not our enemy.[49] The *form* of a statement that the Holy Spirit does things in the world conveys the *content* that He is our

Friend. The Course's words serve as distant metaphors for the real hidden meaning contained in Wapnick's interpretation.

The end result of this is that because Wapnick does not feel bound to the surface form of the words and the direct, literal content they point to, he has tremendous license in interpreting them—as I mentioned above, rejecting intellectual analysis opens the door to subjectivity. In my reading of his interpretations of Course passages, I have found that this leads to two tendencies on his part. First, he has a tendency to virtually ignore the words, often using them simply as a springboard to digress into a discussion of a favorite topic of his, such as the metaphysics of the separation, the darkness of the ego, or the unreality of the world. Second, even when he does pay some attention to the words, he has a tendency to overlook what they literally say in their immediate context, and instead interpret them in light of the broad context of his duality-as-metaphor stance. This frequently leads him to conclude that what the words *really* mean is in direct contradiction to what they *literally* mean.

The tendency to digress

One example of Wapnick's tendency to digress is his commentary on M-4.II, the Manual's discussion of honesty as a characteristic of the advanced teacher of God.[50] Here, I will cite the pertinent lines from the Manual, and then Wapnick's entire commentary on those specific lines, which immediately follows them:

> Honesty does not apply only to what you say. The term actually means consistency. There is nothing you say that contradicts what you think or do; no thought opposes any other thought; no act belies your word; and no word lacks agreement with another. (M-4.II.1:4-6)

> [Wapnick's commentary]: Right at the beginning the ego thought opposed the Holy Spirit's thought, so that the split mind became a battlefield, a place of opposition. From the ego's point of view, it is at war with God, it is opposing God. And the ego tells one lie after another, first by making up a God Who is angry, and then by making up a world that the ego tells us will make us safe and protect us from God's wrath. But then it becomes apparent that the world is not a safe place, because everyone in the

169

world suffers pain and everyone dies. This world is hardly safe.

So the ego lies all the way down the line, right from the beginning. It makes up a world out of a lie, the lie being that the world will defend and protect us—the body will protect us. Well, the body is a hell of a thing to protect us—it is always breaking down and eventually it is going to die. From the beginning, one inconsistency follows after another.

Whatever the merits of Wapnick's commentary as a statement of Course theory, it has very little to do with the actual lines being commented on. The actual teaching conveyed by the literal words of the passage—a thought-provoking teaching about the nature of honesty—is not touched upon at all. Instead, Wapnick uses these words as a springboard to talk about one of his favorite topics: the ego's war against God.

The tendency to overlook the literal meaning of the Course's words

Wapnick does address M-4.II's discussion of honesty elsewhere in his commentary. And what he says there is actually a good example of his second tendency: the tendency to overlook the literal meaning of the Course's words and interpret them in light of his duality-as-metaphor stance. Here is what he says:

> Honesty in the Course is not what we think it would be. It is not about behavior or words. It refers to the consistency of what we do or say with what we think. For example, from the world's perspective, visiting a funeral home and looking as if I am sad as I kneel by a coffin and pray for someone who is not even there is dishonest. But it is not dishonest if my behavior is consistent with the loving thought in my mind. My behavior is a way of joining with the others who are there grieving. And that is what makes my behavior consistent with the thought in my mind.

Compare this to M-4.II.1:4-6, quoted above. When the Course passage speaks of "consistency," it is clearly talking about what we often refer to as "integrity" magnified to an absolute degree: our thoughts, words, and behavior are in absolute accord. Our minds are totally unconflicted and at peace, and so we always say what we really think, we always tell the truth, and we always practice what we preach. In short, we are totally honest in every sense of the word, *including* on the level of words and behavior. After all, if honesty "does not apply *only* to what you say" (M-4.II.1:4, emphasis mine), then it must apply to what you say—it simply isn't *limited* to what you say.

But notice how Wapnick, presumably to preserve his duality-as-metaphor stance, strips out the form elements. He says honesty is "not about behavior or words," but is *only* about the loving content in our *minds*. "Consistency" means that anything we do behaviorally is "honest" as long it is consistent with a loving intent. And while the funeral example Wapnick gives is fairly benign in and of itself, the principle it exemplifies is disturbing in its implications: as long as our intent is "loving" (how can we be certain of this?), anything we say or do is "honest," even if it is actually *dishonest* on a form level. And so, a passage that, when taken literally, unequivocally advocates honesty on all levels has become, in Wapnick's de-literalized interpretation, a passage that leaves the door wide open for *dishonest* words and behavior in the name of "love." Wapnick's "real" meaning, a meaning stripped of form elements like words and behavior, contradicts what the passage actually says about the nature of honesty.

Another example of Wapnick's tendency to overlook the literal meaning of the Course's words is his assertion that the Holy Spirit is only the memory of God in the Son's mind, not a real, personal Being. In one of Wapnick's discussions of this idea, he presents what he calls a "summarizing passage about the creation of the Holy Spirit, made up of different statements from the text."[51] Here is his summarizing passage:

> [The Holy Spirit] came into being with the separation as a protection, inspiring the Atonement principle at the same time....The Voice of the Holy Spirit is the Call to Atonement, or the restoration of the integrity of the mind....He is the Call to return with which God blessed the minds of His separated Sons....The Holy Spirit is God's Answer to the separation; the means by which the Atonement heals until the whole mind returns to creating. The principle of the Atonement and the separation began at the same time. When the ego was made, God placed in

171

the mind the Call to joy....[This] is given you by God, Who asks you only to listen to it.

(T-5.I.5:2,4; T-5.II.2:2,5-3:2,6)

What do these Course lines, which Wapnick himself has quoted, tell us about the Holy Spirit? They tell us that the Holy Spirit is a Person[52] (referred to as "He," as always in the Course) Who "came into being with the separation," a Person Whose Voice calls us to accept the Atonement, the antidote to the separation. They also tell us that He came into being as a result of God Himself intentionally *responding* to the separation; notice the references to God blessing our separated minds with the Call to return, giving us an Answer to the separation, and placing the Call to joy in our minds.

Moreover, the immediate context of these lines makes it clear that the Holy Spirit is a *creation* of God, and thus eternal: the very paragraph from which Wapnick draws his first two quoted lines assures us that "what God creates is eternal" (T-5.I.5:6), and therefore the Holy Spirit will remain with us forever in Heaven, even after the separation is over (see T-5.I.5:7). In short, the plain literal language of these lines depicts the Holy Spirit the way the Course always depicts Him: as a personal Being intentionally created by God in loving response to the separation.

Wapnick, however, completely disregards what these lines literally say. Immediately after quoting them, he gives us his own interpretation of what they really mean:

> On a more sophisticated level, however, and one consistent with the inherent non-dualistic thought system of *A Course in Miracles*, we can better understand the Holy Spirit to be the memory of God's perfect Love that "came" with the Son when he fell asleep. In this sense then the Holy Spirit is not really a Person Who was specifically and intentionally created by God, but an ongoing Presence that lies within each seemingly fragmented mind; a distant memory of our Source that continually "calls" out to us like a forgotten song.[53]

Wapnick's interpretation simply replaces the picture of the Holy Spirit that these lines literally present—a picture that is absolutely consistent with everything the Course says about the Holy Spirit—with his own picture of the Holy Spirit as the memory of God, a picture that cannot be found in the Course at all. Thus, his interpretation replaces what the Course *always* says about the Holy Spirit with something the

172

Course *never* says about Him. And on what basis does Wapnick overrule the Course's own words? He presents no hard evidence for the validity of his interpretation here. The one and only reason given for his view is that it is "consistent with the inherent non-dualistic thought system of *A Course in Miracles*." In other words, his duality-as-metaphor interpretive stance automatically overrules what the words of the Course itself literally say.

One final example of Wapnick's tendency to overlook the literal meaning of the Course's words—especially those words that seem to place importance on "dualistic" form—also has to do with the Holy Spirit. This example is his curious assertion that the Workbook places much greater emphasis than the Text does on asking the Holy Spirit for specific help with our external lives. He claims that in the Text, "this idea of asking the Holy Spirit for specific help with one's external life is barely touched upon."[54] This assertion is in keeping with his view that the Workbook contains more Level Two "metaphorical" language than the Text, which contains more of the pure Level One "literal" language.[55]

I call this assertion "curious" because it is utterly untrue. Robert Perry once collected together every passage he could find on the Holy Spirit either guiding our earthly decisions or doing things in our lives, and he found that the Text actually has the *most* references to this idea. The Manual has the second most, since it deals with the teacher of God carrying out his function in the world, which is meant to be done under the Holy Spirit's guidance. Finally, there is the Workbook, which actually has the *fewest*. Wapnick has apparently either overlooked entirely the Text's many references to the Holy Spirit's activity in our lives, or dismissed those references as metaphor. For the sake of brevity, I will include just one of them here: "In time, He [the Holy Spirit] gives you all the things that you need have, and will renew them as long as you have need of them" (T-13.VII.12:4; see all of T-13.VII.12-13).

The impact of applying Wapnick's duality-as-metaphor stance to study

The bottom line is that applying his duality-as-metaphor stance to the words of the Course causes Wapnick to toss out huge swaths of the Course's teaching as unworthy of serious analysis because they are only "metaphorical." For him, in contrast to Jesus' statement to Helen quoted above, every word is *not* meaningful. Once he has removed all the "metaphor," all he has left as serious teaching is the few Level One words and concepts he considers literal, which isn't much. Left with nothing else, Wapnick repeats a few basic ideas—generally metaphysical theory—over and over. The richness of the Course's teaching has been replaced by a flat, repetitive message. The symphony of the Course has been reduced to a few, oft-repeated notes.

The place of the Text in the program

The Text has a significant place in Wapnick's vision of the program. I think Wapnick would agree with us that the Text represents the first element of the program, in which our minds are introduced to the Course's thought system. Indeed, I think for him it is the primary element, as we will see.

Workbook for Students

In broad terms, the Circle and Wapnick agree that the purpose of the Workbook is to practically apply the thought system we studied in the Text. He affirms with us that the Workbook aims "at training the mind 'along the lines the text sets forth' (W-In.1:4)."[56] However, I am virtually certain that he would disagree with our contention that the purpose of the Workbook is to be a training manual for the Course's form of spiritual practice. The reasons for this will become apparent below.

Applying Wapnick's duality-as-metaphor stance to practice: de-emphasizing the Workbook's literal practices

The major disagreement between Wapnick and the Circle concerning the Workbook can be stated very simply: We at the Circle place great importance on developing a structured spiritual practice rooted in the specific instructions given to us in the Workbook. Wapnick, on the other hand, does not seem to place much importance on this at all.

Wapnick does speak in general terms about the importance of "the practical application of the Course's theoretical ideas."[57] He also says on rare occasions that "[the Workbook] needs to be practiced as the instructions indicate,"[58] and admits that "some structure is obviously necessary,"[59] especially for beginners. But these rare positive

174

references to the Workbook's structured practice are buried within pages and pages of material that explicitly or implicitly warns *against* placing importance on such practice. I think his duality-as-metaphor stance is at the heart of this: just as he cautions against hewing too closely to the literal form of the Text's words, so he cautions against hewing too closely to the literal form of the Workbook's practices.

Wapnick's de-emphasis on practice is evident in the amount of space he devotes to it in his writings. He devotes far more space to Text theory than to Workbook practice. For example, in *The Message of 'A Course in Miracles,'* he spends hundreds of pages talking about Course theory in great detail (largely from the Text), but has only a brief twelve-page section devoted specifically to the Workbook and how to practice it. There are other references to Workbook practice scattered throughout the two volumes, but those references are a distinct minority, and often put a negative spin on it—for instance, a section in *All Are Called* entitled "Our Special Relationship with the Workbook: The Tyranny of Rituals." Finally, I have read hundreds of pages of Ken Wapnick's writings, and I have yet to find a single positive reference to the *specific practice instructions* for a Workbook lesson.

Examples that illustrate Wapnick's de-emphasis on Workbook practice

I will now go through a series of examples from Wapnick's writings that illustrate his basic stance toward Workbook practice. They reveal a consistent pattern of greatly minimizing the importance of doing the Workbook's structured practices—a stance that is in stark contrast to the stance of the Workbook itself. We will see that even in those rare instances where Wapnick affirms the value of Workbook practice, he heavily qualifies his affirmation with warnings against taking it too seriously, lest we succumb to the ego's infatuation with form.

The Workbook brings up an authority problem with Jesus

In *Few Choose to Listen*, Wapnick discusses how the Workbook can bring up an authority problem with Jesus. He tells us that this authority problem can take two forms: we can either "openly rebel by *not* doing the exercises as they are given,"[60] or we can "become totally submissive and docile, doing *exactly* what Jesus says."[61] The first form is trying to avoid doing the Workbook (or doing it sloppily by skipping around, missing practice periods, and such); the second form is trying to do the Workbook perfectly. It seems to me that Wapnick has set up a real no-win situation here. Whether we do a terrible job or a great job of doing the exercises as given, we have an authority problem with Jesus either way.

I'm sure that the first form does happen, since it is definitely true that we tend to resist doing the lessons as instructed. I'm a bit more skeptical about the second form, simply because my impression is that only a small minority of Course students have really tried to do the Workbook perfectly. Besides, I'm not so sure that trying to do the lessons perfectly is necessarily an authority problem. I think it is actually quite appropriate to *try* to do the lessons perfectly, as long as we do that not to please a heavenly authority but to free our minds, and as long as we are gentle with ourselves when we fall short, which we will almost inevitably do.

The danger of using an alarm wristwatch to remind ourselves to practice

Wapnick's main emphasis is on the second form of that authority problem with Jesus, and he goes on to discuss what he considers to be a particularly insidious manifestation of it: using an alarm wristwatch to remind ourselves to practice. He dismisses this practice aid with mocking sarcasm: "The wristwatch enables students to train themselves, like Pavlov's dogs, to 'salivate' the workbook lesson whenever the alarm goes off."[62] In his view, this particular form of practice reminder causes the Workbook's goal of mind training to be "totally sabotaged and undermined."[63]

But why would the Workbook's goal necessarily be undermined? Wapnick's main concern here is that using a wristwatch reminder will turn the exercises into rote repetitions of meaningless form. This, he believes, will compromise the Workbook's ultimate goal of training us to think of God without reminders, just because we *want* to think of Him. But using an external reminder to practice won't turn that practice into rote form, as long as we do the *practice itself* in the right spirit, once we are reminded to do it.

Moreover, the whole reason for the Workbook's structured practices is that we aren't yet at a point where we can think of God all the time without reminders. If we could do that already, we wouldn't need the Workbook's structure. It is precisely because our minds aren't habitually focused on God that the Workbook gives us the discipline of practicing at specific times. Such time-dependent practice is not the ultimate end toward which the Workbook aims, but it is a vital means to that end, particularly for beginners. Lesson 95 puts it this way:

> Regularity in terms of time is not the ideal requirement for the most beneficial form of practice in salvation. It is advantageous, however, for those whose motivation is inconsistent, and who remain heavily defended against learning.　　　　　　　　　　　　　　(W-pI.95.6:2-3)

In other words, ideally our motivation to practice should be internal. We should want to practice simply in order to receive the benefits of practice: deepening of our learning, greater peace and joy, and faster progress to God. However, though this is the ideal motivation, the simple fact is that as beginners, we have a tremendous resistance to practice. And so, as a temporary measure, we need external motivators like an external book telling us to practice by an external clock. This will keep us going until a more consistent internal motivation develops in us as a result of our experiencing the benefits of practice.

Thus, when the Workbook says something like "practice every half hour" and tells us this practice is required, it is setting up a regimen in which we practice not because we want to (though certainly it's good if we *do* want to), but simply because the half hour has come around. And how are we going to know when the half hour has come around if we don't have some sort of reminder, even if the reminder is nothing more than having a clock nearby? It is just common sense that if we're doing a structured practice that requires us to practice at specific times in the midst of our busy daily lives, we will need *some* external reminder if we're going to do much practice at all. But Wapnick's argument against practice reminders, if taken to its extreme, would force us to completely do away with setting any times for Workbook practice.

Quite simply, there is absolutely nothing in the Workbook that counsels against using a practice reminder such as an alarm wristwatch. I personally think that such reminders can be extremely useful, and I suspect Jesus would agree, given the importance he places on doing the practices at their proper times. In fact, since the Workbook does mention several times the idea of practicing "as the hour strikes" (W-pI.137.13:1, et al.)—an obvious reference to a chiming clock—I think we can safely say that Jesus has no problem with this sort of reminder.

The danger of ritual

Wapnick's antipathy toward alarm wristwatches reflects his larger concern that regular, structured Workbook practice will degenerate into meaningless *ritual*: an empty exercise in form. He is greatly concerned that students will think that just by doing a particular practice at a particular time, they will be magically saved. In the section of *All Are Called* mentioned above, the one carrying the forbidding subtitle "The Tyranny of Rituals," Wapnick mentions that the structure of the Workbook "*could* easily lend itself to ritual."[64] No doubt this is true, and worthy of mention, but Wapnick emphasizes this danger out of all proportion. In discussing his own personal practice, he makes the pregnant comment that "I do nothing in a regular, ritualistic way,"[65] which leads me to suspect that there is little real difference in his mind between a *regular* practice and a *ritualistic* one.[66]

The main problem with Wapnick's emphasis is that it is the exact opposite of the Workbook's own emphasis. There are only *two* references in the entire Workbook to the danger of its practices becoming ritualistic, while there are countless references to the importance of doing its practices as given. And neither of the two anti-ritual references discourages regular, structured practice in any way. The first (W-pI.1.3:5) is part of a description of a practice in which we are to apply the idea for the day ("Nothing I see…means anything") randomly to whatever our eyes light on. It simply warns against obsessively attempting to apply the idea to every single thing in our field of vision. This is hardly a warning against regular practice in general.

The second (W-pI.rIII.In.2:4) actually occurs in the context of a discussion that stresses the *importance* of regular practice. This is the very discussion in which, as I quoted above, we are urged to follow the practice instructions "just as closely as [we] can," and are told that "your practicing can offer everything to you." The specific issue being addressed in this discussion is that of missed practice periods. It begins by acknowledging the fact that there are times when missed practice periods are truly unavoidable, and goes on to assure us that it is no big deal when this happens:

> Learning will not be hampered when you miss a practice

period because it is impossible at the appointed time. Nor is it necessary that you make excessive efforts to be sure that you catch up in terms of numbers. Rituals are not our aim, and would defeat our goal.   (W-pI.rIII.In.2:2-4)

The message here is that in those situations where we simply *have* to skip practice periods due to our life circumstances, it is counterproductive to "make excessive efforts" to make them up. (Notice, though, that this does not rule out making *reasonable* efforts to make them up.) Frantically trying to catch up would be ritual: practicing just to fulfill form requirements, so we can check it off on our practice scorecard.

However, as the discussion continues, we are told that missing practice periods due to *unwillingness to practice* rather than truly unsuitable life circumstances is quite a different matter. If this is the reason for our lapse, "learning *will* be hampered" (W-pI.rIII.In.3:1; emphasis mine). In this case, the advice we are given is quite different:

Those practice periods that you have lost because you did not want to do them, for whatever reason, should be done as soon as you have changed your mind about your goal.   (W-pI.rIII.In.4:1)

In other words, these practice periods we *should* try to make up, as best we can. Thus, even in one of the rare places where the Workbook warns against making practice ritualistic, it still places a heavy emphasis on practice. Here, practicing in a ritualistic way simply means practicing in a way that is obsessively concerned with fulfilling the form requirements. But practicing in a nonritualistic way does not mean abandoning the form requirements. As we can see, it still entails seeing those form requirements as an important aspect of the program—even to the point of making up missed practice periods.

Even the Manual reference that Wapnick often cites to warn against practice routines (read: rituals) is, in my opinion, not quite as anti-routine as he seems to think:

Routines as such are dangerous, because they easily become gods in their own right, threatening the very goals for which they were set up.   (M-16.2:5)

Now, if this line were really a blanket condemnation of all routines, then it would invalidate the entire Workbook, which is full of practice routines. But notice that it doesn't speak against "routines"; it speaks against "routines *as such.*" In other words, it speaks against routines done just for the sake of having routines, routines as ends in themselves. But using flexible routines as practice aids is not an issue here. In fact, this section (M-16) goes on to lay out the flexible practice routine of post-Workbook practice I mentioned above, which is rooted in the basic structure of practice laid out in the Workbook: morning and evening quiet times, frequent reminders, and response to temptation throughout the day. We follow this routine not just for the sake of having a routine, but because a loose practice structure is still conducive to our learning at this stage of our growth.

It is easy to see how the Workbook's practice routines could be done in a rote way that inappropriately focuses on the form of the practice at the expense of its underlying content. The above discussion of missed practice periods alluded to this problem. But this problem is avoided not by de-emphasizing the practice, but simply by recognizing that in the Workbook, form is a *vehicle* for content. The Workbook sees its practice forms and routines as *means* to embrace its ideas and train our minds, rather than ends in themselves. The way to avoid ritual, then, is simply to see the Workbook's practice routines as means rather than ends.

To conclude this discussion of ritual, it might be helpful to summarize what our three "anti-ritual" lines, read in their immediate context, have said about what kind of practice is ritualistic and what is not:

Line	Ritualistic practice	Nonritualistic practice
W-pI.1.3:5	obsessively trying to apply the lesson to literally everything in our visual field	applying the lesson randomly to whatever our eyes light on
W-pI.rIII.In.2:4	making excessive efforts to make up practice periods that we missed because circumstances truly did not permit us to do them	making up practice periods that we missed because we didn't want to take the time

Line	Ritualistic practice	Nonritualistic practice
M-16.2:5	engaging in a practice routine just for the magical value of having a routine	engaging in a flexible practice routine based on the routines we learned in the Workbook, because such a routine is still conducive to our learning

In each case, we see that *ritualistic* practice is not equated with *regular* practice; indeed, the practice described in the "Nonritualistic practice" column is actually quite regular. Thus, there is no conflict whatsoever between the Course's rare cautions against ritual and its frequent admonitions to do the regular, structured practice it lays out for us. Wapnick's concern about the dangers of ritual is simply not shared by the Course.

The purpose of the Workbook: to forgive ourselves for not doing it

Wapnick not only minimizes the importance of doing the Workbook as instructed, but even claims that the whole purpose of the Workbook is to forgive ourselves for *not* doing it. He makes this point repeatedly, in different forms. This is the message he draws from the following line from Lesson 95:

> Let us therefore be determined...to be willing to forgive ourselves for our lapses in diligence, and our failures to follow the instructions for practicing the day's idea.
>
> (W-pI.95.8:3)

Based on this, Wapnick's conclusion is that the healthiest way to do the Workbook "is to see the purpose of the workbook lessons as being to forgive oneself when one inevitably fails to do the lesson perfectly."[67] This, he says, is "in keeping with the whole tone and nature of Jesus' instruction."[68] He even goes so far as to say that since the Workbook's purpose (in his view) is to flush out the ego, "seeking to avoid making mistakes (by doing the lessons perfectly) very craftily undercuts Jesus' goal for his students."[69]

Needless to say, Jesus certainly *does* want us to forgive ourselves when we fail to follow his instructions. But there are several problems with Wapnick's line of reasoning here. In my opinion, embracing

181

Wapnick's idea that the whole purpose of the Workbook is to forgive ourselves for not doing it is a recipe for disaster, because it can very easily lead to the complete abandonment of practice. Therefore, I want to address this issue at some length.

First and foremost, Wapnick's line of reasoning is faulty because his use of the line from Lesson 95 totally violates the immediate context of that line. Like the Workbook references to ritual discussed above, this is a good example of the importance of interpreting Course lines in light of their immediate context. What is the context here? Amazingly, the line Wapnick uses as an argument against placing undue importance on doing the structured practices is actually part of an extended discussion of *the importance of doing the structured practices.*

Lesson 95 is part of a series of Lessons (Lessons 93-110) that have us practice the first five minutes of every waking hour. This is perhaps the most demanding series of lessons in the entire Workbook, because they require us to do a lot of practicing in the midst of our busy lives. Since Jesus understands how difficult this is for us, he wants to explain why he is giving us such a strict practice regimen. The reason, in a nutshell, is that our minds are still very much untrained, and therefore "structure…is necessary for you at this time" (6:1; all of the paragraph-sentence references that follow come from Lesson 95). Structured practice is what trains our minds, and the more structure, the better. So, we really need to keep to the structure we are given for this series of lessons:

> We will, therefore, keep to the five-minutes-an-hour practice periods for a while, and urge you to omit as few as possible. Using the first five minutes of the hour will be particularly helpful, since it imposes firmer structure.
>
> (W-pI.95.7:1-2)

But of course, precisely because our minds are untrained, we won't always keep to the structure—we will miss practice periods. And so, Lesson 95 goes on to address this issue. It points out that when we miss practice periods, we have a tendency to give up on practice entirely, "to regard the day as lost" (7:4). We use our practice mistakes as a convenient excuse to bail out of practice. Because Jesus really wants us to practice, this excuse-making is something he wants us to avoid: "Do not…use your lapses from this schedule as an excuse not to return to it again as soon as you can" (7:3). To make such an excuse represents "a refusal to let your mistake be corrected, and an unwillingness to try again" (7:5).

This is where forgiveness comes in. The line that counsels us to forgive ourselves for our practice lapses occurs in paragraph 8, the paragraph immediately following the lines I just quoted. Forgiving ourselves for our practice mistakes is the way to correct our mistake and undo our "unwillingness to try again." Paragraph 9 then concludes the discussion by expanding on Jesus' purpose for this forgiveness:

> When you fail to comply with the requirements of this course, you have merely made a mistake. This calls for correction, and for nothing else. To allow a mistake to continue is to make additional mistakes, based on the first and reinforcing it. It is this process that must be laid aside, for it is but another way in which you would defend illusions against the truth. (9:1-4)

This passage, read in light of the preceding discussion, makes it clear that forgiving ourselves for our practice mistakes is meant to facilitate the larger goal of keeping us on our practice schedule. The "requirements of this course" are the *required practice periods*. The "mistakes" are *missed practice periods*. Failing to do the required practice periods *is* a mistake (9:1), a mistake that needs correction (9:2) if we are to succeed in training our minds as Jesus wants us to do.

But even though missing practice periods is a mistake that needs correction, it is *merely* a mistake (9:1). It is not a sin. And seeing our practice lapses as forgivable mistakes rather than unforgivable sins is the key to keeping our practice alive. If we heap guilt on ourselves for the mistake of not practicing, we will likely give up on our practicing, thereby making that mistake permanent (9:3). "It is this process that must be laid aside" (9:4), and it is laid aside through forgiveness. If instead of heaping guilt on ourselves, we forgive ourselves for the mistake of not practicing, we can more easily move on from it and return to our practice. This return to practice *is* the correction of our mistake. Obviously, the way to correct the mistake of missing our practice periods is to resume our practice periods. Through forgiveness, we will not give our missed practice periods the "power to delay our learning" (8:4), because we will not use them as an excuse to stop practicing.[70]

And so, Jesus' point here is not that we should forgive ourselves for failing to practice because this is the whole purpose of the Workbook. Instead, it is that we should forgive ourselves for failing to practice because *this enables us to continue our practice. This* is what is "in keeping with the whole tone and nature of Jesus' instruction." Nowhere in the Workbook, or anywhere in the Course, does it ever say or imply that the purpose of the Workbook is to forgive yourself for not doing it. Nor does it ever say, as Wapnick does, that trying to do the lessons perfectly is a crafty way to undercut Jesus' goal for us. On the contrary, the Workbook always emphasizes the importance of doing the lessons as instructed, to the best of our ability.

Besides what we have just discussed, there are at least a couple of other reasons why Wapnick's "forgive ourselves for not doing it" idea does not hold up under close scrutiny. First, it contradicts Wapnick's own rare statements that Jesus really wants us to do the Workbook exercises as instructed. How can Jesus' purpose for us be both to *do* the lessons and to *fail* to do them?

Second, this idea just doesn't make logical sense. Let us imagine, just for the sake of argument, that I somehow managed to do the Workbook perfectly—not just in the sense of fulfilling all the form requirements, but in the sense of really doing all of the required practices in such a way that I truly absorbed their content. Jesus would see this as a good thing, right? Not according to Wapnick's logic. According to that logic, I really blew it by doing the Workbook perfectly, because I lost the opportunity to flush out my ego and forgive myself. Ironically, by following Jesus' own instructions for practice really well, I "craftily undercut" his goal for me! I find this very hard to believe.

The primary Course practice: looking at the ego with the Holy Spirit or Jesus

As I mentioned above, Wapnick considers flushing out the ego so we can forgive ourselves to be a major purpose of the Workbook: "The lessons provide a classroom in which the student's ego can 'act up,' so that its thought system can at last be recognized and chosen against."[71] I get the impression that to Wapnick, the whole purpose of all of the rich variety of practices in the Workbook—the practices I listed earlier, practices that Wapnick never specifically talks about—is not the stated purpose Jesus often gives for them. Instead, their purpose is simply to scare up our egos so we can do the *real* Course practice: "Looking with the Holy Spirit's or Jesus' non-judgmental gentleness at our ego thought system."[72]

I think it is safe to say that this practice is *the* central practice of the Course in Wapnick's view. He mentions it countless times, calling it "the essence of forgiveness,"[73] "the essence of the Atonement,"[74] and "the heart of the healing process."[75] Emphasizing the same practice in slightly different words, he says, "Our attention should always be placed on bringing the ego's thoughts of specialness to the Holy Spirit's thoughts of forgiveness."[76] Wapnick does use other words to describe Course practice: he refers to things like choosing the Holy Spirit instead of the ego as our teacher, taking Jesus' hand, accepting the Atonement, and the three steps of forgiveness.[77] But it seems clear to me that these are all basically different forms of looking without judgment at the ego with the Holy Spirit or Jesus. My impression is that when Wapnick stresses the importance of applying the Course to our lives, he means doing this practice. Everything boils down to this.

This is a helpful practice, and it *is* in the Course. Looking fearlessly with unflinching honesty at the ego is definitely an important aspect of the Course's path. But boiling everything down to the single formula of looking at the ego with the Holy Spirit or Jesus leaves us with a dramatically stripped-down version of the Workbook. I think Jesus gives us such a variety of practices in the Workbook for a reason: While the content of the ego's thought system is ultimately all the same, it takes many varied forms in our lives. Thus, if we are to practice the Workbook with "great specificity" (W-In.6:1), as its Introduction advocates, we need varied forms of practice to address our specific needs. This is what will allow us to generalize the lessons to include everything (W-In.6:2).

What the Workbook says about Lessons 181-200 applies, I believe, to *all* of the Workbook lessons:

> Each contains the whole curriculum if understood, practiced, accepted, and applied to all the seeming happenings throughout the day. One is enough. But from that one, there must be no exceptions made. And so we need to use them all and let them blend as one, as each contributes to the whole we learn.   (W-pI.rVI.In.2:2-5)

In boiling down the rich variety of the Workbook's practices to

185

looking at the ego with the Holy Spirit or Jesus, Wapnick essentially takes one socket wrench out of the Workbook's immense toolbox, and throws the rest of the tools away.

The de-emphasis on practice in Wapnick's Workbook commentaries

It should be clear from all the examples we have examined here that however much Wapnick may claim he values the Workbook, his consistent pattern is to devalue its practice. Perhaps nowhere is this clearer than in my final example: his recent series of audiotapes entitled *The Workbook Lessons of 'A Course in Miracles': The Study and Practice of the 365 Lessons.*[78]

I purchased Volume I of this series because we at the Circle had heard from various sources that Wapnick had recently developed a new interest in Workbook practice, and we wanted to see if this was true. We figured that if there was *anyplace* where Wapnick actually talked about the specific practices of the Workbook, a tape set subtitled *The Study and Practice of the 365 Lessons* would have to be it. And so, I listened to his commentaries on the Workbook's Introduction and sixteen different lessons scattered through Lessons 1-60. What I heard confirmed everything I've said in this essay about Wapnick's emphasis.

He begins by saying that his purpose in these tapes is to help Course students "see the importance of applying the daily lessons to their everyday lives." So far, so good. He also says, "In general, I read and commented on the lessons line by line, but when this did not seem necessary, I focused only on the key paragraphs and passages."

But as I listened to the tapes, it soon became clear to me what material "did not seem necessary" for Wapnick to read: *the practice material*. He *completely skips* the vast majority of the practice instructions, along with any material stressing the importance of following those instructions. Instead, he uses the lessons almost exclusively as a springboard for long discourses on Course theory and metaphysics. On the rare occasions that he does refer to practice material, it is usually because the material either lends itself to a discussion of theory, or can be interpreted in a way that de-emphasizes the importance of doing the practice. For instance, he mentions the cautions against straining, and the injunctions to not feel distressed if we don't remember to practice. Amazingly, in a tape series subtitled

The Study and Practice of the 365 Lessons, Wapnick focuses virtually exclusively on *study,* and doesn't ever talk about the specific *practice* of the lessons!

I could cite many examples of this, but perhaps the most striking ones are his commentaries on Lessons 27 and 40, two lessons that strongly emphasize regular, frequent practice. In Lesson 27, he skips over 2:2-3:6, and in Lesson 40, he skips over the *entire lesson,* with the exception of the first sentence. The material that Wapnick omits from these lessons gives us the specific practice instructions for each lesson, and also emphasizes the following points:

- Frequent repetitions of the idea for the day are necessary—up to four times an hour for Lesson 27, six times an hour for Lesson 40

- It is important to set a regular time schedule for these repetitions, and adhere to it whenever possible (emphasized in both lessons)

- Whenever we forget to practice, we should try again (emphasized in both lessons)

- We need to practice frequently in order to get the most benefit (Lesson 27)

- Our frequency of practice is the measure of how much we really want to have vision (Lesson 27)

- It is easy to do the required practice, even when we are engaged in other activities (Lesson 27)

- We can practice well under any circumstances if we really want to (Lesson 40)

- We should not miss a practice period just because circumstances don't allow us to close our eyes (Lesson 40)

- Even if only a short period of time is available to us, we can still do a shorter version of the practice (Lesson 40)

The only practice material that Wapnick mentions in these two lessons is one sentence from Lesson 27: "You will probably miss several applications, and perhaps quite a number" (4:4). His comment on this sentence: "So [Jesus is] telling you, 'Don't feel guilty when you forget. I expect you to forget.'" That's the major point Wapnick wants us to get. Of course, the point about not feeling guilty is perfectly valid, but it is only a small part of the picture of practice presented by the lesson. He doesn't even mention the sentence immediately following 4:4, which stresses the importance of getting right back onto our practice schedule once we've noticed our practice lapse.

If there are any doubts about where Wapnick's emphasis lies concerning the Workbook, his commentary on these lessons should put those doubts to rest. We are not to take seriously the structured practices Jesus gives us, nor are we to take seriously his repeated emphasis on doing the practices as instructed. Instead, we are to forgive ourselves for *not* doing the practices as instructed, because that is the whole point of the Workbook.

The impact of applying Wapnick's duality-as-metaphor stance to practice

In our opinion, Wapnick's views concerning Workbook practice, if taken to heart, will almost certainly lead to serious negative consequences for our journey through the Course. Jesus really wants us to develop a habit of regular practice, but we have a great deal of resistance to practice. Everyone who has attempted to go through the Workbook has found this out firsthand. Our experience at the Circle has echoed the experience of many people in other spiritual traditions: because resistance to practice is so strong, the habit of regular, disciplined spiritual practice simply does not take hold unless we have a great deal of encouragement and support. Without that support, our practice is unlikely to survive.

Wapnick's view of practice, however, not only fails to encourage our practice, but actually *discourages* it. His constant de-emphasis of the importance of practice gives us the perfect excuse not to do it; indeed, I would go so far as to say that his stance pretty much guarantees that we *won't* do it. And if, as Jesus emphasizes, Workbook practice is truly vital to our progress in the Course's program—if our practicing truly can offer everything to us—then adopting Wapnick's stance will effectively cause us to fail in a crucial element of the path to salvation Jesus has given us.

Should the Workbook be gone through more than once?

Wapnick's answer to this question is "No. The workbook for students is set up as a one-year training program, and there is no reason for a student to deviate from that."[79] He says that the Workbook should be done only once, and "probably should be done relatively early in a student's work with the Course."[80] He does say that it is okay to go through the Workbook again if the student finds it helpful. However, he strongly warns against "possible, if not probable ego involvement"[81] in this decision—specifically, ego involvement in the form of "urging repeated run-throughs of the Workbook exercises in the magical hope that 'this time, I'll get it right.'"[82]

No doubt this kind of ego involvement is possible, but I think Wapnick overstates the point. There is certainly nothing inherently ego-based about wanting to practice something repeatedly in order to get it right. Imagine a piano teacher telling her pupil, "Unfortunately, you didn't play that piece very well, but I warn you against doing repeated run-throughs of it. If you do, that's probably your ego magically hoping that 'this time I'll get it right.'" Here, as elsewhere, Wapnick's emphasis discourages the practice of the Workbook.

I have already discussed the Circle's answer to the question of whether to repeat the Workbook, so I will not elaborate on that here.

Post-Workbook practice

Concerning post-Workbook practice, Wapnick does not advocate any kind of practice structure whatsoever for those who have completed the Workbook. He does not acknowledge the post-Workbook practice structure given in Section 16 of the Manual. This comes as no surprise, since he does not see that material as addressing teachers of God who have completed the Workbook, and therefore now need a more loosely structured format for their continuing practice. Instead, he sees it as addressing all Course students who are in the early stages of their growth.[83] This is erroneous in our view, and has the unfortunate effect of essentially removing Jesus' own instructions for post-Workbook practice from the Course.

What Wapnick *does* advocate is much more vague. This is his description of what Course students are to do when they have completed the Workbook:

> Once they are in touch with their right minds and understand the process of forgiveness that the Course sets forth, students are then able to spend the rest of their lives in daily practice with Jesus or the Holy Spirit as their Teachers.[84]

189

What this "daily practice" might look like is never specified, but I think there is little doubt that it is mainly Wapnick's primary practice of looking at the ego with Jesus or the Holy Spirit. As we have seen, this practice is "the essence of forgiveness" and "the heart of the healing process" in his view. He does mention that we can do other practices like meditation if we find them helpful, though he warns against making meditation "a source of dependency."[85] But in the end, it always seems to come down to looking at the ego, and never is there a warning against *that* becoming a source of dependency.

The relationship between the Text and the Workbook

To complete this section on Wapnick's view of the Workbook, I want to discuss his view of the relationship between the Text and the Workbook. As I mentioned above, he and the Circle agree that the purpose of the Workbook is to practically apply the thought system we studied in the Text. He sometimes illustrates the relationship between the two volumes by using the analogy of a class in chemistry or biology:[86] in such a class, one generally has a text in which the theory is presented, and a laboratory section in which the theory is put into practice. I think this is an excellent analogy. So, in Wapnick's view, there is some sense of a process in which theory is translated into practice. He also depicts Workbook practice itself as a process, even citing W-pII.284.1:5-6 as evidence for this, just as we do.[87]

However, in looking more closely at Wapnick's vision of the Text and Workbook, I don't get the impression that the two volumes are equally important components of the process. It seems that the Text and its theory is given far more weight and importance than the Workbook and its practice. In the rest of this section, I will briefly sketch the relationship between them as I understand it.

The Text is central. It presents the theory, which is the real meat of the Course. It "contains the theology, metaphysical foundation, and teachings on accepting forgiveness for our special relationships, on which the curriculum rests."[88] Because of this, it has more of the Level One language that is meant to be taken literally. In addition to theory, in Wapnick's view the Text also emphasizes the *practice* that he considers central: looking at the ego with the Holy Spirit or Jesus. In the Text, Wapnick says, "Students are urged to go to the Holy Spirit (or Jesus) with their guilt and judgment, so that together they can look at the ego and let it go."[89]

The Workbook, on the other hand, clearly has a lesser role. For one thing, in Wapnick's view, it doesn't give us nearly as much insight into Course theory as the Text does. There *is* theory in the Workbook, to be sure, but he considers it insufficient: "In short, students wishing to know what *A Course in Miracles* teaches, would hardly find such information in the workbook."[90] Why not? Because, as we've seen, Wapnick believes that the Workbook contains much more Level Two "metaphorical" language than the Text does. In his eyes, the Workbook is filled with "metaphors" like the Holy Spirit helping us with the specifics of our lives, and the prayers to God in Part II. The prayers, in particular, cannot be taken too seriously, since in Wapnick's view the Course clearly teaches that "God does not hear our prayers."[91] In short, the Workbook simply doesn't present the "straight stuff" theory as deeply and consistently as the Text does, and thus is not as reliable a source for Course theory.

The Workbook also has a lesser role than the Text because, as we've also seen, Wapnick does not place a great deal of emphasis on Workbook practice. The Workbook should be done just once, fairly early in our journey with the Course. During that one run-through, we shouldn't take the practice instructions too seriously. Instead, we should regard the purpose of the Workbook as to give us an opportunity to flush out the ego, look at it with the Holy Spirit or Jesus, and forgive ourselves for not doing the Workbook as instructed. Once we are done with the one-year training program of the Workbook, we are to spend the rest of our lives doing the same practice of looking at the ego with the Holy Spirit or Jesus.

We are also to spend the rest of our lives studying Course theory. While practice of the Workbook is just a one-year affair, Wapnick clearly sees study of Course theory to be a lifelong pursuit. Indeed, even though he sees the Workbook as insufficient in itself as a source of Course theory, he does recommend that Course students "read carefully through the workbook itself at some point after they had gone through the lessons, as they would do with the text." If they do so, they will find "a depth of teaching that can easily be overlooked as one does the lessons in the one-year training program."[92] In short, once we are done with the Workbook, we are to read it for its theory, as we would the Text—it becomes a kind of mini-Text.

We at the Circle agree that the study of Course theory is a lifelong pursuit, and that the Workbook does contain a remarkable depth of teaching that should be studied. However, in our view, Wapnick's vision of the relationship between the Text and the Workbook illustrates the point I made earlier: Wapnick doesn't seem to see a truly distinct and essential role for each volume. He doesn't see each volume as representing a different basic activity that builds on the previous ones, but instead sees each volume as presenting us with the same basic activities.

And now that we have examined Wapnick's view of the Text and the Workbook, we have a good idea of what those basic activities are. They amount to two: the *study* of Course theory, and the *practice* of looking at the ego with the Holy Spirit or Jesus. Though Wapnick acknowledges that the form and focus of each volume is certainly different, it seems that for him each volume really can be reduced to these two basic activities.

The place of the Workbook in the program

All in all, the Workbook really seems to have a fairly minor place in Wapnick's vision of the program. While there are a number of points of agreement between the Circle's and Wapnick's views of the Text, there are far fewer when it comes to the Workbook. Wapnick's minimizing of the importance of Workbook practice is strikingly different from the Circle's strong emphasis on Workbook practice. And without a regular regimen of practice, it is difficult to see how the thought system introduced to us in the Text can really penetrate deeper into our minds.

Manual for Teachers

When it comes to the Manual, one really has to stretch to find areas of agreement between the Circle and Wapnick. The most I can say is that in *very* general terms, both parties agree that the Manual is for teachers of God, and that at least one purpose it has is to summarize some of the Course's teachings. However, I am certain Wapnick would disagree with our description of the Manual's main purpose: to serve as an instruction manual for more experienced Course students who are now ready to take up their function of extending healed perception to others. The reasons for this will become clear as we proceed.

Applying Wapnick's duality-as-metaphor stance to extension: de-emphasizing literal extension to others

The central disagreement between the Circle and Wapnick concerning the Manual, like our disagreement concerning the Workbook, can be expressed very simply: We at the Circle place great importance on extending to others in thought, word, and deed as the final phase of the Course's program. Wapnick, on the other hand, does not seem to place much importance on this at all, to the point that it is essentially absent from his vision of the Course's program.[93]

Now, it must be said that Wapnick does speak favorably at times of extending love to others in the world.[94] For instance, the conclusion of *All Are Called* is entitled "Being Kind." In that conclusion, Wapnick says that "this simple rule ['Be kind']...should also be the guiding principle of students of *A Course in Miracles* seeking to learn and practice Jesus' teachings of forgiveness."[95] But as with his references to doing the Workbook as instructed, his references to extending to others in the world are rare, and buried within material that strongly warns against placing importance on such extension. Once again, I think his duality-as-metaphor stance is at the heart of this: just as he cautions against hewing too closely to the literal form of the Text's words and the Workbook's practices, so he cautions against getting caught up in the form of helping others outside ourselves—the literal form of what the Manual is calling us to do.

As with the Workbook, we can see where Wapnick's heart is concerning extension by noting how much space he devotes to it in his writings. It isn't much. For example, in the brief four-page section devoted to the Manual in *Few Choose to Listen*—the only section in the entire two-volume set that discusses the Manual at any length—there is only *one sentence* that speaks at all positively of extending to others in the world. This sentence is buried in material that speaks clearly and forcefully *against* this kind of extension. It is a weak qualifier of that material, a sentence which reads: "This does not mean that people may not be guided on the behavioral level to heal, help, or teach others."[96]

But it doesn't even work as a qualifier, for it directly contradicts Wapnick's own stance in three ways. First, the Holy Spirit and Jesus don't guide behavior in Wapnick's view, so how could we possibly be "guided on the behavioral level"? Second, even if such guidance *were* possible, Wapnick says on the previous page that the teacher of God's "behavior [is] essentially irrelevant."[97] If behavior is essentially irrelevant, why would the Holy Spirit or Jesus bother to guide it? Finally, also on the previous page, Wapnick claims that it is an egoic distortion of the Manual to believe that the Course student "is asked by Jesus *behaviorally* to teach other students, heal the sick, or preach to the world."[98] If it is only an egoic distortion to believe that Jesus asks us to teach and heal behaviorally, how can Wapnick then say that we *may* be guided to do so? Wapnick's weak qualifier granting a place for extension in the world is thus soundly overruled by the very material it attempts to qualify. There is no doubt where Wapnick's inclinations lie.

The diminished role of the Manual

Given his antipathy toward extension, it is difficult to see exactly where the Manual fits in Wapnick's scheme of things. The roles of the Text and Workbook are fairly well defined in his vision: in broad terms, the Text is for study, and the Workbook is for practice. (As we've seen, however, he strongly de-emphasizes the practice, and once we're done with the Workbook's one-year training program, it too is for study.)

But Wapnick's thumbnail descriptions of the Manual's purpose are rather vague and nondescript, making the Manual seem almost a kind of afterthought. In one of those descriptions, for instance, he says that the Manual "provides a summary of *some* of the themes and principles of the text....organized in question and answer form."[99] In another, he says that the Manual "serves as a summary of many of the Course's teachings, as well as helping to define what Jesus means by *a teacher of God*."[100]

Wapnick tends to stress the "summary of the Course's teachings" aspect in his thumbnail descriptions, and I have yet to find a specific reference in any of his works to the Manual's own description of its purpose (M-In.4, quoted in part above). Thus, Wapnick's descriptions focus on a purpose the Manual itself regards as *secondary*, mentioned only briefly in the last section, while overlooking the purpose the Manual itself regards as *primary*. That primary purpose is to serve as an instruction manual for teachers of God, a manual that will describe who they are, list their qualifications, explain what they do in the world, and give them counsel on how to do it.

In short, since teachers of God as extenders of healed perception to others have no place in Wapnick's vision of the program, the Manual itself does not really seem to have a place. In his words, it is simply "a most useful adjunct to the other two books."[101] His use of the word "adjunct" is telling; my dictionary defines "adjunct" as "something added to another thing but not essentially a part of it." This suggests that the Manual, in Wapnick's view, does not really have an essential part to play in the Course.

We don't actively extend healing to others; we just accept the Atonement for ourselves

While extending to others is the most important step of all in the Circle's vision of the Course's program, it is effectively ruled out of Wapnick's vision because, in his view, there is *no such thing* as extending to others. He says, "One does not heal *others*, minister to *others*, or teach *others*; one simply accepts the truth within oneself by realizing the illusory nature of the ego."[102] He goes on to say that "one cannot heal others because ultimately, if the world is an illusion, who is there to help?"[103] In a nutshell, "Teachers of God need merely accept the Atonement for themselves, and…salvation of the world depends on their simply doing just that *and only that.*"[104]

The view presented here is fairly simple: Because the world I see is an illusory projection of my own mind, the *only* thing the Course wants me to do is accept healed perception into my own mind. "Extension" just spreads from there automatically by osmosis, since we all share the same mind. One must admit that this view does have a kind of inner logic to it. The Course *does* say that the world is an illusory projection of our minds, that we must accept the Atonement for ourselves, and that the automatic transfer of the Atonement to other minds is one form that extension takes. There are even a number of Workbook lessons that talk about how much our brothers will benefit if we accept that day's lesson fully into our own minds.[105] It seems a logical conclusion that all we have to do is accept healed perception in the privacy of our own minds, and that's it.

The problem with this conclusion, however, is that the Course itself does not reach the same conclusion. Instead, it asserts again and again that active extension to other people in thought, word, and behavior is crucial to the salvation process. True, the world is an illusion and there are ultimately no separate "others" out there, but in the Course's view, helping those we perceive as others in this illusory world is *how we learn that.*

To cite just one example of this: I have referred to the Course idea of a "holy encounter," a brief interaction between two people in which healing is exchanged. The following passage describes what such a holy encounter ultimately teaches us:

> You once believed that, when you met someone else...he *was* someone else. And every holy encounter in which you enter fully will teach you this is not so.
> You can encounter only part of yourself because you are part of God, Who is everything. (T-8.III.6:7-7:1)

In other words, it is through earthly extension to others—a holy encounter between two apparently separate people—that we ultimately learn that there is no real separation. Through exchanging healing with others, we learn that the world is an illusion, that the "others" we see are really part of us, and that we are all ultimately one.

I discussed Course evidence for the importance of earthly extension above, so I won't go into great detail about it here. But I do want to address briefly an idea that Wapnick often uses as evidence for his views: the idea that our only responsibility is to accept the Atonement for ourselves. Wapnick seems to believe that this well-known Course idea means that we should just accept Atonement into our own minds and *do nothing else*. But in my opinion, it does not mean that at all.

To see what it really means, we need to look at the Course's first statement of the idea: "*The sole responsibility of the miracle worker is to accept the Atonement for himself*" (T-2.V.5:1). Notice that this line refers specifically to the "miracle worker." We've already seen that a miracle worker is not just someone who accepts miracles into his own mind, but also someone who *extends miracles to others*. Therefore, what this statement really means is that the miracle worker's only responsibility is to accept the Atonement into his own mind, *so that he can extend it to others*. Indeed, the Course specifically calls the recipient of the miracle worker's activity a "miracle receiver" (T-1.VII.3:10; T-2.V.3:2). And paradoxically, it is only by extending miracles to others that the miracle worker fully and completely accepts the Atonement for himself: "Through miracles you accept God's forgiveness [the Atonement] by extending it to others" (T-1.I.21:2).

The danger of "spiritual specialness"

In Wapnick's view, any belief that we may actually have a Course-sanctioned role of extending to others in the world is an insidious ego ploy that he calls "spiritual specialness."[106] What this means is that any belief that the Holy Spirit has chosen us "to do *holy, special, and very important work* in this world"[107] is *always* nothing more than the ego's desperate attempt to cling to specialness in a "spiritualized" form. This must be so, because the Holy Spirit does not actually guide behavior, and the world is an illusion anyway.

This view is in direct contrast to the Course, which emphasizes that the Holy Spirit has given *all* of us holy, special (in the sense of "unique," not "better than others"), and important work to do in this world—what the Course calls our "special function":

> Such is the Holy Spirit's kind perception of specialness; His use of what you made, to heal instead of harm. To each He gives a special function in salvation he alone can fill; a part for only him. Nor is the plan complete until he finds his special function, and fulfills the part assigned to him, to make himself complete within a world where incompletion rules. (T-25.VI.4:1-3)

But to Wapnick, we apparently have *no* special function in this world, at least not as the Course uses the term. His duality-as-metaphor stance forces him to redefine the Course term "special function," stripping out the elements in the above description that speak of us having unique, specially assigned individual roles in salvation.

In Wapnick's redefinition, he simply equates our special function with our *general* function of forgiveness. Two examples of this redefinition are from places where he is commenting on passages—including the one above—that actually describe our special function as our unique, individual role in salvation. In one place, he refers to "our 'special function' of forgiveness,"[108] and in the other, he says, "This special function of forgiveness belongs to everyone."[109] A third example is from his *Glossary-Index for 'A Course in Miracles,'* where he says, "Our 'special function' is to forgive our special relationships."[110] The bottom line here is that our special function has nothing to do with having a unique and important role in God's plan for salvation. To believe that it does is to fall into the trap of "spiritual specialness."

The term "teacher of God" does not describe a distinct role; it simply refers to any Course student

Wapnick's antipathy toward extension basically invalidates the Manual's entire purpose of instructing teachers of God in their role of extending to others. Since in his view one "does not heal *others*, minister to *others*, or teach *others*," Wapnick completely rejects the idea that the distinct earthly roles of *teacher of pupils* or *healer of patients* are discussed at all in the Manual, even though these roles are central to the Manual. The "teacher of pupils" role, in particular, is ruled out on principle because, in his view, "*A Course in Miracles* is inherently a self-study curriculum."[111]

Wapnick, in fact, doesn't see the term "teacher of God" as referring to a distinct developmental stage in one's spiritual growth at all. In his view, the term "teacher of God" refers simply to *any Course student.* It is "Jesus' term for his students,"[112] "the Course's term...for those who pursue *A Course in Miracles* as their spiritual path."[113] He shares the common idea in the Course community that *everyone* is a teacher of God (and given his influence, perhaps contributed to the popularization of that idea). Since everyone is a teacher of God in this view, a person does not become such a teacher by reaching a more advanced stage of development, nor by actually teaching others in some way. Rather, a person is made such a teacher simply by being a student of the Course. "Teacher" is apparently a metaphor that really means "student."

The danger of helping and joining with others

A major ramification of Wapnick's stance is that the two essential ingredients of salvation in the Circle's vision of the Manual—helping those who call for help, and joining in holy relationships dedicated to the goal of healing—play no part in his vision. He's not against helping others and joining with them behaviorally; it's just that he doesn't see this as a vital part of the Course's program. Instead, he sees it as a tremendous temptation to engage in "spiritual specialness."

Wapnick's de-emphasis on helping and joining others is evident in his writings. Concerning helping, we have already seen his statement that there is no point in helping because "ultimately, if the world is an illusion, who is there to help?" He adds, "Needless to say, the whole concept of *helping* presupposes a dualistic universe, of which God

198

knows nothing."[114] Concerning holy relationships, in his view the Course term "holy relationship" isn't about two people joining at all, but simply refers to *one* person joining with another *in his own mind.*[115] The entire idea of mutual joining has been removed.[116]

One result of Wapnick's de-emphasis on mutual joining is that he warns strongly against joining in Course groups. I mentioned above the Circle's belief that because of the Course's strong emphasis on mutual joining, joining together in such groups can be a very helpful aspect of walking the Course's path. Not so for Wapnick, who devotes an entire chapter of *Few Choose to Listen* (Chapter 6) to the dangers of external joining with others. He concedes that meeting in Course groups is not inherently wrong,[117] but also says that such groups "are totally irrelevant to the Course's curriculum, and reflect the anthropomorphic projections onto a God Who now thinks like a dualistic ego, believing in external joining."[118] We must constantly guard against "the magical belief in the efficacy of Course groups meeting together."[119] Such joining is not true joining at all.

If mutual joining with others is not true joining, then what is? According to Wapnick, "Jesus' words about joining with our brothers are metaphors for the greater joining in the *mind.*"[120] And what is this "greater joining in the mind"? Is it joining with the minds of our brothers, which the Course does indeed regard as the internal joining that should always be behind our external joining? No—at least not directly. Instead, Wapnick says, "It cannot be said too often that the only true joining—and the real focus of Jesus' teachings in *A Course in Miracles*—is the joining with him or the Holy Spirit in our minds."[121]

Where, then, does joining with our brothers fit in? In Wapnick's view, the experience of joining with our brothers is simply a by-product of joining with our inner Teachers in the privacy of our own minds.[122] Joining with the Holy Spirit or Jesus "should *always and only be* the Course student's focus."[123] Jesus' "sole emphasis in *A Course in Miracles*...is on the individual student's relationship with the Holy Spirit."[124] In fact, Wapnick equates "joining" with his central Course practice of looking at the ego with the Holy Spirit or Jesus: "Joining means looking without judgment at *one's own belief in sin* projected onto another, the operational definition of looking with Jesus or the Holy Spirit."[125] In Wapnick's view, then, the Course's constant references to mutually joining with our brothers are simply metaphors for an internal process that has nothing to do with actually joining with our brothers.

Now, certainly the Course wants us to join with Jesus and the Holy Spirit, but that is definitely not Jesus' "sole emphasis." And certainly external joining with our brothers, in and of itself, is not true joining; to be true joining, external joining must be an expression of internal joining, the joining of minds. But that being said, such external expression of our internal joining is vital.[126] All of Wapnick's warnings against extension in the world and mutual joining with others are utterly contrary to the Manual, and indeed to all of the Course material. Extension in the world is absolutely essential to the Course's path.

One of the reasons I quoted those passages from the *Psychotherapy* supplement earlier is that they make the "in the world" aspect totally unequivocal. They are not just talking about a person helping or joining with another within his own mind. Within their immediate context as part of the *Psychotherapy* supplement, they are talking about a specific worldly situation: a psychotherapist and her patient joining together at the psychotherapist's office in the common goal of healing the mind of the patient, an act which will ultimately heal the mind of the therapist as well. The Manual's discussions of the teacher of God are referring to the same types of real-life external situations: teachers getting together with pupils, healers meeting patients, people joining together in myriad forms for the purpose of sharing healed perception with one another.

I want to say one more thing about those *Psychotherapy* quotes, specifically about the statement that "two come very close to God in this attempt [to help and heal], however limited, however lacking in sincerity." This line speaks volumes about the emphasis the Course material places on helping and healing others in the world, an emphasis that is the exact opposite of Wapnick's. It is clear from everything Wapnick says on the topic that he sees the impulse to extend help and healing to others in the world as primarily an ego impulse to make the error real and engage in "spiritual specialness." In his few positive comments on helping others, he acknowledges that it *might* be a genuine spiritual impulse. But it is clear that he believes this impulse is *almost certainly* ego, and so he strongly discourages us from making too much of it.

This line from *Psychotherapy*, however, turns the emphasis completely around. It clearly depicts the impulse to extend help and healing to others as a *holy* and *spiritual* impulse. It is so holy and spiritual that even when it is tainted by ego elements—when it is limited and insincere to some degree, which most of the time it probably is—it is still so holy that we "come very close to God in this attempt." This line grants that the ego can certainly distort the desire to help, but also strongly encourages us to follow that desire anyway, because "nothing in the world is holier" (P-2.V.4:2). In short, while Wapnick's emphasis is on the distortion of the helping impulse, the Course's emphasis is on the holiness of it. And which emphasis is more likely to inspire us to be truly helpful to others?

The impact of applying Wapnick's duality-as-metaphor stance to extension

We have seen the impact of Wapnick's stance throughout this discussion of the Manual, but I would like to summarize it here. Wapnick simply can't see extension in a very positive light, because his duality-as-metaphor stance forbids it. Looking at the Manual through the lens of this stance, Wapnick strips out its very heart: teachers of God teaching and healing in the world; extending healed perception to others in every way; helping others who ask for help; joining with others in the holy relationships that, by virtue of that very joining, undo the ego's thought system of separation in both teacher and pupil alike. Needless to say, this has a tremendous impact both on the Manual's role in the Course's program, and on our own journey through that program. I will expand on this in my next point.

The place of the Manual in the program

For all intents and purposes, the Manual *has* no place in Wapnick's vision of the program. Extension as described in the Manual is not the final step in his version of the program, and cannot be. While Text study plays a significant role in Wapnick's vision, and Workbook practice plays at least some role (albeit a very limited one), extension to others as described in the Manual simply plays no meaningful role at all. This is easily the most significant difference between Wapnick's vision of the program and the Circle's, and it is a critical one. Without extending to others, our learning will never become complete.

201

THE BIG PICTURE:
HOW DOES EACH VISION SEE THE
DEVELOPMENTAL PROGRESSION
OF THE COURSE'S PATH?

Now that we've seen both the Circle's and Ken Wapnick's visions of the Course's program, I think it should be clear that they are profoundly different visions. This difference becomes especially apparent when we examine how each vision sees the developmental progression of the program. So, now I would like to focus on the "big picture" described by each vision, the developmental progression it sees unfolding for Course students as they go through the three volumes.

The Circle

In the Circle's view, *the three volumes represent three distinct activities—study, practice, and extension—which lead us through the inner process of progressively internalizing the Course's thought system.*

Before going on, a couple of qualifications of the above summary statement are in order. First, I want to reiterate my statement that each volume includes all three elements of study, practice, and extension. Certainly, Jesus wants us to engage in all three activities throughout our journey with the Course. When I say that the Text represents study, the Workbook represents practice, and the Manual represents extension, I am simply talking about the primary emphasis of each volume, the primary role each volume is intended to fulfill.

Second, even though the three activities follow each other in a progressive, logical sequence—study is the foundation of practice; study and practice are the foundation of extension—it does not necessarily follow that the three volumes must be done in order. It is true that the way the Course is written assumes that we will go through the volumes in order: the later volumes remind us of things that we are expected to remember from the earlier ones. However, the Course also suggests that some students might benefit from going through the volumes in a different order (see M-29.1:5-7). And of course, the volumes may be gone through concurrently. The crucial point, I think, is that regardless of what order we actually go through the volumes, the overall developmental progression we follow will most likely follow the general pattern of study leading to practice leading to extension. It is the purpose of the volumes to guide us through this progression, regardless of what order we actually go through them.

With these qualifications in mind, and with the additional understanding that the journey of any given Course student may not be as neat and linear as the "ideal" version I present below, let's look at each volume and its role in our developmental progression.

The journey through the Course's program logically begins with the Text. Ideally, the Course would have us begin under the tutelage of a personal Course teacher, but whether we have a teacher or not, our primary focus at the beginning is *study*. Our first priority as we begin the Course is simply to take this new and radical thought system into our minds, and we do that through study. Through studying the Text, we introduce ourselves to what will eventually become our new thought system. This activity of study is our primary means of learning at this point. Students in a college program must begin by learning the theoretical foundation of their chosen field. In like manner, we as Course students must begin by learning the theoretical foundation of the Course. This is the first step in our developmental progression.

Once we have gained some basic understanding of the Course's thought system through study, we progress to the next phase, represented by the Workbook. We go through the Workbook as instructed. We continue our study, but as we progress on our journey, slowly but surely our primary focus becomes *practice*. Our priority now is to deepen our understanding and living experience of the Course's thought system, and we do that through practice. Through doing the Workbook, we develop a regular, structured, multi-faceted spiritual practice, and learn how to apply the Course's thought system to our individual lives. This activity of practice is our primary means of learning at this point. Students in a college program must build on their theoretical understanding of their chosen field by putting that theory into practice through lab work, internships, and such. In like manner, we as Course students must build on our theoretical understanding of the Course by putting it into practice through using the tools the Workbook gives us. This is the second step in our developmental progression.

Once we have deepened our understanding of the Course's thought system through practice, we progress to the final phase, represented by the Manual. We become beginning teachers of God, and assume our function of extending to others. We continue our study. We also continue our practice, following the basic framework of practice we learned in the Workbook. But as we progress on our journey, slowly but surely our primary focus becomes *extension*. Our priority now is to *fully* embrace the Course's thought system as our own, and we do that by extending healed perception—forgiveness, miracles—to others. Through working with the Manual, we learn how to fulfill our function of extension, and thus reinforce the Course's thought system in our minds. This activity of extension is our primary means of learning at this point. Students in a college program eventually graduate and go out into the world to extend what they have learned through teaching, working in their chosen fields, being of service to others, and such. In like manner, we as Course students eventually "graduate" from the Text and Workbook (in the sense that we have gone through both volumes—we will continue to work with them), and then go out into the world to extend healed perception to others in thought, word, and deed. Through fulfilling this function of extension, we gradually develop into advanced teachers of God, and eventually attain true perception completely and awaken to God. This is the third and final step in our developmental progression, the step that makes our learning complete.

Ken Wapnick

In Ken Wapnick's view as I understand it, *the three volumes represent the same basic activities—the study of Course theory, and the practice of looking at the ego with the Holy Spirit or Jesus—which are the sole means of internalizing the Course's thought system.*

Even though Wapnick claims that the Course's curriculum represents a kind of progression in which each volume plays a distinct role, this simply does not seem to be the case when we look more closely at his vision. Instead, we see the same basic activities emphasized throughout: studying Course theory and looking at the ego with the Holy Spirit or Jesus. While Wapnick does talk about other things in his writings, these two activities are so heavily emphasized that I think his entire vision of the Course's program really comes down to this.

The Text is clearly the central volume for Wapnick, precisely because it both presents the Course's theory and, in his view, strongly emphasizes the practice of looking at the ego with the Holy Spirit or

Jesus. The Text, and Course theory in general (especially metaphysics), is Wapnick's major focus. The other two volumes have secondary roles, which for all intents and purposes simply echo the role of the Text.

The Workbook is just a one-year training program, the purpose of which is to flush out the ego so we can look at it with the Holy Spirit or Jesus, and forgive ourselves for not practicing. Once we are done with this one-year training program, we are to spend the rest of our lives studying the Workbook "as [we] would do with the text," and continuing the same practice of looking at our ego and forgiving ourselves, with the Holy Spirit and Jesus as our Guides.

The Manual has an even lesser role. It is basically nothing more than a Q & A book, a "useful adjunct" that "provides a summary of *some* of the themes and principles of the text." And joining with others—a central theme of the Manual—has nothing to do with actually going out into the world to extend healed perception to others, but instead is nothing more than a metaphor for looking at the ego with the Holy Spirit or Jesus.

We internalize the Course's thought system solely through using the three volumes to facilitate our two basic activities. This is the way that we eventually attain true perception completely and awaken to God.

Comparing the big picture of the two visions

In this brief overview, we can clearly see the difference between the Circle's vision and Wapnick's. The Circle's vision sees the developmental progression of the Course's path as one in which we progressively internalize the Course's thought system through engaging in different, sequentially unfolding activities represented by the Course's three volumes. But Wapnick's vision sees the developmental progression as simply one in which we gradually internalize the Course's thought system through engaging in the same two basic activities of Course study and looking at the ego with the Holy Spirit or Jesus.

Wapnick's vision, then, basically sets aside the whole logical sequence suggested by the volumes, the sequence one normally expects in a course with a text, a workbook, and a teacher's manual. The Course, which was dictated to two professors, is clearly modeled on a college course. The Circle's vision fits this basic model. But while

Wapnick does sometimes compare the Course to a college course, his vision does not present a genuine parallel with such a course, in which we learn the theory (text), apply it in practice (workbook), and then graduate and teach what we learned to others (teacher's manual). Rather than working through the volumes with an eye to the unfolding developmental process of study, practice, and extension that those volumes take us through, in Wapnick's vision we simply skip around from volume to volume as needed to facilitate our two basic activities.

In sum, it seems to me that this is one more place where our different interpretive stances lead to different ways of seeing the Course. For the Circle, the Course is literally a *course*. It is not exactly the same as a college course, but it does follow the same basic form, and its author expects us to take that form seriously. Jesus really wants us to *take* this Course as it is laid out. He really wants us to be diligent students of the Text, dedicated practitioners of the Workbook, and eventually devoted teachers guided by the Manual. It is through actually taking this course as given that we learn its curriculum and awaken to God.

But for Wapnick, it seems that the "Course" part of the title *A Course in Miracles* is more of a broad metaphor for the learning process. Yes, the Course is similar to a college course in some respects, but we shouldn't take that form too seriously. We shouldn't study the literal words of the Text too closely, we shouldn't do the literal practices of the Workbook too regularly/ritualistically, and we certainly shouldn't become literal teachers of the material, however much the Manual may seem to suggest it. Instead of taking the form of the Course seriously, we should just treat it as a loose framework for facilitating the activities of studying the theory and looking at the ego. This is all Jesus wants us to do; this is all we *need* to do to learn its curriculum and awaken to God.

WHICH VISION WILL BETTER ENABLE THE COURSE'S PROMISES TO BE FULFILLED IN THE LIVES OF ITS STUDENTS?

We are at last ready to answer the final question of this essay. To phrase that question another way: Since the Course's program is the answer to the question of how to *take* this course, which vision of that program will better enable Course students to *pass* this course?

The Circle's vision will truly enable Course students to pass this course.

We believe that the Circle's vision goes a long way toward capturing the essence of the remarkable spiritual program that Jesus gave us in the Course. It is a truly integrated program in which each volume plays a distinct and essential role. It takes us through a systematic process in which the thought system of the Course enters the soil of our minds through study, grows through practice, and bears fruit through extension to others. This program is remarkably rich, multi-faceted, and complete. Though none of us at the Circle is a spiritual giant, our attempts to implement the Course's program in our own lives have led to powerful positive results. Our own experience has convinced us that this program will truly enable us to pass this Course. It will truly enable the Course's promises to be fulfilled in the lives of all its students.

Wapnick's vision is extremely unlikely to enable Course students to pass this course.

Wapnick's vision, in our opinion, fails in many crucial respects to capture the essence of the program Jesus gave us in the Course. The main reason for this is his duality-as-metaphor interpretive stance, which again and again forces him to strip out or greatly minimize anything in the program that seems to regard "dualistic" form as important. We can see this at work in his picture of each of the three volumes:

> *Text:* He does urge study, but this study is crippled by his strong caution against getting trapped by the literal form of the words, since that would raise verbal forms to the status of truth. This reduces the Text to a constant repetition of a few of Wapnick's favorite metaphysical themes.

> *Workbook:* He does say we should practice, but this practice is crippled by his strong caution against getting

trapped in the form of doing the practice, since that would give an empty, ritualistic form saving power. This reduces the Workbook to an ego-uncovering device which, like any challenging situation in our lives, scares up our ego so we can look on it with the Holy Spirit or Jesus and forgive ourselves.

Manual: He does say that we *might* be guided to extend help to others, but this extension is effectively canceled out by his strong caution against getting trapped in the form of helping others, since that would make real the error that there is a world outside ourselves. This reduces the Manual to a Q & A book that just summarizes a few basic ideas of the Text.

What gets lost every step of the way is the vibrant *richness* and *variety* of the Course's program. The richness of the Text's detailed, multi-faceted teaching is replaced by a repetition of a few basic metaphysical principles. The richness of the Workbook's treasure chest of practices is replaced by the single practice of looking at the ego with Jesus or the Holy Spirit—a practice that isn't even a significant part of the Workbook. The richness of joining in mutual relationships rooted in the goal of extending healing to the world is replaced by the single act of accepting the Atonement by joining with the Holy Spirit and Jesus in the privacy of our own minds. The result is a program that simply leaves out too much that is essential. Thus, in our opinion, Wapnick's version of the Course's program is extremely unlikely to enable Course students to pass this Course. It will make it very difficult for the promises of the Course to be fulfilled in the lives of its students.

This may seem like an overly strong statement, but to us it is simply the logical outcome of Wapnick's leaving so much of Jesus' program out of his vision. The Course tells us, in a line I quoted above, that it is a unified curriculum "in which nothing is lacking that is needed, and nothing is included that is contradictory or irrelevant" (W-pI.42.7:2). Applying this statement to the program, it means that the Course's program has everything we need, and every element of the program is necessary to our salvation (at least if we want to find salvation through the Course's system). Throughout this essay, we have seen that the Course material considers each element of the program to be vital. We have seen that study is required if we want to pass the Course (*Absence from Felicity*, p. 285), practice is required in order to "make the goal of the course possible" (W-In.1:2), and extension to others is required because "there is no other way to find your Self" (P-2.V.8:8). In short, salvation depends on our doing the entire program.

If this is so, then removing major elements from the program, as Wapnick does, has disastrous effects. If salvation depends on studying and understanding the full depth of meaning contained in the words of the Text, developing a regular habit of spiritual practice as instructed by the Workbook, and extending healed perception to others as described in the Manual, then what will happen if we don't do these things? If salvation in the Course's system comes from doing its program, what will happen if we take to heart the vision presented by Wapnick, who emphatically warns us away from most of the program?

Why is this not more apparent in the Course community?

It seems obvious that Wapnick's vision will make it very difficult for Course students to truly reap the benefits the Course promises. Why, then, is this not more apparent in the Course community, a community that still seems to be heavily influenced by Wapnick's views? In our opinion, a major reason for this is something that I mentioned at the very beginning of this essay: not much has been said or written about the Course's program. The program has not been discussed much in Course circles, so Course students do not know much about it. As a result, Course students generally are not doing the Course's own program (as we envision it), so they are not reaping the Course's benefits to the degree that they could. Thus, they have no real standard of comparison between Wapnick's views and the program given in the Course.

However, we at the Circle look forward to a future in which the program will receive the attention it deserves. We hope that this will lead to more students following the program as Jesus instructed. We hope that this, in turn, will eventually lead to the Course's path producing advanced teachers of God who are true lights to the world. If this happens, then the benefits of doing the Course's program as given will become obvious, and students will have a real standard of comparison by which to measure the effectiveness of Wapnick's approach. At this present juncture in the Course's history, then, students are for the most part unaware of the Course's own alternative to Wapnick's approach, and thus the relative ineffectiveness of his approach is not apparent. Yet we hope for a different future.

CONCLUSION

In his interview with Ian Patrick, Ken Wapnick speaks very movingly of his encounters with Mother Teresa. He relates how much her forgiving love inspired him, and calls her "a spokesperson for the love of Jesus."[127] I too have always been greatly inspired by Mother Teresa. But as I read Wapnick's words about her, I felt a real sense of irony: as much as Wapnick admires her, it seems to me that his version of the Course's program would make it unlikely that we could ever become like her.

I say this because Mother Teresa herself followed an "organized, well-structured and carefully planned program" for her own spiritual growth. And while Roman Catholicism is certainly different from the Course in many respects, her program nonetheless included all three elements of study, practice, and extension in large measure. It was a program of *study*: she was no scholar, but certainly her education as a nun required her to read the scriptures and learn the basic thought system of her faith. It was a program of *practice*: all her life, she followed a very regular, rigorous, structured spiritual practice—she actually spent more time per day in prayer and spiritual practice within her convent than she did working in the outside world. Above all, it was a program of *extension*: she didn't just look at her ego and forgive in the privacy of her own mind, but instead extended herself in every way imaginable, devoting her life to loving service to the poor of Calcutta, as well as to the entire world. It was indeed her love in action that inspired everyone, including Wapnick, to regard her as a living saint. She was recognized by all as a living, breathing miracle worker.

Wapnick asks, "How many *A Course in Miracles* students would you want to put next to her, as an example of love and egoless expression?"[128] His implied answer is "Not many," and I agree with him. But I don't think that number will grow if we say that the Course is full of metaphor. It won't grow if we don't take the Course's literal words and practices seriously. It definitely won't grow if we tell ourselves not to take all those injunctions to help others in the world literally, lest we fall into the trap of "spiritual specialness." Instead, I think the only way we can become miracle workers like Mother Teresa is the same way she did: follow a rigorous spiritual program of careful study, regular practice, and active extension to others. As Course students, this means that we need to follow the program of the Course. I believe that if we do this, we will ultimately become the miracle workers this course in miracles was intended to produce: miracle workers who, like Jesus two thousand years ago, will teach the saving message of God's Love and extend healing to all who come to us for help. Through Jesus, the Holy Spirit asks each and every one of us: "Are you ready yet to help Me save the world?" (C-2.9:1). Let us become ready through using the means Jesus has given us. Let us really *take* his course in miracles, and by so doing, join him in bringing God's healing light to a dark and suffering world.

Notes

[1] In this essay, I will draw heavily from two main works of his: his series of articles on the Circle's website (www.circleofa.com) entitled "The Spiritual Program of *A Course in Miracles*," and his article entitled "How Can *A Course in Miracles* Accomplish Its Purpose?" (*A Better Way*, Issue #18, also available on the Circle's website). All Robert Perry quotes in this essay come from these two sources. I encourage you to consult these works for a more in-depth treatment of what I will cover all too briefly here.

[2] See Robert Perry's essay entitled "How Metaphoric Is the Language of the Course?" on page 61 of this book for an in-depth exploration of this crucial issue.

[3] The Course speaks of what we might call *internal* miracles (accepting healed perception from the Holy Spirit or Jesus into our own minds) and *interpersonal* miracles (extending healed perception to others as the Holy Spirit or Jesus directs—being a "miracle worker"). Both are important; internal miracles are the prerequisite for interpersonal miracles. But based on our research, the Circle's view is that the vast majority of references to "miracle" in the Course refer to *interpersonal* miracles. This is especially evident in the fifty miracle principles in the first section of the Text (T-1.I); for instance, see principles 8, 9, 11, 16, 18, 21, and 24.

[4] *Absence from Felicity*, by Ken Wapnick, p. 258.

[5] *Ibid.*, p. 258.

[6] *Ibid.*, p. 285.

[7] *Bringing the Course to Life: How to Unlock the Meaning of 'A Course in Miracles' for Yourself*, by Allen Watson and Robert Perry.

[8] *Absence from Felicity*, p. 234.

[9] One result of the Circle's work in this area is the three-volume series of books entitled *A Workbook Companion: Commentaries on the Workbook for Students from 'A Course in Miracles,'* by Allen Watson and Robert Perry. (Volume I, unfortunately, is out of print as of the date of this writing.) These books have proven to be the most popular of all the Circle's books. Robert Perry also has an excellent booklet on how

to practice, entitled *The Workbook as a Spiritual Practice.*

[10] As an aside, the post-Workbook practice described here is the form of practice that I am doing at present. I have found it to be a very effective form of practice.

[11] Here is a list of those occurrences: T-13.X.10:1-2; T-26.V.6:1-4; W-pI.37.Title-2:1; W-pI.64.4:1-4; W-pII.256.1:1-2; and P-2.V.8 (three occurrences in this paragraph). Some of these are more focused on *inward* extension to others (say, of forgiveness), and others are more focused on one's function of *outward* extension to others (as an expression of inward forgiveness). In addition to these occurrences, there are other Course references that present the same basic idea that extending to others is the only way to salvation. These references say of this idea that it is "the only way" (T-6.III.4:3), that "there is only one way" (T-7.VII.10:9), that "this is the way, and the only way" (T-9.II.12:4), that "there is one way, and only one" (W-pI.186.5:1), and that "there is no other choice of pathways" (P-2.VII.9:8).

[12] For an examination of the Manual's description of this role, see Robert Perry's article "The Evidence in the Manual for the Teacher-Pupil Relationship," on the Circle's website. Here is a brief excerpt from that article, describing this role: "The teacher qualifies to be a teacher by having reached a certain level of development [M-1.1:2]. Having qualified, the teacher will teach a particular path; in this case, *A Course in Miracles* [M-1.3:1; M-1.4:1]. He will teach the Course to certain pupils, who are selected for him because the Course is the path they need to learn [M-2.1:1-2] The common goal that will knit them together and make their relationship holy is the goal of learning *A Course in Miracles* [M-2.5:3-4; M-2.5:7]."

[13] For an examination of the Manual's description of this role, see Robert Perry's article "The Teacher of God as Spiritual Healer," on the Circle's website. Here is a brief excerpt from that article, describing this role: "A teacher of God comes to a 'patient' [thirteen occurrences of the word 'patient' in the Manual, all in sections describing the role of healer]....This patient has a 'presented problem' [M-21.5:3], which is some form of physical sickness. The teacher then attempts 'to be a channel for healing' [M-7.2:1] to the patient. The Manual expects that he will often succeed—the patient will be healed. This is indicated by the fact that two entire sections address what to do when a healing appears to fail, when there is the appearance of 'continuing symptoms' [M-7.4:1]. If the Manual expected the sickness to simply continue as before, why devote so much attention to what to do when it actually *does* continue?"

[14] My main sources for Ken Wapnick's vision are his books *The Message of 'A Course in Miracles'* (a two-volume set), and *The Most Commonly Asked Questions about 'A Course in Miracles'* (co-written with his wife, Gloria). I have also consulted a number of other sources, which will be indicated as I cite them. I have found that all of his more recent works present the same basic vision of the Course and its program (though his works written before the mid-1980's have some significant differences).

[15] That section is Chapter 1 of *The Message of 'A Course in Miracles,' Volume Two: Few Choose to Listen*, by Ken Wapnick.

[16] See Robert Perry's essay entitled "How Metaphoric Is the Language of the Course?" on page 61 of this book for a much more in-depth exploration of Wapnick's interpretive stance. That essay presents two arguments Wapnick makes for his stance that the Course is mainly metaphor, arguments which contradict one

another. The first argument, "Wapnick's argument #1," is that *all* words must be metaphors, because words cannot describe ultimate reality. The second argument, "Wapnick's argument #2," concedes that *some* words *can* be literal, which contradicts argument #1. My brief account here of Wapnick's stance follows argument #2.

[17] *Few Choose to Listen*, p. 94.

[18] For a brief summary of what Wapnick means by "Level One" and "Level Two," see *Commonly Asked Questions*, p. 120.

[19] *Few Choose to Listen*, p. 69.

[20] The phrase "duality as metaphor" comes from the title of a Ken Wapnick taped workshop on this topic, *Duality as Metaphor in 'A Course in Miracles.'*

[21] To my knowledge, Wapnick never puts it exactly this way, but the following quote certainly expresses the basic idea: "Teachers of God need merely accept the Atonement for themselves, and…salvation of the world depends on their simply doing just that, *and only that*" (*Few Choose to Listen*, p. 32).

[22] "The Uniqueness of *A Course in Miracles*," by Gloria and Ken Wapnick; *The Lighthouse*, Vol. 13, No. 1 (March 2002), p. 1.

[23] *Commonly Asked Questions*, p. 122.

[24] *Ibid.*, p. 122.

[25] *Few Choose to Listen*, p. 35.

[26] *Ibid.*, p. 13.

[27] *Glossary-Index for 'A Course in Miracles,'* 4th Ed., by Ken Wapnick, p. 1.

[28] *Ibid.*, p. 1.

[29] *Few Choose to Listen*, p. 13.

[30] *Ibid.*, p. 17.

[31] *Ibid.*, p. 19.

[32] *Glossary-Index*, p. 1.

[33] *Ibid.*, p. 1.

[34] *Few Choose to Listen*, p. 37.

[35] *The Lighthouse*, Vol. 13, No. 3 (September 2002).

[36] "How to Approach ACIM," p. 1.

[37] *Ibid.*, p. 1.

[38] *Ibid.*, p. 1.

[39] *Ibid.*, p. 1.

[40] *Ibid.*, p. 2.

[41] *Ibid.*, p. 2.

[42] *Ibid.*, p. 3.

[43] *Ibid.*, p. 1.

[44] For more on the Course as a work of art, see my articles entitled "Appreciating the Masterpiece, Part 1" and "Appreciating the Masterpiece, Part 2," in *A Better Way*, Issues #27 and #28. In Part 2, I cite a number of art experts from various disciplines (music, visual art, literature), all of whom stress the connection between analysis of an artwork and deeper appreciation of it. Here is one example, from a college literature textbook entitled *The Bedford Introduction to Literature*:
To discover the insights that literature reveals requires careful reading and sensitivity. One of the purposes of a college introduction to literature is to cultivate the analytic skills necessary for reading well....

The more sensitively a work is read and understood by thinking, talking, or writing about it the more pleasurable the experience of it is.

[45] "How to Approach ACIM," p. 1.

[46] *Ibid.*, p. 1.

[47] *Few Choose to Listen*, p. 55.

[48] *Ibid.*, p. 43.

[49] *Commonly Asked Questions*, p. 89; see also *Few Choose to Listen*, p. 29.

[50] "What It Means to Be a Teacher of God" (transcript of FACIM workshop), available on the FACIM website at http://www.facim.org/excerpts/togseries.htm. All quotes in the following discussion of "honesty" are from "Part IV" that transcript, available at http://www.facim.org/excerpts/s5e4.htm.

[51] *All Are Called*, p. 32.

[52] Of course, He does not have the form and limits we normally associate with the word "person." The idea here is simply that He is, in some real if inscrutable sense, a Person—a Being with personal qualities.

[53] *All Are Called*, p. 33.

[54] *Few Choose to Listen*, p. 29.

[55] For Wapnick's discussion of the different emphases of the Text and Workbook, see the question "Why do the text and workbook have different focuses, and at times seem to be saying different things?" (*Commonly Asked Questions*, pp. 118-121).

[56] *Few Choose to Listen*, p. 20.

[57] *Ibid.*, p. 30.

[58] *Commonly Asked Questions*, p. 123.

[59] *All Are Called*, p. 329.

[60] *Few Choose to Listen*, p. 24.

[61] *Ibid.*, p. 24.

[62] *Ibid.*, p. 25.

[63] *Ibid.*, p. 25.

[64] *All Are Called*, p. 329.

[65] "In Conversation with Ken and Gloria Wapnick—Part 2," by Ian Patrick; *Miracle Worker: Magazine of the UK Miracle Network*, Issue 27, March/April 1999, p. 8.

[66] Wapnick's students seem to share his tendency to make no distinction between "regular" and "ritualistic" practice. I know of at least one Wapnick student who, when referring to practice, always says "ritualistic" when he means "regular." In general, it seems that Wapnick's students have picked up his implicit message that regular practice is frowned upon.

[67] *Few Choose to Listen*, p. 26.

[68] *Ibid.*, p. 26.

[69] *Ibid.*, p. 26.

[70] There are three other passages in the Course that give us this same basic pattern of forgiving ourselves for a mistake *so that* we can then correct (or let go of) the mistake. These passages are T-31.IV.10:4-11:1; W-pI.99.7:4-6; and W-pI.200.3:4-5. Forgiving ourselves for the mistake, then, is the first step in a two-step process. This first step is meant to prepare us for the actual correction of the mistake—the second step. As the Text points out (T-19.III.1-3), labeling something as an unforgivable sin leads to the keeping of it, while labeling it as a forgivable mistake leads to the correction of it.

[71] *Few Choose to Listen*, p. 27.

[72] *Glossary-Index*, p. 137.

[73] *Ibid.*, p. 137.

[74] *Ibid.*, p. 137.

[75] *All Are Called*, p. 227.

[76] *Commonly Asked Questions*, p. 126.

[77] For a discussion of the three steps of forgiveness, see *All Are Called*, pp. 204-11.

[78] All Wapnick quotes in the following discussion of this tape set are from *The Workbook Lessons of 'A Course in Miracles': The Study and Practice of the 365 Lessons, Volume I*, by Ken Wapnick.

[79] *Commonly Asked Questions*, p. 116.

[80] *Ibid.*, p. 116.

[81] *Few Choose to Listen*, p. 22.

[82] *Ibid.*, p. 22.

[83] See *All Are Called*, p. 330.

[84] *Commonly Asked Questions*, p. 115.

[85] Ibid., p. 76. This is part of Wapnick's answer to the question "What is the role of meditation in practicing *A Course in Miracles?*" (p. 74; the quotes that follow in this endnote are also on that page). His short answer to this question is as follows: "Meditation as such is not an integral part of the Course's curriculum." Thus, unlike the Circle, Wapnick does not see meditation as a specific practice taught in the Workbook (a practice that is also included in the post-Workbook practice instructions in M-16—clearly, Jesus wants us to continue this practice after the Workbook). Instead, Wapnick suggests that the term "meditation" could be applied more loosely to *all* of the exercises in the Workbook—exercises that he says "are only meant for a one-year period."

[86] See, for instance, *Few Choose to Listen*, p. 28.

[87] *Ibid.*, p. 27.

[88] *Commonly Asked Questions*, p. 118.

[89] *Few Choose to Listen*, p. 29.

[90] *Ibid.*, p. 20.

[91] *Commonly Asked Questions*, p. 120.

[92] *Ibid.*, p. 123.

[93] For more on how the Circle and Wapnick regard extending to others, see the concluding essay of this book, entitled "What Would the Course Have Me Do? Applying the Circle's and Ken Wapnick's Visions to a Specific Situation" (p. 219).

[94] It must also be said that Wapnick placed considerably more importance on extension in his works written before the mid-1980's, particularly *Forgiveness and Jesus* and *Christian Psychology in 'A Course in Miracles.'* This emphasis, however, has been absent from his work for quite some time.

[95] *All Are Called*, p. 368.

[96] *Few Choose to Listen*, p. 33.

[97] *Ibid.*, p. 32.

[98] *Ibid.*, p. 32.

[99] *Ibid.*, p. 31.

[100] *Commonly Asked Questions*, p. 114. There *is* a more detailed description of the Manual's purpose in *Few Choose to Listen* (p. 16), which says that, among other

things, the Manual includes "specific teachings that relate to how a teacher reacts and behaves in the world." But even here, the behavior element is heavily qualified.

[101] *Few Choose to Listen*, p. 31.

[102] *Ibid.*, p. 33.

[103] *Ibid.*, p. 33.

[104] *Ibid.*, p. 32.

[105] See, for instance, W-pI.62.4:3; W-pI.97.5; W-pI.106.9:2; W-pI.107.10:3; W-pI.108.10; W-pI.109.6-7; W-pI.132.16:1; W-pI.137.10:1; and W-pI.rV.In.10:7.

[106] *Few Choose to Listen*, p. 137. See the entire discussion of spiritual specialness in pp. 137-142.

[107] *Ibid.*, p. 137.

[108] *Ibid.*, p. 86.

[109] *All Are Called*, p. 340.

[110] *Glossary-Index*, p. 78.

[111] *Commonly Asked Questions*, p. 131.

[112] *Few Choose to Listen*, p. 13. Immediately after this reference, Wapnick contradicts what he just said by quoting M-16.3:7, which says a teacher of God is (among other things) a person who has completed the Workbook—which means the teacher of God cannot simply be *any* Course student.

[113] *Ibid.*, p. 16. I should add that Wapnick does see the term "*advanced* teacher of God" as referring to a developmental stage in one's spiritual growth. Oddly enough, though, in his one extended discussion of the advanced teacher of God in *The Message of 'A Course in Miracles'* (the section entitled "On Being an Advanced Teacher of God," in *All Are Called*, pp. 355-359), he does not discuss the Manual's own descriptions of the advanced teacher of God at all (there is only one passing reference to M-4). Instead, he simply equates the advanced teacher of God to Plato's notion of the philosopher-king.

[114] *Ibid.*, p. 34.

[115] See *Glossary-Index*, p. 102. It should be noted that in earlier editions of the *Glossary-Index*, Wapnick did say that the holy relationship is a relationship between two people, but this has since been changed.

[116] Wapnick even claims that the material in the Course that emphasizes mutuality— two people joining in a relationship and forgiving one another—was not intended to be taken as literal teaching, but is just an artifact of language reflecting the fact that the Course was originally dictated to *two* people: Helen and Bill (see *Few Choose to Listen*, pp. 59-60).

[117] *Ibid.*, p. 174.

[118] *Ibid.*, pp. 140-141.

[119] *Ibid.*, p. 183.

[120] *Ibid.*, p. 167.

[121] *Ibid.*, p. 169.

[122] *Commonly Asked Questions*, p. 126: "Since…the Holy Spirit is in all the minds of the separated Sons, by joining with Him…one has *already* joined with everyone." See also *Few Choose to Listen*, p. 169, where Wapnick says that joining with Jesus and the Holy Spirit in our minds allows us to remember "the *greater joining*…of Christ with Christ," and "it is this joining (the *cause*) that automatically becomes

reflected in our experiencing a joining with others (the *effect*)."

[123] *Ibid.*, p. 126.

[124] *Ibid.*, p. 127.

[125] *Few Choose to Listen*, p. 169.

[126] In calling it "vital," I am not saying that every single time we join with someone in our minds, we must express it outwardly. In some cases, the Holy Spirit may not guide us to do anything outwardly. What I am saying is that in general terms, outward expression of our healed perception—extending to others, joining with them—is a vital element of the Course's path.

[127] "In Conversation," p. 8.

[128] *Ibid.*, p. 8.

What Would the Course Have Me Do?

Applying the Circle's and Ken Wapnick's Visions to a Specific Situation

by Greg Mackie

A dirty, disheveled, homeless man comes to your door on a cold winter night. He says he desperately needs something to eat and a place to stay for the night. All the homeless shelters are full; you are his only hope. As a Course student, what should you do?

Course students often wonder how to make the Course practical. Given this concern, how would each vision of *A Course in Miracles*—the Circle of Atonement's and Ken Wapnick's—have us apply the Course to specific situations in our daily lives, especially situations in which we are called upon to help others? In this concluding essay, I would like to address this important question, using the above example of the homeless man at your door.

THE CIRCLE'S VISION

The following three points are a broad outline of what we believe the Course would have you do in the encounter with the homeless man:

1. Do Course practice to heal your perception, in the understanding that this mental healing—a miracle—will be mentally extended to this man in some way.

2. Ask the Holy Spirit or Jesus for guidance about how to behaviorally extend your healed perception to this man in the way that will benefit him the most.

3. Behaviorally extend your healed perception to this man, in whatever way your guidance directs.

These points are expanded upon below. Of course, in the actual situation, you wouldn't do all of the various practices listed; you probably wouldn't have time for more than a few. In such a situation, I often pick just one practice—something quick and simple—and stick with that. The idea is simply that you think of the situation in terms of these three broad points, and select whatever practices work best for you.

1. Do Course practice to heal your perception, in the understanding that this healing—a miracle—will be mentally extended to this man in some way.

This point consists of three elements: using the practices the Course itself provides, allowing your perception of this man and his situation to be healed, and mentally extending this healing to this man in some way.

Use the practices the Course itself provides to help you with this situation.

This is a crucial point. In our view, if the Course is your path, you are using its program of study, practice, and extension, which means among other things that you are developing a regular, structured spiritual practice. You are either going through the Workbook or doing post-Workbook practice. You have either established or are in the process of establishing a regular regimen of morning and evening quiet times, remembering God on the hour, reminding yourself of God frequently through the day, and quickly responding to the temptation to listen to the ego.[1]

Ideally, your response to the homeless man is built upon the foundation of that practice. So, if you are going through the Workbook, you might apply today's lesson to this situation—a number of Workbook lessons provide specific practices to use when you feel upset, or have some difficulty facing you. If you are doing post-Workbook practice, you might apply whatever practice you are doing that day, or perhaps use something from your "problem-solving repertoire" (W-pI.194.6:2) of Course practices. Or you might have a Course practice come to your mind spontaneously. The key point is that whatever you do flows from your daily work with the program given in the Course's own pages. The Course provides literally hundreds of practices for situations like this. Below, I'll provide some examples.

Allow your perception of this man and his situation to be healed.

As every Course student knows, healing your own perception is key. As you see this ragged, smelly, homeless man at your door, you will likely feel distressed. You will also be tempted to believe that this distress is a product of the situation itself, rather than your perception of it. It is easy to forget that the world you see is an illusion, the distress you are feeling is coming only from your own mind, and you have the power to change your mind. So, you might use a practice like this one, a composite of three Workbook practices that we are instructed to use when confronted with a situation that disturbs us:

> *I have invented this situation as I see it. There is another way of looking at this. I could see peace in this situation instead of what I now see in it.*
> (W-pI.32.6:3; W-pI.33.3:4; W-pI.34.5:4)

You may be quite convinced that your perception of the situation is correct, and that you know exactly what to do about it. For instance, you may believe that homeless people are lazy parasites who sponge off of decent working people. You may believe that they need to be turned away with "tough love" so they can learn to take care of themselves. In the Course's view, however, you don't have a clue. So, to let go of your own preconceived notions about the homeless man standing in front of you, you might use a practice like this one from the Text:

> *I do not know what anything, including this, means. And so I do not know how to respond to it. And I will not use my own past learning as the light to guide me now.*
> (T-14.XI.6:7-9)

Of course, your distress and your distorted perception are products of the ego. You need to look at your ego thoughts squarely and deal with them, because otherwise they will sabotage your attempts to do the right thing for this man. So, you might use this practice, one of my personal favorites, to gently but firmly dismiss ego thoughts:

> *This thought I do not want. I choose instead* _____
> [a Course-based thought]. (W-pI.rVI.In.6:2-3)

The thoughts you really want come from the Holy Spirit or Jesus, so your next step may be to ask Them how to perceive this man and his situation. How well you hear Their response depends upon your willingness to hear. But to the degree you are willing to open your mind to Them, They give you the blessing of true perception, which reveals who this man really is behind his rough exterior: a holy Son of God. No matter how much he appears to suffer, his true Self is forever changeless, limitless, and joyous. No matter how distressing his outer situation appears to be, it is an illusion with no ultimate affect on his reality.

As you allow your perception to be healed, you see the entire situation in a whole new light. Instead of seeing it as a difficult encounter that interrupted a comfortable night at home, you see it as a holy encounter that has the potential to develop into a holy relationship. Instead of seeing this man's request of you as an imposition, you see it as a call for healing and help, a call for love, a call you want to answer *with* love. And instead of seeing this man as a nuisance who certainly has nothing to offer *you*, you see him as the Christ, a beloved brother who is quite literally your savior. To reinforce this new perception, you might use a practice like the following:

> Let me behold my savior in this one.   (W-pI.78.7:3)

Mentally extend this healing—a miracle—to this man in some way.

There is not a firm distinction between the previous step and this one: on a deep level, when you allow your perception to be healed, it extends to others without your effort. This is what we might call *passive* extension, the automatic transfer of healed perception from one mind to another. You accomplish this just by doing practices like the ones described above.

Yet the Course very much encourages *active* extension as well. One form of this active extension is the mental extension of a healing thought to another person. The Course, especially the Workbook, has a number of specific practices to help you do this. So, as you interact with the homeless man, you might silently say a prayer for him, or silently extend affirmations of love and healing to him with Course practices such as the following (of course, it doesn't matter if you don't know his name):

> Let peace extend from my mind to yours, [name].
>
> (W-pI.82.2:2)

222

You stand with me in light, [name]. (W-pI.87.2:3)

2. Ask the Holy Spirit or Jesus for guidance about how to behaviorally extend your healed perception to this man in the way that will benefit him the most.

The other form of active extension is behavioral extension—what the Course calls "the action aspect of the miracle" (T-1.III.8:4). Behavioral extension is not required in every situation, but in this situation, you obviously have to do something. The Holy Spirit and Jesus are your guides for what to do. Because They perceive the situation correctly, They know what behavioral response will best communicate your healed perception to this man. Your job is simply to ask, and trust that you will receive a response.

One of my favorite lines for asking is actually directed to God. As you contemplate what to do for the homeless man, you might use this simple line to ask God for guidance about how to help him:

> What should I do for him, Your holy Son?
>
> (S-2.III.5:1)

3. Behaviorally extend your healed perception to this man, in whatever way your guidance directs.

Once you have guidance about what to do, the only thing that remains is to act on it. Whatever guidance you receive—whether it is to give this man food, invite him in, or express love in some other way—do as you are directed.

This point may seem so obvious that it need not be said, but I think it is a helpful reminder. In my experience, it is very easy to get guidance but fail to act on it. Yet acting on it is very important. This man needs your loving behavior in order for your healed perception to really get through to him. You need it as well, because it reinforces that healed perception in your own mind. So, in your encounter with him, you might want to remind yourself of just how important your behavioral response is, both for his salvation and your own:

> Only by answering this man's appeal for help can I be helped. (based on T-12.I.5:6)

To conclude, I will mention one more practice that encompasses many of the elements we have discussed: the "be truly helpful" prayer

223

from the Text. I have used this prayer countless times in helping situations, and it has never failed to lift my mind and make me a more effective helper. I can think of nothing better than to repeat this prayer as you decide what to do for the homeless man at your door:

> *I am here only to be truly helpful.*
> *I am here to represent Him Who sent me.*
> *I do not have to worry about what to say or what to do,*
> *because He Who sent me will direct me.*
> *I am content to be wherever He wishes, knowing He*
> *goes there with me.*
> *I will be healed as I let Him teach me to heal.*
>
> (T-2.V.A.18:2-6)

KEN WAPNICK'S VISION

The following three points are a broad outline of what we believe Wapnick's vision of the Course would have you do in the encounter with the homeless man:

1. Look at the ego with the Holy Spirit or Jesus, in order to heal your perception that this man's situation is a problem outside your own mind.

2. Do *not* ask the Holy Spirit or Jesus for guidance about how to behaviorally respond to this man, since They do not guide behavior.

3. With your perception healed, you will automatically know what to do behaviorally for this man; you do what any normal person would do.

These points are expanded upon below. Most of the Wapnick quotes are taken from his tape set entitled *True Empathy: The Greater Joining.*[2] I chose to draw from this tape set because in it, Wapnick uses numerous examples to illustrate how we as Course students should respond to others in need. One example he uses is a social worker helping the homeless.[3]

1. Look at the ego with the Holy Spirit or Jesus, in order to heal your perception that this man's situation is a problem

outside your own mind.

This point consists of two elements: the problem as Wapnick sees it, and the solution to that problem.

The problem is that you are seeing a problem outside your own mind and taking it seriously; in so doing, you are listening to the ego and making the error real.

In Wapnick's view, the only real problem in any situation is the ego-based belief that there is a problem outside your mind, and the feeling of concern that stems from that belief:

> I know I'm trapped [in the ego] when I make some aspect of the physical or psychological world real—I take something here seriously; I feel there is a problem outside that has to be corrected or someone out here who has to be helped and I'm the one who is going to do it or see that it is done, and that becomes my motivation. I am seeing through the eyes of the ego...because I am seeing something that is literally not here. There is no problem here.[4]

Applying this idea to an encounter with someone who has cancer, Wapnick says, "The problem is not the person who is dying of cancer. The problem is my *concern* over the person who is dying of cancer."[5]

So, in your encounter with the homeless man, the real problem isn't the suffering he is experiencing, but your *concern* about that suffering, a concern that comes completely from your own mind. Such concern is totally unwarranted, because the whole situation is pure illusion. Not only is the physical world an illusion, but the man himself is nothing more than a lifeless marionette manipulated by the decision maker in the mind. As Wapnick says, paraphrasing Shakespeare, "'All the world's a puppet stage, and all the people in it are merely puppets.'"[6] Therefore, "there is no problem here." The only thing that has to be healed is your *belief* that there is a problem here. The homeless man himself has nothing to do with it.

Moreover, your distress about this situation is really a projection of your distress about your original decision to separate from God. Using the example of concern about stray cats that are outside on a rainy night, Wapnick says:

I can see the stray cats as a mirror of myself. I believe I am a stray and that I am all alone in a world that doesn't care about me, a world that is governed by a God Who doesn't care about me….That is how my ego sees things, because that is what my ego is—a belief that I am separated from God and alone.[7]

The problem, then, is that you are projecting outward your own mental distress about the separation, which causes you to see it as a problem that needs to be solved "out there." This is what is really going on in the situation with the homeless man—again, the man himself has nothing to do with it. He is just a convenient movie screen on which you project a problem that stems solely from your own mind. By seeing the problem outside yourself, you have fallen for the ego's ruse and made the error real.

The solution is to look at the ego with the Holy Spirit or Jesus.

As I mentioned in my essay on the Course's program, Wapnick regards this practice is the primary Course practice, "the essence of the Atonement."[8] Taking the homeless man's problem seriously by getting concerned about it is an indicator that you have "turned away from the Holy Spirit in [your] mind, dropped the hand of Jesus, [and] turned towards the ego."[9] What's more, by projecting the problem outward, you have denied the fact that you made the problem by listening to your ego. Fortunately, however, you have the power to change your mind, and the way to do that is to step back from your investment in the ego and look at it dispassionately with the Holy Spirit or Jesus:

If the problem is defined as not looking, then the solution is clear—we look. Not looking at the ego means we have listened to the ego and have turned away from the Holy Spirit. Therefore, looking at the ego means that we are dropping the hand of the ego and are looking with the Holy Spirit, Who tells us, "Look at all this—it is nothing more than a silly dream in which absolutely nothing has happened."[10]

What we are asked to do, which is a point I'll come back to over and over, is simply to look at the investment we have in making sickness and judgment real. And we are asked to look at it with Jesus or the Holy Spirit next to us, which means that we look without judgment.[11]

In reading these descriptions of the process as Wapnick sees it, it is important to remember that he does not regard the Holy Spirit and Jesus as real Beings. As we've seen throughout this book, he believes that the Holy Spirit and Jesus are illusions, merely symbolic reflections of the memory of God that we brought with us into the dream. Thus, these descriptions do not literally mean that you are to look at your ego with a real divine Helper by your side. Rather, these are metaphorical descriptions of a process that can be more accurately described as looking at the ego while trying to recall a distant memory of the truth.

When you look at the ego with Jesus or the Holy Spirit (or, as Wapnick also describes it, when you "join with Jesus or the Holy Spirit"),[12] the entire process that set up the problem is reversed. You withdraw your projection from the homeless man's situation, realize that your distress is coming from your own mind, and change your mind. Now you see the situation with Their vision, and so now you see it very differently:

> Now I see—not people in pain, physically or emotionally, not some problem in the world—I see others calling out for the Love of God that they believe they have separated from and which they believe they will never, ever more rejoin.[13]

You are no longer concerned about the homeless man's external situation, because you realize that isn't the problem. Instead, you see a man who believes that he has separated from God, and who is therefore calling for the Love of God. You also see that his call is yours—remember, everything you're seeing comes from your own mind—and therefore in answering his call, you are answering yours:

> I know that your sickness and your pain came from your call for the Love of God, which is the echo of my call for the Love of God. I am not taken in by the dream anymore. It is not the dream I want to help, it is the call for the Love of God that I want to answer. And I understand that by answering your call for the Love of God, I am also answering my own.[14]

How do you answer this man's call for the Love of God? In Wapnick's view, you *don't* answer it through the kind of active mental extension described above in the Circle's vision—for him, all mental extension is passive. Why not extend healing actively? For starters, the inherent unity of minds renders it pointless: "We do not join in an active way, because we are already joined."[15] Moreover, such active extension is actually an ego ploy designed to reinforce the idea that the problem is outside your mind, an idea which makes the error real:

> When we become involved with beaming light into people who have cancer, or into parts of the world that are in conflict, we are seeing darkness outside. We are seeing the world as real.[16]

Therefore, all you do is look at the ego with the Holy Spirit or Jesus. This is how you fulfill your sole responsibility of accepting the Atonement for yourself—"taking the hand of Jesus represents accepting the Atonement."[17] Once you take care of your own mind, everything else happens automatically without you doing anything:

> Since there is no one out there anyway, I am really forgiving myself....Rejoining with the Holy Spirit automatically, inevitably, and simultaneously affects everything in my perception and experience.[18]

2. Do not ask the Holy Spirit or Jesus for guidance about how to behaviorally respond to this man, since They do not guide behavior.

This follows from Wapnick's fundamental metaphysical premise, which we have seen throughout this book. In *True Empathy*, he states it in this way:

> It is important to understand that God does not even know about this world, and that Jesus and the Holy Spirit do not do anything with the dream. If They did, They would share it, which would mean that the dream had a cause and would be real.[19]

In addition, as I mentioned above, Wapnick regards the Holy Spirit and Jesus as illusions. Therefore, asking them for advice on what to do for the homeless man is not only futile, but is just one more way in which the ego deceives you into making the error real:

> Rather than drag Jesus down from the mind into the world and have him fix it, I want to come up to where he is, in my mind. He can't help me in the world, because if he

228

could he would be as insane as I am, since there is no world here.[20]

We all tend to bring the Holy Spirit into the suffering here and have Him fix it. We don't want to ask Jesus how to help other people. That's another red flag signaling that we have fallen into the ego's trap. Whenever we ask Him what we should do for someone, or what should be done for us on the level of the body, the ego has been our companion and not the Holy Spirit.[21]

3. With your perception healed, you will automatically know what to do behaviorally for this man; you do what any normal person would do.

Once your perception is healed by looking at the ego with the Holy Spirit or Jesus, everything you do will be kind and loving. Guidance is unnecessary; the right thing will just happen without your effort:

> By joining with [the Holy Spirit], I automatically know what to do for you on the level of behavior or form that would be of help. I don't have to ask about it because it will automatically come through me.[22]

"Automatically" is an important word for Wapnick, one that he repeats again and again. Just as your healed perception automatically goes everywhere without any active mental extension on your part, so loving behavior automatically flows from you without any active asking for guidance. It is a totally passive process; you do nothing.

This does not mean, however, that you do nothing behaviorally. As Wapnick stresses, "Doing the Course right…does not mean that I turn my back on people's suffering, or that I do not do something for the homeless."[23] Instead of turning your back, you simply "do what most normal people would do,"[24] acting in "whatever form would be most helpful."[25] So, you might respond to the homeless man at your door by giving him food, inviting him in, or helping him in some other way.[26] The difference is that now you are no longer doing it from the ego's motivation of making the error real. Instead, you are doing it in order to demonstrate to this man that God loves him, and that he can choose to reject the ego and accept God's Love, just as you have:

> What I am really doing by ending another's physical pain

is giving a message that says God is not angry at you, and by my love and my peace I am reflecting for you the love and peace that is inside you. Just as I was able to make a choice not to make your error real, not to make guilt or sin real, so can you make the same choice.[27]

A COMPARISON OF THE TWO VISIONS

Now that we have both views of what the Course would have you do in the encounter with the homeless man, we are ready to compare them.

Similarities

In broad terms, I see two similarities:

1. Your inner mental work, focused on healing your own perception of the homeless man's situation, is a vital part of the process.

Both approaches regard this as crucial, and the mental healing process described by both has many ideas in common:

- The entire physical world is an illusion caused solely by our perception.
- Your distress about the situation comes solely from your own mind.
- You have the power to change your mind.
- Looking at your ego and letting it go is an important part of healing your perception.
- You need to join with the Holy Spirit or Jesus (in some sense) in order to perceive the situation correctly.
- When your perception is healed, you see the situation as a call for love, a call that you want to answer with love.

2. Truly loving, compassionate behavior toward the homeless man is a positive and desirable result of the process.

Both approaches consider loving behavior in this situation to be a good thing. Both see it as a means of communicating and demonstrating your healed perception to the homeless man in a way that is most helpful to him.

Differences

In broad terms, I see four differences:

1. The Circle's approach makes constant use of the tools the Course itself provides. Wapnick's approach virtually ignores those tools.

In the Circle's approach, you come to the situation with a foundation of regular, structured practice, which provides you with a variety of practice tools from the Course itself. But in Wapnick's approach, regular, structured practice is discouraged (as we saw in my essay on the Course's program), and the Course's own practice tools are disregarded. I listed many Course practices when I went through the Circle's vision above. But I didn't list any when I went through Wapnick's vision, for the simple reason that Wapnick himself virtually never refers to such practices. For him, applying the Course to the situation essentially means nothing more than looking at the ego with the Holy Spirit or Jesus.

2. In the Circle's approach, you have active help from Heaven and should therefore ask for it. In Wapnick's approach, you have no help from Heaven and should therefore not ask for it.

The reasons for this difference have been discussed throughout this book, so I won't elaborate on them here. All I will say here is that as much as Wapnick stresses that "we cannot do without the Holy Spirit's help,"[28] for all practical purposes, in Wapnick's system we don't *have* the Holy Spirit's help. If the Holy Spirit is just the memory of God within you, a memory that doesn't actively do anything for you but just passively awaits your decision to access it, then it's all up to you. You have to make this decision all by yourself. God doesn't even know about your situation, and so no one in Heaven can help you. You're totally on our own in this world. I find this a chilling and very lonely state of affairs.

3. The Circle's approach involves both looking within and actively extending outward to the homeless man. Wapnick's approach involves virtually nothing but looking within.

In the Circle's approach, you do the inner work of acknowledging your responsibility for your perception, withdrawing your projections, confronting your ego, and so on. But there is also a strong component of actively extending outward to this man: mentally sending him healing thoughts and prayers, seeing him as a real Son of God who needs your help, and behaving lovingly toward him. Both the inner work you do and the outer extension of it are aimed at healing your mind *and* his mind. Extending healing to him is a vitally important aspect of the Course's path, because it both helps him and reinforces your own healing.

But in Wapnick's approach, the process is virtually all inward. It's all about what happens in the privacy of your own mind. Yes, as we've seen, in Wapnick's approach answering the homeless man's call for love is in some sense answering your own, and loving behavior can demonstrate healed perception to him. But as we've also seen, you don't actively extend to him; everything you do is simply a passive, automatic by-product of your inner work. Even loving behavior is not really an active interaction between two real Sons of God, but is instead just two puppets seeming to "interact" on the puppet stage of the world. Real interaction simply doesn't happen in this world, because "there is no one out there anyway."

Thus, though Wapnick occasionally suggests that there is value in doing something for others, this is effectively canceled out by his contention that there *are* no others. Though he sometimes speaks of a positive role for loving behavior, this is effectively canceled out by his contention that "behavior [is] essentially irrelevant."[29] The work you do is not aimed at healing both your mind and the homeless man's mind, but instead is all about healing your own mind, and nothing else.[30] Extending healing to him cannot, then, really be a vitally important aspect of the Course's path. If there is really no one out there to help, how could helping him reinforce your own healing?

4. In the Circle's approach, the desire to help the homeless man out of concern for him is at heart a holy impulse that should be acted upon. In Wapnick's approach, the desire to help the homeless man out of concern for him is almost certainly an unholy ego impulse that should be treated with great suspicion.

I discussed this in my essay on the Course's program, but because

I think it is the heart of the matter, I want to spend some more time with it here. In the Circle's view, the concern you have for the homeless man could come from either of two sources. (Of course, it may well be a mix of the two.) One source is the ego: your concern could be false empathy, which is nothing but hate wearing a loving mask. But the other source is the Holy Spirit: your concern could also be a genuine concern that is truly rooted in God's Love, a holy caring that is actually the template for the ego's grossly distorted version.

As much as the Course discourages the ego's version of concern, it strongly encourages the Holy Spirit's version. Indeed, the Course itself is the product of this truly loving concern, and is drenched with the spirit of it. Jesus says, "As a loving brother I am deeply concerned with your mind" (T-4.IV.2:9). He speaks of the Holy Spirit's limitless "concern and care for you" (T-15.VIII.1:5). He says that the sane "look on stark insanity and raving madness with pity and compassion" (T-19.IV(D).11:2). He has us repeat the phrase "Helpfulness created me helpful" (W-pI.67.2:5), since helpfulness is an "attribute which is in accord with God as He defines Himself" (W-pI.67.2:7). He teaches, in the *Psychotherapy* supplement, that "nothing in the world is holier than helping one who asks for help" (P-2.V.4:2). He implores us to help our brothers in the world, appealing to our innate compassion:

> Look about the world, and see the suffering there. Is not your heart willing to bring your weary brothers rest?
> (W-pI.191.10:7-8)

But in Wapnick's view, concern is *always* a sign of the ego. Recall his statement above that *concern* about the cancer patient is the real problem. Remember also his contention that anytime I see "someone out here who has to be helped and I'm the one who is going to do it," I am trapped in my ego. For him, being concerned about the homeless man is a sure sign that you are making the error real. Since there is really no one out there, any concern you have is just a projected concern about yourself, which you fix not by helping the man at your door, but by going to the Holy Spirit or Jesus in your mind. Anything else is taking the hand of the ego.

As we've seen, it's not that Wapnick is against helping others. While he regards concern as a sure sign of the ego, he does not see *all* desires to help as inherently egoic. He speaks highly of Mother Teresa, and claims that his approach will end up making us "much more compassionate, loving, and sensitive to the needs of others—not

233

less."[31] Perhaps this is true, but Wapnick's tone when he speaks about helping others is not encouraging. *True Empathy* is filled with statements like the following:

> You do not have a *need* to help anybody else.[32]

> We do not have to do anything about people's problems.[33]

> It is always the ego that wants to do something.[34]

> We must not succumb to the temptation to do something.[35]

> Our responsibility is not to alleviate people's suffering in the world.[36]

> Our one responsibility according to the Course...has nothing to do with alleviating pain.[37]

> My concern about you, my investment in helping you, my empathy, my sympathy, my compassion for you...arise only from the ego's point of view.[38]

Wapnick's overall tone when he speaks of helping others in the world is captured well in the following quote:

> [The ego] makes up a world of pain and suffering, and tells us we will be the good people, and we will undo pain and suffering in the world. These are the do-gooders in the world. That is why Jesus says, "Trust not your good intentions. They are not enough" (T-18.IV.2:1-2). It is the well-intentioned people who are the most terrible people in the world. They are the ones you have to watch out for, because they seem to be something other than what they are. An ill-intentioned person is a blessing, because you know exactly what you are up against. I am not saying that such a person is all-loving, but at least you know what you are getting. With Hitler, you knew exactly what you were getting right from the beginning. With the ego's version of love you don't know. That is what special love is. These are the people who are always trying to help others.[39]

Now, Wapnick is speaking here of "the ego's version of love," so this is not a blanket indictment of all attempts to help others. However, the withering statements about "do-gooders" and "well-intentioned people" being "the most terrible people in the world" are telling. They make it clear that in Wapnick's eyes, *most* people who care about the world and want to help others are trapped in their egos. And let's face it: if you believe that your desire to help another person is most likely a terrible, ego-driven impulse more insidious than Hitler's megalomania, are you very likely to act upon that desire?

AS A COURSE STUDENT, WHAT SHOULD YOU DO?

Whatever the Circle of Atonement and Ken Wapnick say about this question, how you answer it in the specific situations of your life will, of course, be up to you. In closing, I invite you to reflect on the example we have examined, and consider which approach—the Circle's, Wapnick's, or none of the above—speaks to you the most. Which approach do you think would best enable you to respond to the homeless man in a truly helpful way? If you were in his place, which approach do you think you would find most helpful to you? Finally, based on your own study of the Course and the material presented in this book, which approach do you think best answers this essay's title question: "What would the Course have me do?"

Notes

[1] See my essay on p. 145 entitled "The Spiritual Program of *A Course in Miracles*: The Circle's Vision and Ken Wapnick's Vision Compared" for more information on the Circle's vision of the Course's program.

[2] These quotes are drawn from a written transcript of that tape set, which is available on FACIM's website at www.facim.org/excerpts/teseries.htm. The page at that URL contains 23 links numbered with Roman numerals, which take you to the 23 parts of that transcript. In subsequent references in this essay, I will indicate the part from which a particular quote was taken, i.e., "Part XV."

[3] Other examples he uses include responding to a loved one in pain, taking care of a sick cat, being concerned about stray cats outside on a rainy night, helping a person dying of cancer, and visiting someone in the hospital.

[4] *True Empathy*, Part III.

[5] *Ibid.*, Part VIII.

[6] *Ibid.*, Part II.

[7] *Ibid.*, Part VI.

[8] *Glossary-Index for 'A Course in Miracles,'* 4th Ed., by Ken Wapnick, p. 137.

[9] *True Empathy*, Part V.

[10] *Ibid.*, Part XI.
[11] *Ibid.*, Part IX.
[12] *Ibid.*, Part VI.
[13] *Ibid.*, Part III.
[14] *Ibid.*, Part XXII.
[15] *Ibid.*, Part X.
[16] *Ibid.*, Part XXI.
[17] *Ibid.*, Part XIII.
[18] *Ibid.*, Part XIII.
[19] *Ibid.*, Part XVI.
[20] *Ibid.*, Part V.
[21] *Ibid.*, Part V.
[22] *Ibid.*, Part V.
[23] *Ibid.*, Part VIII.
[24] *Ibid.*, Part XXII.
[25] *Ibid.*, Part XX.
[26] Different people, of course, may choose different behavioral responses, and this illustrates one of the problems I see with Wapnick's approach: in many situations, it is not at all obvious "what most normal people would do." Many situations present us with a number of legitimate behavioral possibilities, but in Wapnick's approach we don't have a guide to help us choose, because the Holy Spirit or Jesus do not give us behavioral guidance. We are really on our own in deciding what to do.
[27] *True Empathy*, Part III.
[28] *Ibid.*, Part IX.
[29] *The Message of 'A Course in Miracles,' Volume Two: Few Choose to Listen*, by Ken Wapnick., p. 32.
[30] Elsewhere, Wapnick expresses his emphasis as follows: "Teachers of God need merely accept the Atonement for themselves, and…salvation of the world depends on their simply doing just that, *and only that*" (*Few Choose to Listen*, p. 32, emphasis Wapnick's).
[31] *True Empathy*, Part XXI.
[32] *Ibid.*, Part IV.
[33] *Ibid.*, Part IV.
[34] *Ibid.*, Part IV.
[35] *Ibid.*, Part XXI.
[36] *Ibid.*, Part V.
[37] *Ibid.*, Part XIII.
[38] *Ibid.*, Part XXII.
[39] *Ibid.*, Part II.

Index of Key Issues

After the initial listing, A Course in Miracles *is referred to as "ACIM."*

238

239

The Circle's Mission Statement

To discern the author's vision of *A Course in Miracles* and manifest that in our lives, in the lives of students, and in the world.

1
To faithfully discern the author's vision of *A Course in Miracles*.

In interpreting the Course we strive for total fidelity to its words and the meanings they express. We thereby seek to discover the Course as the author saw it.

2
To be an instrument in Jesus' plan to manifest his vision of the Course in the lives of students and in the world.

We consider this to be Jesus' organization and therefore we attempt to follow his guidance in all we do. Our goal is to help students understand, as well as discern for themselves, the Course's thought system as he intended, and use it as he meant it to be used—as a literal program in spiritual awakening. Through doing so we hope to help ground in the world the intended way of doing the Course, here at the beginning of its history.

3
To help spark an enduring tradition based entirely on students joining together in doing the Course as the author envisioned.

We have a vision of local Course support systems composed of teachers, students, healers, and groups, all there to support one another in making full use of the Course. These support systems, as they continue and multiply, will together comprise an enduring spiritual tradition, dedicated solely to doing the Course as the author intended. Our goal is to help spark this tradition, and to assist others in doing the same.

4
To become an embodiment, a birthplace of this enduring spiritual tradition.

To help spark this tradition we must first become a model for it ourselves. This requires that we at the Circle follow the Course as our individual path; that we ourselves learn forgiveness through its program. It requires that we join with each other in a group holy relationship dedicated to the common goal of awakening through the Course. It also requires that we cultivate a local support system here in Sedona, and that we have a facility where others could join with us in learning this approach to the Course. Through all of this we hope to become a seed for an ongoing spiritual tradition based on *A Course in Miracles*.

Books & Booklets in This Series

Commentaries on *A Course in Miracles*
by Robert Perry, Allen Watson & Greg Mackie

1. **Seeing the Face of Christ in All Our Brothers** *by Perry*. How we can see the Presence of God in others. $5

3. **Shrouded Vaults of the Mind** *by Perry*. Draws a map of the mind based on the Course, and takes you on a tour through its many levels. $5

4. **Guidance: Living the Inspired Life** *by Perry*. Sketches an overall perspective on guidance and its place on the spiritual path. $7

8. **A Healed Mind Does Not Plan** *by Watson*. Examines our approach to planning and decision-making, showing how it is possible to leave the direction of our lives up to the Holy Spirit. $5

9. **Through Fear to Love** *by Watson*. Explores two sections from the Course that deal with our fear of redemption. Leads the reader to see how it is possible to look upon ourselves with love. $5

10. **The Journey Home** *by Watson*. Presents a description of our spiritual destination and what we must go through to get there. $8.50

11. **Everything You Always Wanted to Know About Judgment but Were Too Busy Doing It to Notice** *by Perry and Watson*. A survey of various teachings about judgment in the Course. $8

12. **The Certainty of Salvation** *by Perry and Watson*. How we can become certain that we will find our way to God. $5

13. **What Is Death?** *by Watson*. The Course's view of what death really is. $5

14. **The Workbook as a Spiritual Practice** *by Perry*. A guide for getting the most out of the Workbook. $5

15. **I Need Do Nothing: Finding the Quiet Center** *by Watson*. An in-depth discussion of one of the most misunderstood sections of the Course. $5

16. **A Course Glossary** *by Perry*. 158 definitions of terms and phrases from the Course for students and study groups. $7

17. **Seeing the Bible Differently: How *A Course in Miracles* Views the Bible** *by Watson*. Shows the similarities, differences, and continuity between the Course and the Bible. $6

18. **Relationships as a Spiritual Journey: From Specialness to Holiness** *by Perry*. Describes the Course's unique view of how we can find God through the transformation of our relationships. $11

19. A Workbook Companion Volume I *by Watson and Perry.* Commentaries on Lessons 1-120. $16

20. A Workbook Companion Volume II *by Watson and Perry.* Commentaries on Lessons 121-243. $16

21. A Workbook Companion Volume III *by Watson and Perry.* Commentaries on Lessons 244-365. $18

22. The Answer Is a Miracle *by Perry and Watson.* Looks at what the Course means by miracles, and how we can experience them in our lives. $7

23. Let Me Remember You *by Perry and Watson.* Regaining a sense of God's relevance, both in the Course and in our lives. $10

24. Bringing the Course to Life: How to Unlock the Meaning of *A Course in Miracles* **for Yourself** *by Watson and Perry.* Designed to teach the student, through instruction, example and exercises, how to read the Course so that the experience becomes a personal encounter with the truth. $12

25. Reality and Illusion: An Overview of Course Metaphysics *by Perry.* Examines the Course's lofty vision of reality, its account of the events which gave birth to our current existence, and how the Course views the relationship between ultimate reality and the illusory world of separation. $11

26. How Can We Forgive Murderers? And Other Answers to Questions **about** *A Course in Miracles* *by Mackie.* Insightful answers to perplexing Course questions, and practical tips for how to apply those answers to your personal life. $15

27. One Course, Two Visions: A Comparison of the Teachings of the **Circle of Atonement and Ken Wapnick on** *A Course in Miracles by Perry, Mackie & Watson.* An in-depth exploration and comparison of two very different visions of the Course. E-book only. $7.95

For shipping rates, a complete catalog of our products and services, or for information about events, please contact us at:

The Circle of Atonement
Teaching and Healing Center
P.O. Box 4238
W.Sedona, AZ 86340
(928) 282-0790, Fax (928) 282-0523
E-mail: info@circleofa.com
Website: www.circleofa.com

About the Authors

 Robert Perry brings to *A Course in Miracles* many years of private study and public teaching. He began teaching at Miracle Distribution Center in 1986, and has since then taught throughout North America and around the world. His teaching grows out of his dedication to the Course as his own path and his desire to assist others on this path. Over the years he has become a respected voice in Course circles and has written for many Course newsletters and magazines. Robert is the founder of the Circle of Atonement and the author of numerous books and booklets based on the Course, including the popular *An Introduction to "A Course in Miracles."*

 Greg Mackie has been a student of *A Course in Miracles* since 1991, and a teacher for the Circle of Atonement since 1999. In addition to writing his "Course Q & A" page on the Circle's website, he has assisted in teaching Allen Watson's weekly in-depth Course class in Portland, Oregon. Greg also writes regularly for the Circle's newsletter, *A Better Way*. He sees his primary function as helping to develop a tradition of Course scholarship.

 Allen Watson is a staff writer and teacher with the Circle of Atonement, and is the author, or co-author with Robert Perry, of several popular books on the Course, as well as numerous articles in Course magazines and newsletters. He is well known around the world for his helpful daily commentaries on the Workbook lessons, which are on the Internet and in book form (*A Workbook Companion*, *Volumes I*, *II*, *& III*). Also on the Internet are his Electronic Text Classes—detailed, section-by-section commentaries on the Text. Allen's gifted and spirited writing and teaching help students to unlock the meaning of the Course for themselves.